Religion in American Politics

Religion in American Politics

A SHORT HISTORY

Frank Lambert

 PRINCETON UNIVERSITY PRESS

Princeton and Oxford

Published by Princeton University Press, 41 William Street,
Princeton, New Jersey 08540
In the United Kingdom: Princeton University Press, 6 Oxford Street,
Woodstock, Oxfordshire OX20 ITW
press.princeton.edu

Second printing, and first paperback printing, 2010
Paperback ISBN: 978-0-691-14613-3

The Library of Congress has cataloged the cloth edition of this book as follows

Lambert, Frank, 1943–
Religion in American politics : a short history / Frank Lambert.
p.   cm.
Includes bibliographical references and index.
ISBN 978-0-691-12833-7 (hardcover : alk. paper)
1. Christianity and politics—United States. I. Title.
BR516.L36 2008
322'.10973—dc22   2007026054

British Library Cataloging-in-Publication Data is available

This book has been composed in Adobe Garamond

Printed on acid-free paper. ∞

Printed in the United States of America

10   9   8   7   6   5   4

FOR BETH

CONTENTS ▦

ACKNOWLEDGMENTS ▨

This book is a collaborative effort from conception to publication. Its initial inspiration came from Brigitta van Rheinberg, then Executive Editor and now Editor-in-Chief at Princeton University Press, who called and asked whether I would be interested in writing a book on religion and American politics. Before that conversation, I had not been considering such a project; afterward, I was hooked. Brigitta's enthusiasm for the possibilities of such a book sparked my interest and resulted in my submitting a proposal. Having worked with Brigitta on a previous book, I was confident that the project would proceed under her sure guidance, and I have not been disappointed.

Doug Hurt, Head of the Department of History at Purdue University, has supported this effort from its beginning. A productive scholar in the history of the American West and American agriculture, he well understands the intellectual and practical process of historical investigation and writing. Through his good offices, I enjoyed a research leave, and, through his interest as a colleague and friend, I received ongoing encouragement.

A number of dedicated, conscientious librarians, most of them anonymous to me, played an inestimable role in the research for this book. In particular, Larry Mykytiuk, History and Political Science Librarian at Purdue University, has been tireless in acquiring materials that have supported my work.

Librarians at the University of Virginia, the University of North Carolina, and George Washington University were also especially helpful.

I am appreciative of those who have heard or read portions of the manuscript. I am indebted to the staff at Gunston Hall Plantation in Virginia for enabling me to test some of book's themes at the 2006 Liberty Lecture Series: "Faith of the Fathers." And I appreciate the insightful comments of the anonymous readers who vetted the manuscript for Princeton Press. Their thoughtful suggestions have made this a better work. I am also indebted to Lauren Lepow, Senior Editor at Princeton Press, for bringing greater clarity and expression to the text through consummate copyediting.

I am most thankful to my wife, Beth, who, as always, has supported my work with patience, understanding, and grace. While experiencing the highs and lows one encounters in research and writing, I could always count on her for much-needed perspective and unfailing love.

INTRODUCTION ▨

From the birth of the republic, religion and politics have operated most of the time in separate spheres. Fearing sectarian strife in a society characterized by religious pluralism, delegates to the Constitutional Convention in 1787 opted against a federal religious establishment, giving the government no power over religion and religion no official role in the state. Indeed, one of the exceptional features of the American Revolution was the separation of church and state. Separation did not, however, mean that religion was regarded as unimportant in the new nation; on the contrary, many deemed it to have a mission far more important than that of politics. Samuel Williams, pastor of the First Church in Bradford, Massachusetts, discussed the proper place of religion and the delicate relationship between the church and civil society in a 1779 sermon. He declared that "religion is a *private* thing." It was, in his words, a "personal transaction between God and a devout soul," and he added, "society can have nothing to do with it."[1] Until 1965, Jerry Falwell, the Lynchburg, Virginia, Baptist minister who helped make the Religious Right a political force in the 1970s, expressed similar sentiments. "Preachers are not called upon to be politicians," he insisted, "but soul winners. Nowhere are we commissioned to reform the externals."[2]

However, religion does have, and always has had, a public dimension. In that same sermon in 1779, Williams asserted that "religion is also a *public* concern." More pointedly, he asserted that the Christian religion is "well adapted to do the most essential service to Civil society" through its moral teachings.[3] Most of the time, religious influence is exerted primarily in the private sphere, within the walls of churches, synagogues, and mosques, and within families of the faithful. But as religion shapes individual character and moral development, it thereby influences public affairs, albeit in an indirect way. Through moral instruction, religion informs the values, priorities, and decisions of citizens and officeholders as they enter the voting booth and the statehouse. On occasion, such as when Falwell mobilized his Moral Majority, religious groups become more directly involved in the political process. At those times, they behave much like other interest groups. They lobby Congress to enact or oppose specific legislation, participate in electoral politics on behalf of candidates who support their agendas, and offer the full range of their institutional resources to sympathetic political parties.

One early instance of religious involvement in politics began on July 4, 1827, when Ezra Stiles Ely addressed a patriotic crowd gathered at the Seventh Presbyterian Church in Philadelphia. A prominent Calvinist minister in the city, Ely was sorely displeased with the republic's godless drift in recent years, and he blamed the nation's immorality on its leaders, men given to secular freethinking, deism, and Christian heterodoxy. He was active in a campaign led by the major Protestant denominations to overturn the 1810 federal law mandating Sunday mail service, an act that to him underscored the country's moral decline. In Ely's eyes, the problem and its solution were evident: a "Christian nation" was being led by un-Christian men, and Christian voters must elect Christian legislators and executives. He stated his case clearly: "We are a Christian nation: we have a right to demand that all our rulers in their

2

conduct shall conform to Christian morality; and if they do not, it is the duty and privilege of Christian freemen to make a new and a better election." To mobilize Christians and return the nation to its religious foundation, Ely proposed "a new sort of union, or, if you please, a Christian party in politics." He insisted that his was no pipe dream, that Presbyterians alone could deliver a half million votes, and if the Baptists, Methodists, and Congregationalists joined the new party, they could restore America's Christian heritage.[4]

Reaction to Ely's call was swift and largely negative. Predictably, "freethinkers," as secularists of the day were known, opposed the scheme for a Christian Party. But so did many Christians, who viewed it as a threat to religious liberty. "The cry of war is already sounded by the enemies of our religious freedom," trumpeted the Universalist magazine *Olive Branch*, adding, "It is time the lines were drawn between the friends and enemies of a national religious establishment." Many evangelicals, including some of his fellow Presbyterians, also spoke out against Ely's "immoderate" stance and called his plan a blatant sectarian attempt "to obtain civil domination."[5]

The most recent manifestation of a religious coalition's concerted effort to shape American politics is the rise of the Religious Right. Reacting to what many conservative evangelicals thought was an assault on American moral values during the 1960s, Reverend Jerry Falwell organized the Moral Majority in the 1970s and called for like-minded Christians to "take back" the country from secular humanists who ran the government. They decried court decisions banning prayer in public schools and denounced the judicial imposition of a "wall" separating church and state that had the effect of virtually removing religion from the public square. But the issue that galvanized religious conservatives more than any other was the Supreme Court decision in *Roe v. Wade* (1973) declaring unconstitutional most laws prohibiting abortion and making the decision to terminate a pregnancy the mother's choice. Through effective use of the Internet and cable television, the Religious Right energized millions of conservative evangelicals who had long shunned electoral politics, believing that their focus should be on eternal spiritual matters, not transitory things of this earth. Falwell's Moral Majority became the heart of what Richard Nixon had envisioned as a "Silent Majority" of Americans who were fed up with "liberal" social policies that trampled on traditional family values. Much of the GOP's recent success, beginning with the election of Ronald Reagan in 1980, can be accounted for by the Religious Right's energetic participation.

The rise of the Religious Right as a political force has attracted much scholarly attention. Indeed, the impressive literature on religion and politics in the United States over the past twenty-five years has focused primarily on the post–World War II period with special attention given to the politicization of religion embodied in the Religious Right.[6] Scholars portray the period as unique in the history of religion in American politics, a dramatic break with past religious excursions in politics. Sociologist of religion and director of the Center for the Study of Religion at Princeton University Robert Wuthnow sees the postwar period as the "restructuring" of American religion, a transformation that has altered the way religious groups engage the public on moral issues. Among the major changes he cites is the emergence of "big government" with its enormous social, educational, and medical programs that meet needs formerly satisfied by religious organizations. Thus, increasingly, religious groups must engage in the political process in order to carry out their mission of serving the poor and aiding the afflicted, and to ensure that government policies conform to moral principles. Moreover, Wuthnow notes the breakdown of religious denominations that used to be the major vehicles of public expression and action; more recently these have been replaced by larger coalitions organized around ideology, seen in the emergence of the Religious Right—and, in opposition to the Right, the reemergence of the Religious Left.[7]

While acknowledging the restructuring of American religion, this book takes a longer look at the question of religion in American politics, that is, one with a broader chronological sweep. Viewing religion in politics in historical terms, it begins with the birth of the republic in the late eighteenth century and examines the intersection of religion and politics at several moments throughout the nation's history up to the present. Though discontinuity is evident in the changing composition of the religious culture over time and in the receptivity of political parties to religious agendas, so is continuity. Change in historical and social contexts is inevitable, and those changes must be detailed to frame specific attempts by religious groups to reshape the country's political and cultural direction. But while religious agendas differ according to particular social changes defined by a historical moment, certain religious claims and moral visions recur. Though separated by more than a century and a half and operating in vastly different contexts, both Ely and Falwell made the same claim that America was a Christian nation, and that their coalitions represented moral visions rooted in that claim.

The political movements inspired by Ely and Falwell and the opposition they sparked illustrate the two main arguments of this book. The first is that religious coalitions seek by political means what the Constitution prohibits, namely, a national religious establishment, or, more specifically, a *Christian* civil religion. Religious groups become politically active because of their dissatisfaction with prevailing public policy. In some instances, such as those which motivated Ely and Falwell, the federal government, through specific legislation and court decisions, seems to be leading the country away from its religious heritage and moral foundation. In others, such as the rise of the social gospel movement in the late nineteenth century and the civil rights movement in the mid-twentieth century, it is the inaction of the government to deal with social injustice that stirs religious groups to political activism. Whatever the grievance, politically active religious groups are inspired by a particular vision of America as a Christian nation. Some, like the Religious Right, want to restore the country to its Christian origins. Others, like the Southern Christian Leadership Conference, Martin Luther King, Jr.'s organization during the civil rights movement, want America to become in fact the Christian nation that it has never been. Depending upon their particular notions of the nation's religious heritage, religious groups develop moral agendas that become the centerpieces of their political campaigns. They then must find a political party willing to adopt their agendas and find candidates who will embrace their values and express their visions. On occasion, as in the case of Ely, they attempt to operate as a separate party; more often, as in the case of Falwell, they work within an existing political party.

The book's second argument is that religion in American politics is contested. That is, any religious group's attempt to represent the nation's religious heritage or claim to be its moral conscience is sure to be met with opposition from other religious groups as well as from nonreligious parties. In American political culture, religion matters, and politicians often recognize its influence by invoking the name of God in public addresses. However, any reference to a particular religion, such as a presidential candidate's speaking in the name of Christ, is viewed as sectarian. Further, some construe as partisan any religious group's pronouncements on public affairs, no matter if couched in universal language. Pluralism explains part of the resentment. Each religious body has its own notions concerning public and private morality and is against claims purporting to represent all people of faith. Religious individualism also plays a role. Some persons embrace the idea that religion is strictly a private concern and, therefore, corporate religious statements have no place in the public square. Thomas Jefferson was of that mind, declaring himself to be of a "sect by myself," a sentiment shared by Thomas Paine, who avowed, "My mind is my own church."[8]

While powerful and persistent in shaping the nation's culture, religion is not the only influence on morals. Secular notions and material interests exert enormous influence on the nation's political culture, and often they collide with religious agendas. Science, for instance, offers hope for medical breakthroughs in stem-cell research, research that transgresses the moral teachings of some religious groups. And merchants offer consumers ever-expanding choices that promise to satisfy every conceivable appetite, including those that some religions deem sinful. The result is sometimes a clash between the country's secular laws, which reflect the tenets of liberal capitalism and the free exchange of goods, and the "higher laws" that religious groups cite to condemn certain goods and services offered in the marketplace. As the Frenchman Alexis de Tocqueville observed in the 1830s, "the law permits the American people to do everything, religion prevents them from conceiving everything and forbids them to dare everything."[9] Thus, in a secular and material culture that emphasizes individual liberty and freedom of choice, religious moral codes that threaten liberty or restrict choice face certain opposition.

Questions of religion and politics in the United States date to the birth of the republic. In 1776, delegates to state constitutional conventions debated such fundamental issues as government support of churches and rights of dissenters, and nowhere were these matters more hotly contested than in Virginia. Patrick Henry and James Madison staked out the positions that framed the debate and still account for the contention surrounding religion in American politics. As a member of the Virginia House of Delegates, Henry in 1784 opposed the establishment of the Episcopal Church, as some had advocated, as a violation of the "liberal principle" that animated the new republic, but he thought it wise for the state to support the "Christian Religion": not any particular sect, but Christianity in general. He believed that despite sectarian differences all Christians could agree on the fundamental principles of Christianity, and that those principles constituted the moral foundation of republican virtue. Madison demurred, opposing the proposal on the grounds that Christianity could not be defined to the satisfaction of all. There were numerous sects in pluralistic America, he argued, and they disagreed with each other on basic assumptions of faith and practice. What authority defined Christianity, he asked? Was it the Bible, and if so, which edition and what translation? Within the Bible, which books were deemed to be canonical and which apocryphal? And whose interpretation of those sacred writings should prevail: the Trinitarian's, the Socinian's, the Arian's? A worse prospect inherent in Henry's scheme, Madison thought, was what might happen if Christians could not agree on a common definition of their faith. Then the matter would fall to the government, and who in government, he wondered, would determine its meaning as a guide for ordering civil society. Would it be legislatures or judges or magistrates?[10]

With the 1785 passage of the Virginia Act for Religious Freedom, Madison's position prevailed in Virginia and became the model for the federal constitution as well: no religious establishment of any kind and freedom of religion as a right that government cannot abridge. For Madison, the new republic's religious pluralism, if unfettered by government interference, would contribute to a moral society while at the same time guaranteeing religious liberty. He reasoned that myriad competing sects would vigorously promote their own interests, and would in the process spread religion to every man, woman, and child, while checking ambitions of any rival group that might attempt to foist its views on the whole. Patrick Henry remained unconvinced. He feared that left to voluntary support, religion would languish, to the detriment of society. Better, he argued, that the public support religion. He had a different view of religious pluralism; he believed that the various sects shared common Christian beliefs that could form the basis of a Christian establishment. Religious groups purporting to speak for "Christian America" subscribe to Henry's vision as they seek to shape public policy according to their moral agendas. Those who oppose them claim, as Madison did, that there is no agreed-upon "Christian America," and that representations of the nation as such are partisan.

Social scientists and historians often express surprise that religion persists as a topic of public debate in the United States. Foreign observers in particular are astonished that Americans, whom they regard as the most materialistic people on earth, are at the same time so openly spiritual and express their spiritual concerns in politics. Further, they are perplexed at seeing religion and politics so enmeshed in a country committed to the doctrine of separation of church and state. Part of the explanation lies in the theoretical lens through which they view American politics. Embracing secularization theory as an explanatory framework, they conclude that when society becomes more secular—as manifested by a powerful, expansive state, a vigorous capitalist economy, and a supreme confidence in science—religion is relegated to the private sphere, becoming the keeper of traditions that have little if any impact on modern culture.

But that theory fails to account for the continued vitality of religion in the United States, as attested to by rising rates of church adherence, and the vigor with which religious groups pursue their agendas through political means. An alternative framework, and the one that informs this book's investigation, is the theory of religious economy. According to this sociological perspective, the presence of a multitude of religious groups, each free to pursue its own moral vision and each relying only on its own members for support, ensures a vigorous competition among those groups. To attract and retain members, they appeal to a variety of interests and tastes and employ innovative strategies for recruiting new devotees. In recent years, we have seen the rise of so-called megachurches located in suburban communities and offering an optimistic message, music with a rock beat, and social and educational opportunities for all ages. Many of these churches, often aligned with the Religious Right, make full use of cable television and the Internet to reach a wide audience. Those same tools prove to be effective means of mobilizing the faithful behind specific public policy initiatives and particular candidates for office.

This brief history explores religion in American politics by examining some of the public moments when religion and politics have intersected. Organized chronologically, it attempts to capture the circumstances and character of religious activism within particular historical periods. Each of the eight chapters examines moral issues within specific contexts, an exploration that addresses the character and composition of the prevailing religious pluralism, the coalition or coalitions that emerge to give voice to a moral vision in the political arena, and the political expression of that vision. The book begins at the founding of the republic with the question of the optimal role of religion in American public life, and ends in the twenty-first century with moral questions debated by the Religious Right and the Religious Left. ·

Anyone writing on religion and politics must begin with clear definitions. In this book religion is defined as a set of beliefs in a transcendent God, grounded in an authoritative sacred text, and expressed by a body of believers through the performance of certain rituals and adherence to a specific moral code. It is not used in a broad functional sense in which anything that demands one's devotion counts as religion, such as nationalism or even fashion; the belief in a transcendent god must be at the center. Politics is defined as both the process that establishes priorities, formulates policies, and allocates resources among competing interests, and the political culture that informs the underlying assumptions, beliefs, and values of voters and politicians. This book examines how religion engages in the political process in pursuit of specific policy and electoral outcomes, and how it shapes the political culture as well.

Meanings also change over time. For example, the phrase "Christian America" has resonated differently to a range of groups at various times. In the early nineteenth century it meant "Protestant America" or, more specifically, "Evangelical America." As Catholics became a major presence in American religion in the late 1800s, "Christian America" for some took on a more expansive meaning to include all Christians, including Catholics. However, fundamentalists narrowed the meaning in the early twentieth century, insisting that "Christian" meant subscribing to a number of specific beliefs. As the country grew more secular in the twentieth century, some religious conservatives redefined "Christian America" to mean "Judeo-Christian" or "theistic" America as opposed to "secular" or "nontheistic" America. In its latest meaning, "Christian America" is a contested term debated by the Religious Right and the Religious Left.

Religious groups themselves are often conflicted over what they are called. Consider the term "evangelical." For some, it is a broad designation for all Protestants whose faith centers on the Bible and whose mission is to "win souls" for Christ. In that sense, it has come to include all those groups outside "mainline" Protestantism, the phrase used to characterize older, more traditional denominations such as Episcopalians, Congregationalists, and Presbyterians. However, many evangelicals are uncomfortable with being lumped with "fundamentalists," who insist that only those subscribing to certain fundamentals of faith can be properly designated Christian. Recently, evangelical leaders have debated whether evangelicalism should be "a big tent, open to more divergent views, or a smaller, purer theology." And politics complicates the issue. Evangelicals are divided over such questions as whether they should engage in activism concerning global warming and immigration, or whether they should retreat from politics altogether.[11]

The presence of a wide spectrum of religious groups in the United States poses an additional challenge for the student of religion and politics. Though not every group is active in the political process, all have views concerning public matters. However, the goal of writing a brief treatment of the subject precludes any attempt to be inclusive. Rather, the aim here is to identify the major coalitions that claim to speak for religion in politics. Such a strategy runs the risk of distorting the positions of individuals and specific groups. For instance, fundamentalists are subsumed in this book under the heading "Religious Right" or "religious conservatives" though we know that fundamentalists do not constitute a monolithic bloc. The labels used herein are by and large political tags that come out of historical engagements, such as that between modernists and fundamentalists. Locked in battle over rival claims, each side has been quick to label the other and ascribe certain views to it. Further, each side has pigeonholed whole groups of people into one faction or the other, regardless of whether the designation fit or was accurate.

The individuals and groups highlighted in this book are drawn predominantly from the Christian faith, and, more specifically, from Protestant Christianity. This selection does not minimize the contributions of non-Christians and non-Protestants in political contests; rather, it reflects the historical predominance of Protestants in the nation's religious heritage and their claims to speak for that heritage. Because Protestantism prevailed at the nation's founding, Protestants are most likely to demand that voters restore America as a "Christian nation."

Providential and Secular America: Founding the Republic

During the Revolutionary era, patriot ministers reminded Americans that God was sovereign over the new republic. In a 1774 sermon, Rev. Samuel Sherwood of New York asserted that God is the "sovereign Lord and supreme Ruler of all things" who "has the great affairs of the kingdoms and empires of the earth, in his own hands; and can dispose of them as seems good unto him." God's preference, Sherwood argued, was for godly rulers to govern according to God's law; however, he pointed out that the Almighty "made mankind rational creatures; and left them to choose" what they deemed best for their circumstances. Sherwood made clear his choice: civil rulers must be "men of uprightness and integrity; men of real piety and religion; who fear the Lord, and keep up a proper awe and reverence of him upon their minds." Further, their governance should be "duly regulated by Christian principles and rules."[1] He pointed out in another sermon that, under God, Americans had a special obligation to follow his law because the United States was an exceptional land. "This American quarter of the globe," he claimed, "seemed to be reserved in providence, as a fixed and settled habitation for God's church."[2] Sherwood considered the United States to be the New Israel, and that the nation should conduct its public affairs as such.

Sherwood's vision for a Christian America was far from the minds of politicians in Philadelphia who were preoccupied with more pressing military and diplomatic matters. Indeed, while Sherwood pleaded for a Protestant America, Congress dispatched American diplomats to Paris for the purpose of negotiating a defense and commercial treaty with France, a Catholic power. Though many congressmen, like Sherwood, also recognized God's providence, they interpreted it differently. They believed that geopolitics sometimes required alliances with Catholics and non-Christians, and they deemed their pact with France to be providential. Indeed, by 1781, they viewed it as decisive in defeating the British. It was a French fleet that cut off Cornwallis's attempts to escape at Yorktown, forcing the general to surrender to Washington. To the congressmen, military and political necessity, not religious purity, defined what was providential. For American merchants, independence meant the opportunity to trade in markets throughout the world, not just within the British Atlantic. After 1783, they dispatched ships to the Mediterranean where they dealt with Catholic and Muslim traders and explored markets in Asia; there they sought exchanges with Confucian, Hindu, and Buddhist partners.

When delegates to the Constitutional Convention completed their work in 1787, there was no hint of a Protestant America. The Constitution virtually ignored religion and made no acknowledgment that the United States was a Protestant, or even a Christian nation. Fearing sectarian strife and church-state oppression, the delegates granted Congress no powers regarding religion. The result was that religion remained within the purview of the states, and several states, especially in New England, continued to support religious establishments. But there would be no national establishment.

Such an outcome was troubling to many Americans who envisioned a Christian America, if not a Protestant republic. Upon first reading a draft of the new Constitution, they were appalled at the absence of any acknowledgment of divine providence. New Englanders, in particular, objected because providence was deeply embedded in their Puritan heritage. Why, they asked, would a people who owed so much to God's favor refuse to acknowledge the debt in its principal founding document? The failure to mention the Almighty's influence was, to say the least, the height of ingratitude.

This chapter examines the tension between sacred and secular conceptions of the new republic by first exploring the cultural matrix in which Americans worked out a sense of national identity and purpose. Three major influences—Protestant Christianity, liberal republicanism, and commercial libertarianism—commingled and sometimes clashed in shaping that culture. In a diverse society where both sacred and secular ideas prevailed, conflict was inevitable. The chapter then explores the arena in which debate occurred: a religious pluralism where all faith groups were placed on equal footing as a result of the Constitution's ban on a religious establishment and thus were free to offer competing visions of religion and its place in public life. Was America a Christian nation, and, if so, should Christianity not play a preeminent role in public affairs? Or was America a bold liberal experiment in religious liberty where pluralism and tolerance were valued above orthodoxy? And whose religious freedom was at stake? Was the emphasis on religious freedom for Christian sects to practice their faith as they wished, or was it on individuals to choose what, if any, faith to embrace? The chapter ends by looking at how religion and politics commingled in the presidential campaign of 1800 when some pro-Federalist ministers declared Thomas Jefferson unfit for the presidency because of his religious beliefs.

American Culture—Sacred and Secular

From the earliest English settlement, Americans viewed them-selves within the great stream of salvation history: a New World people who were fully committed to completing the Protestant Reformation. One of Americans' most powerful and enduring myths is that of God's choosing the American wilderness as the site of a special outpouring of grace. Remote and wild, America was just the spot for God to complete the Protestant Reformation because no one could ascribe a work in such a distant wasteland to any power but God. Unlike Europe, where proud monarchs and even learned theologians might consider themselves to be architects of momentous events, early seven-teenth-century America could make no similar claims. The "City upon a Hill" that arose from the wilderness was entirely the work of God. Massachusetts was nothing less than the New Israel, a chosen people with whom God had entered into a covenant that promised his blessings as long as the people obeyed his commandments. Experiences and events during the colonial period strengthened and extended the idea of Ameri-cans as God's chosen people. History convinced American Protestants that God favored their land by demonstrating his assistance in their countless struggles against the Catholic pow-ers. When the British and their colonists defeated the French and their Indian allies in the French and Indian War (1754–1763), Americans interpreted the victory as the triumph of Protestants over Papists.[3]

The Protestants who populated British North America were a diverse lot. Men and women from every branch of Protestant-ism immigrated in the seventeenth and eighteenth centuries in the pursuit of a better life. Churchmen and Nonconformists or Dissenters arrived from England; Calvinists and Lutherans of every stripe left the Rhineland, Switzerland, the Low Countries, and Scandinavia; radical Protestants such as Anabaptists, Quakers, and Pietists came from every corner of western Europe.[4] Though these Protestants differed from each other in certain doctrinal matters, they shared some common core beliefs: the sufficiency of scripture as a guide to salvation, the priesthood of all believers, and salvation by the grace of God appropriated through faith alone. They shared something else: an abiding hatred of the Catholic Church. They vilified Catholics as "Papists" and "Romanists" and castigated the Catholic Church as the "Whore of Babylon."[5]

European Protestants found in America a haven of religious freedom. While religious difference often meant persecution in the Old World, differences were accommodated in the New. An abundance of land and the eagerness of colonizers to attract settlers enabled members of a particular faith to establish communities free of harassment. For example, Puritans left England because of persecution and settled in New England, where they organized societies according to their own beliefs, free of superintendence from the Church of England. Indeed, they forbade Anglicans to settle in their midst. The Quaker William Penn became proprietor of a large stretch of woodland in the Delaware Valley and turned it into a haven not only for his coreligionists but for all persecuted Protestants in the Rhineland. The vast amount of land meant that religious disputes could be settled by one party's simply leaving and founding a new colony elsewhere. That was the case when Roger Williams clashed with John Winthrop and the Puritan leadership of Massachusetts; he left and established the colony of Rhode Island in the New England wilderness. As a result of settlement—and, in some cases, resettlement—mainland British North America became home to men and women who spanned the full spectrum of Protestantism.

Rather than leading to bloody wars of religion like those in Europe, religious differences in eighteenth-century America resulted in a pluralistic society where differences were accommodated. Unlike Europeans who recognized liberty of conscience as only the right to *private* judgment, Americans by the time of the War of Independence had expanded it to embrace *public* language and behavior. A series of evangelical revivals in the mid-1700s known as the Great Awakening contributed to that pluralism by elevating personal religious experience above ecclesiastical orthodoxy in matters of salvation. As the bonds of church controls over individuals weakened, so did the civil arrangements, known as religious establishments, by which the state protected and supported one denomination in preference to all others.[6] Giving additional impetus to pluralism were Enlightenment ideas of natural rights. The central notion of the philosophy known as the Enlightenment was the idea that through the use of their reason individuals could understand the laws of nature and use that understanding to harness nature's power for the advancement of human progress. Like the Great Awakening, the Enlightenment challenged ecclesiastical and civil powers that imposed religious uniformity. Thus, fired with ideas that empowered individuals and undermined religious establishments, Americans freely and publicly expressed their beliefs while recognizing that those who disagreed with them deserved the same right.

The War for Independence made Americans think about what they had in common, not what divided them.[7] Indeed, one could argue that by 1776 a common American religion had emerged, a shared faith that lent the new republic a common identity and mission. Despite sectarian differences, the thirteen states were overwhelmingly Protestant, and Protestantism provided the moral foundation for society. In their ardent belief that they were God's chosen people, Americans interpreted his-

tory through a moral lens: good times pointed to divine blessing; bad times indicated divine disapproval. In the fight for
independence, such faith meant that as long as Americans
obeyed God, he would bless their cause. In addition to supplying Americans with a moral compass, the Protestant faith, unlike Catholicism, also promoted religious freedom. Writing at
midcentury, Connecticut Congregational minister Elisha Williams argued that in Protestant states "the sacred scriptures lie
open to the people," but that in Catholic ones the "people's
eyes" are put out and "they are more easily induced to follow
their leaders."[8] Moreover, in Protestant America, citizens practiced their faith under governments that promoted the Christian religion as the bedrock of republican virtue, guaranteed
freedom of conscience to all, and tolerated religious dissent.
And, in a fusion of Christian and republican principles, Americans claimed that God had endowed all humans with certain
inalienable rights, and that no government, including that of
the British, could take them away.

Any notion of Protestant unity in the Revolutionary era,
however, ignores deep divisions among Protestants, schisms
with colonial roots but also exacerbated by the Revolution. Indeed, commentators such as John Adams believed that cultural
and religious differences among the disparate colonies were so
great that any attempt at union would likely fail. Protestants
split into myriad denominations and sects, spawned by doctrinal disputes, ethnic loyalties, and political affiliations. While
most Protestants embraced some form of Calvinism, with its
emphasis on God's grace as the sole instrument in salvation,
others favored a more Arminian stance that allowed for individual free will in the drama of redemption. But, beyond
theological or even denominational distinctions, American
Protestants were most deeply divided over the question of religious authority. The event that created, or perhaps exposed,

the divide was the Great Awakening, which began in the 1740s in the Middle Colonies and New England and spread to the Chesapeake in the 1760s. The central message of the revivalists was the necessity of a "New Birth," a spiritual transformation wrought within the individual by the working of God's grace. What was revolutionary was the notion that the individual experience of the New Birth became authoritative. In the words of the awakeners, the "only thing needful" was personal experience, not belief in a church creed, not acceptance of doctrine, not submission to church authority, not the teachings of learned ministers.[9]

Such a radical empowerment of individuals split churches in colonial America. Congregationalists divided into "New Lights" and "Old Lights," with the former supporting the new teaching and the latter opposing it. Similarly, Presbyterians split into "New Side" and "Old Side" synods. At the center of the dispute was the question of who exercised authority. On the one hand, defenders of the church's traditions and ministerial authority placed confidence in "learning and civility" as hallmarks of an educated clergy. God called certain persons to be ministers of the gospel, Old Lights maintained, and he expected them to be good stewards who studied hard to understand the divine will and presided over the orderly worship of God. God was a God of reason and order, and his ministers must reflect those exemplary traits. On the other hand, revivalists embraced anticlerical ideas against any learned order to mediate the gospel. To them, seminaries were mere factories spewing out theologians, many of whom had never experienced the New Birth, who crafted doctrines that they then imposed on parishioners. Suspicious of what they called religion of the "head," they favored religion of the "heart," the powerful emotional experience that often sent those in the throes of the New Birth into fits of anguish and ecstasy.

The spirit of the American Revolution tilted toward New Light individualism, encouraging an "egalitarian theology" and a "Christianity of the people." Just as republicans challenged the authority of political tyrants, many Protestants revolted against ecclesiastical oppression. Dissenters challenged church establishments that favored one sect over others, and New Lights insisted that, as in politics, in religion all are on equal footing before God. The result was a "revolt against Calvinism" by those who placed greater weight on the authority of private judgment than on that of an educated ministry and the "collective will of the church." This revolution of American religion created a popular theology that blurred the boundaries between sacred and secular. In what historian Nathan Hatch calls "odd mixtures," the crucible of this new American Christianity was a blend of "renewed supernaturalism and Enlightenment rationalism, of mystical experiences and biblical literalism, of evangelical and Jeffersonian rhetoric." With a firm belief in the "primacy of the individual conscience," American Protestants greatly expanded the number of religious options available in the new republic. Armed with the authority of the New Birth, individuals freely interpreted the Bible, chose their own leaders, and shaped their own faith.[10]

Protestantism was, however, but one of several influences that shaped American culture. Indeed, Americans drew upon two powerful sets of secular ideas to declare their independence and craft the Constitution: liberalism and civic humanism. The Enlightenment provided them with the optimistic belief that human reason, if rightly applied, could not only understand the physical and social worlds, but control them for their own benefit. It encouraged individuals to think for themselves, to base their knowledge on observation and experimentation rather than on traditional authority, including that of the church. Its ideal was the free individual who, unfettered by artificial constraints imposed by rulers and religion, enjoyed inalienable rights of life, liberty, and property.[11] In 1776, the Declaration of Independence conceived of self-governing individuals as the architects of the state, agreeing to submit to rulers of their choosing only so long as the governors protected the people's natural rights. That same year, Scottish philosopher Adam Smith published his *Wealth of Nations*, which called for the removal of artificial constraints on trade, thus allowing individuals to pursue their self-interests in a free market governed only by the laws of supply and demand.

When Thomas Jefferson drafted the Declaration of Independence, his inspiration sprang more from the Enlightenment than from Protestantism. Voicing respect for the "opinions of mankind," he offered a logical explanation for the colonies' severing ties with Britain. He began his analysis by asserting that all men possessed certain natural rights granted them by their "Creator," an entity he equated with "Nature's God." His allusions to God were those of a deist who recognized God as Creator, not those of a Protestant affirming personal belief in a saving Christ. The rights of life, liberty, and the pursuit of happiness were part of the natural order, not the result of a divine covenant or special dispensation wherein God granted them to a chosen people. Jefferson found the origins of popular sovereignty in an imagined state of nature. In contrast to the Garden of Eden, where God determined the rules, in the state of nature men and women took control of their destinies, relying on popular, not divine, sovereignty. Voluntarily deciding to forgo some of their freedom in order to enjoy their natural rights in safety and security, they placed themselves under governors of their choosing and demanded that the government protect their rights and property. Far from a divine covenant where God chose a people and commanded them to live under his rule, Jefferson's "natural" people entered into a social contract with their governors, agreeing to obey them so long as the governors protected natural rights. And the people placed conditions on the governors: you stay in power only as long as you safeguard our rights. In the Genesis account of the covenant, God set the conditions, and God could declare the covenant void if the people violated its conditions. Not so here. The people retained the right and duty to revolt against unjust rulers.[12]

While Enlightenment liberalism saw the self-interested, property-owning individual as the best guardian of freedom, civic humanism deemed the community to be its surest safeguard. Embodying ideas that inspired the republic of Renaissance Florence, civic humanism found expression for English republicans during the seventeenth-century Civil War; it was then that some radicals sought to create a more just, equitable society where all would enjoy the blessings of liberty. While English republicans failed to see their dream materialize until the nineteenth century, Americans, ironically, employed those same ideas to overthrow British rule and create a republic in the late eighteenth century. Civic humanism pitted virtuous citizens pursuing the common good against vicious self-interested individuals who did the bidding of venal rulers.[13]

In addition to liberalism and civic humanism, Americans also drew upon English common law to craft the new republic. While some argued, then as now, that the United States was founded on Christian principles, Jefferson pointed out that the Saxon laws forming the foundation of common law predate the arrival of Christianity in England. In an 1814 letter to Dr. Thomas Cooper, Jefferson declared that there was a "space of two hundred years [under Saxon rule], during which the common law was in existence, and Christianity no part of it."[14] It should be noted that Jefferson's claim hardly went unchallenged: among the disputants was the eminent jurist Justice

Joseph Story, who claimed that "Christianity [was] a Part of the Common Law."[15]

Devotees of secular philosophy claimed that morality was independent of Christianity or any other religion. While all religions had moral codes, all people, Jefferson argued, had an innate moral sense that gave them a propensity to do good and shun evil. Following the Aristotelian idea of moral sense, Jefferson wrote in 1787:

> The moral sense, or conscience, is as much a part of man as his leg or arm. It is given to all human beings in a stronger or weaker degree, as force of members is given them in a greater or less degree. It may be strengthened by exercise, as may any particular limb of the body. This sense is submitted indeed in some degree to the guidance of reason; but it is a small stock which is required for this: even a less one than what we call Common sense. State a moral case to a ploughman and a professor. The former will decide it as well, and often better than the latter, because he has not been led astray by artificial rules.[16]

According to this view, moral sense predates religion; religions codify what conscience dictates and what a particular society permits.

While most politicians in the founding era avoided sectarian discourse in discussing public issues, they did give voice to what some scholars have called America's civil religion. Jean-Jacques Rousseau coined the term "civil religion" in his 1762 essay on the social contract, denoting those religious beliefs that a society holds in common, apart from sectarian tenets that are beyond the state's jurisdiction. Those beliefs include the idea of a nation's divine origins and of God's providence in its history. Leaders in the early republic laced their speeches and writings with their firm belief that God had guided the United States through the War of Independence and through the creation of the Constitution. Moreover, the great ideals of the Revolution—life, liberty, equality—became sanctified in the civil religion. The Declaration of Independence, the U.S. Constitution, and the Bill of Rights were canonized as part of "America's Scripture"; George Washington, Thomas Jefferson, and Abraham Lincoln were heralded as its major prophets.[17] According to Robert Bellah, who has written at length on the subject, America's civil religion, "while not antithetical to and indeed sharing much in common with Christianity, was neither sectarian not in any specific sense Christian." It gave religious content to the nation's identity and mission without committing it to a particular religion. Bellah is among those who have noted that, like any religion, the civil religion can lead to idolatry in the form of the worship of the nation.[18]

Americans' dual sacred-secular cultural heritage has several implications for questions of religion and politics. First, it challenges the argument that America was founded as a Christian nation but that, in recent years, secular humanists have pushed religion out of the public square. Sacred claims have long faced challenges from secular interests, even before the Revolution. Writing in the mid-1700s, Jonathan Edwards accused deists of "wholly cast[ing] off the Christian religion," and of "deny[ing] the whole Christian religion" in favor of humanist notions.[19] While Edwards's fear seems overblown, it is true that those claiming Christianity as the nation's religious heritage face rival claims from those who acknowledge America's civil religion as its birthright. Second, America's religious pluralism makes for a competitive, sometimes contentious, struggle among groups to represent the nation's religious heritage. As historian Edmund Morgan has observed, Christian teaching in America is "usually a matter of emphasis."[20] Some emphasize the idea of

America as a chosen nation, a New Israel, shaping its Christian legacy; others stress the notion of America as a haven of religious toleration, rooted in its pluralistic culture.

America's Religious Settlement— A Secular State and a Pluralist Society

Religion was barely mentioned at the Constitutional Convention. Given pervasive and deeply rooted convictions of providence, one would expect to find in the Constitution at least an acknowledgment of God's superintending power or a pledge that political conduct be consistent with scriptural tenets. Computers make possible a close analysis of the delegates' language at the constitutional and ratifying conventions; what a keyword search shows is that law and commerce dominated, while religion was barely mentioned. "Property," "law," "trade," "natural rights," "taxes," and "representation" all yield hits in excess of one hundred. On the other hand, in Philadelphia at the Constitutional Convention Christ was mentioned not once, and just four times in all the ratifying conventions. Similarly, the name of Jesus was not heard in Philadelphia and but twice in the state meetings. Only twice did the constitutional delegates mention scripture or the Bible, while ratifiers referred to them six times. The framers invoked the name of God twelve times, and the ratifiers thirty-six. Several of the references, however, were popular phrases such as "Good God, Sir . . ." and "God knows how many more . . ." rather than reverent invocations.[21]

On two occasions religion became the subject of brief discussion. On June 28, 1787, the convention was at an impasse after five weeks of heated debate on the question of whether representation in Congress should be equal among the states or proportionate to population. With tempers rising along with the summer temperatures, Benjamin Franklin suggested that the body turn to prayer in search of the political wisdom that had thus far eluded them. He reminded his colleagues that in another great crisis, the fight for independence against Britain, Americans had offered prayers, which were "graciously answered," proof of a "Superintending providence in our favor." The aging and venerable Franklin told the delegates that the longer he lived, the more he was convinced that "God governs in the affairs of men."[22] He then proposed that the convention hire a chaplain and begin each session with prayer, something that it had theretofore neglected to do, to its own loss.

In the short but spirited debate on Franklin's prayer proposal, delegates voiced several objections, but the most telling came from Alexander Hamilton. The young New Yorker conceded that perhaps such a resolution might have been proper at the beginning of the convention, but to adopt it in the midst of an important debate would send the wrong message to Americans who had charged the delegates with fixing the federal Constitution. In Hamilton's view, their resorting to prayer now would be an admission to the public that the delegates were incapable of overcoming dissensions and reaching a reasonable compromise. Franklin's proposal failed, and on the original draft of his speech, Franklin noted, "The convention, except three or four persons, thought prayer unnecessary."[23]

Fifty years after the event, William Steele wrote a letter to his son recounting the episode. In his version, Franklin's motion carried, and, buttressed by prayer, the body proceeded to hammer out a compromise. Perhaps James Madison knew of Steele's account or of other versions that may have circulated; in any case, he set the record straight. Drawing on the records of the convention, Madison explained to a correspondent,

Thomas Grimke, what had happened: "The proposition was received & treated with the respect due to it; but the lapse of time which had preceded, with considerations growing out of it, had the effect of limiting what was done, to a reference of the proposition to a highly respectable Committee. This issue of it may be traced in the printed Journal."[24]

The second brief discussion of religion came late in the convention when Charles Pinckney moved to add the wording "but no religious test shall ever be required as a qualification to any office or public trust under the authority of the U. States." Pinckney had included such language in his own draft proposal for a constitution, as had Hamilton in his version. Two years earlier, Thomas Jefferson had incorporated a proscription against religious tests in his bill for establishing religious freedom in Virginia. The state could not, Jefferson wrote, deem any citizen unworthy of public confidence "by laying upon him an incapacity of being called to offices of trust and emolument, unless he profess or renounce this or that religious opinion."[25] Roger Sherman of Connecticut objected to Pinckney's explicit bar on religious tests on the grounds that the language was unnecessary, "the prevailing liberality being a sufficient security against such tests." According to Luther Martin of Maryland, "a great majority of the convention" supported the ban on religious tests "without much debate."[26] Charles Pinckney of South Carolina explained the prohibition of religious tests as a liberal, enlightened measure, "a provision," he declared, "the world will expect from you, in the establishment of a System founded on Republican Principles, and in an age so liberal and enlightened as the present." [27] Some delegates, however, supported the federal religious test ban in order to protect existing state religious tests. Initially Edmund Randolph had worried that the federal Constitution at this and other points interfered with state and individual religious rights. However, he concluded that the test ban really protected officeholders because it precluded their being bound to support any "one mode of worship, or to adhere to a particular sect." Moreover, he pointed out, it protected states in respect to religion; officials were obligated to support the U.S. Constitution only in powers granted to it, not in all other matters, including that of religion.[28]

Delegates wished to keep religion out of their discussions and out of the Constitution because they viewed it as divisive. Their aim was to create a "more perfect Union," and sectarian strife threatened that goal. Many of the delegates had had firsthand experience in state constitutional conventions characterized by warring sects insisting on protecting their particular religious interests. James Madison had been engaged in Virginia's lengthy and acrimonious debate over the place of religion in that commonwealth, dueling with Patrick Henry, who wished to establish the Christian faith. Madison had opposed any establishment, even that of Christianity, because he believed that the result would be the majority's tyranny over the minority. He considered religious sects, including that of Christianity itself, to be special interests that placed their private goals above those of the public good. Later, in *Federalist* Number 10, he explained that perspective. Madison worried about the effects of a "factious spirit," including a "zeal for different opinions concerning religion." The problem with self-interest was that "no man is allowed to be a judge in his own cause, because his interest would certainly bias his judgment, and, not improbably, corrupt his integrity." He feared that if a majority of "the same passion or interest" were able to act in concert, they would then be able to "carry into effect schemes of oppression." Religious groups were as susceptible to exercising the tyranny of the majority as any other interest group, such as the monied or manufacturing or planting interest. "If the impulse and the opportunity be suffered to coincide," he argued, "we well know that neither moral nor religious motives can be relied on as an adequate control."[29]

On September 17, 1787, after four months of debate and compromise, all but three of the delegates signed the engrossed copy of the Constitution. Now for the first time Americans would see their handiwork, and elected delegates to the state ratifying conventions would decide its fate. As in the Constitutional Convention, questions of representation, protection of individual rights, the division of power between the states and the new federal government, and questions of taxation and commerce dominated the discussions. But, in many states, religious questions received considerable attention as well. Three issues in particular were raised. Why did the preamble contain no acknowledgment of God's providence in guiding America or of America as a Christian nation? Could not the ban on religious tests lead to a non-Christian president? And, without the explicit guarantee offered by a Bill of Rights, was religious liberty secure against encroachments of a powerful federal government? What was not at issue was the question of a federal religious establishment. No one wanted to see a particular religion or a specific Christian sect elevated to the status of a *national* church, though many continued to support ecclesiastical establishments at the *state* level.

Madison was pleased with the Constitution's religious settlement and placed great faith in the religious marketplace it presupposed. Scores of competing sects, he thought, would be an effective guarantor of religious freedom. Claims by any one group would be sure to be challenged by others, thus assuring that no one sect could impose its will on the entire nation. At the same time, he was confident that religion would flourish to a far greater extent in an open market than as an arm of the state. In his *Memorial and Remonstrance* (1785), he had argued that Christianity did not need government support to thrive. "It is known," he maintained, "that this Religion both existed and flourished, not only without the support of human laws, but in spite of every opposition from them."[30] He believed that competition bred industry and innovation, which would make religion more attentive and responsive to the people.

Not all accepted Madison's rosy assessment of the religious settlement. William Williams, a Connecticut merchant and delegate to that state's ratifying convention, was appalled at the absence of any acknowledgment of America's dependence on God's providence. While not opposed to popular sovereignty, he thought it important to recognize that the people would govern under the watchful eye of God. Williams's Puritan fore-fathers had been explicit in their reliance on divine guidance. And Congress, just five years earlier, had adopted a seal for the United States that included on its obverse side an unfinished pyramid with an eye in the zenith and, above it, the words *Annuit coeptis*: Providence has favored our undertaking. Surely the Constitution, which was the nation's fundamental docu-ment, should similarly express the widespread belief that God's hand guided events in the new independent republic. To that end, Williams proposed a new preamble that was an affirma-tion of faith:

> We the people of the United States, in a firm belief of the being and perfections of the one living and true God, the creator and supreme Governour of the world, in his universal providence and the authority of his laws; that he will require of all moral agents an account of their conduct; that all rightful powers among men are ordained of, and mediately derived from God.[31]

Such a declaration, Williams thought, would make explicit the fact that America was a Christian nation.

The second provision to which delegates objected was the ban on religious tests. Again, William Williams offered a remedy, advocating a religious test for officeholders that would "require an explicit acknowledgment of the being of a God, his perfections and his providence."[32] Many state constitutions had such provisions, and Williams thought it appropriate that the federal Constitution have one as well.

Nowhere did the ban on religious tests spark more debate than it did in North Carolina. Rev. Henry Abbott, a Baptist minister from Camden, was disturbed by the absence of a religious test. "As there are no religious tests," he reasoned, "pagans, deists and Mahometans might obtain office, and senators and representatives might all be pagans." If so, then, he asked, "by whom were men to swear?—by Jupiter, Juno, Minerva, Proserpine, or Pluto?"[33] James Iredell responded by warning that the imposition of a religious test threatened the right of religious freedom, a right that Abbott and other Baptists had long advocated. Iredell asked, "[I]s it possible to exclude any set of men without taking away that principle of religious freedom which we ourselves so warmly contend for?" His question made the central point of all debates concerning religious liberty: any favoritism toward one sect or religion and any discrimination against any group placed the liberty of all at risk. If the government had the power to favor or discriminate, then today's beneficiaries could never be secure in their position; tomorrow's lawmakers might remove that privilege and grant it elsewhere. Rev. David Caldwell, a Presbyterian minister from Guildford, worried that the absence of the test had the potential to undermine the nation's moral foundation. The ban on a test was, he feared, "an invitation to Jews and pagans of every kind, and that these might endanger the character of the United States." Judge Samuel Spencer countered that religious tests had long been instruments of persecution, that they served only to keep good rather than bad men out of office, and that it was unreasonable to assume that voters would elect anyone without regard to his character. Gov. Samuel Johnston supported Spencer's view, arguing that a "Jew, a Mahometan or a pagan could get office only in one of two ways: either the American people would have to lay aside the Christian religion altogether, or such persons would have to acquire confidence and esteem by good conduct and the practice of virtue." Delegate William Lancaster said that he did not worry that the current generation would elect a non-Protestant to public office, but he was concerned about the "millions not yet in existence," who in four or five hundred years, might, if there were no religious test, elect a Papist or a Mahometan to the presidency.[34]

The third question that vexed many in the ratifying conventions was the lack of a Bill of Rights, especially an explicit safeguard against the federal government's violation of citizens' rights of religious freedom. Delegates were aware that they needed to restrain future generations of Americans, who might not be as liberal and enlightened as they.[35]

Religion and Politics—Whose Christianity?

Though the Constitution separated church and state, it did not keep religion out of politics. And while delegates ignored religion in 1787, voters did not follow suit in the presidential campaign of 1800.[36] Indeed, religion emerged as a central issue when a group of New England Calvinists attacked Thomas Jefferson's religious views, charging that the Democratic-Republican candidate was an "infidel" and an "atheist." By contrast, they depicted their candidate, Federalist incumbent John Adams, as a God-fearing Christian. Jefferson considered himself to be a Christian, albeit one who had little in common with Calvinists.

In a letter to his friend Benjamin Rush written after his election, he affirmed his faith: "I am a Christian, in the only sense in which [Jesus] wished anyone to be: sincerely attached to his doctrines in preference to all others, ascribing to himself every human excellence, and believing he never claimed any other."[37] Jefferson's Christianity consisted of several tenets: religion was a private matter between the individual and God; liberty of conscience was a natural right; moral behavior was more important than doctrinal purity; claims of divine revelation must be subjected to the light of reason; and plural religious perspectives should be tolerated in a free, civil society. By contrast, Calvinists adhered to many beliefs antithetical to those of Jefferson: Christianity was a matter of public as well as private concern; theology matters, and religion is more than good works; religious freedom means freedom from error as well as free expression; divine revelation transcends human reason; and pluralism offends the sovereignty of God.

Calvinist ministers used Jefferson's own writings to condemn him as an unfit candidate to lead a Christian nation. In particular they mined his *Notes on the State of Virginia* for damning evidence. They were offended by passages that affirmed what they believed to be a dangerous pluralism. At one point, Jefferson expressed his admiration for Pennsylvania's toleration. "Religion is well supported," he wrote, "of various kinds, indeed, but all good enough; all sufficient to preserve peace and order; or if a sect arises, whose tenets would subvert good morals, a good sense has fair play, and reasons and laughs it out of doors, without suffering the State to be troubled with it."[38] The Calvinists objected to the notion that any religion was as good as another because they subscribed to the idea of one true faith. They found even more offensive Jefferson's statement on religious liberty: "Let every man speak freely without fear; maintain the principles that he believes, worship according to his own faith, either one God, three Gods, no God, or twenty Gods: and let government protect him in so doing."[39] To his detractors, such a sentiment was proof that Jefferson's pluralism made him either a polytheist or an atheist.[40]

Jeffersonian supporters spoke out against such blatant politicization of religion. Tunis Wortman thought that Federalist attacks on Thomas Jefferson's religious beliefs during the presidential campaign of 1800 violated the constitutional principle of separation of church and state. The New York lawyer thought that church and state "should be kept separate and distinct." He warned his fellow Americans not to commingle the two, arguing that "the church will corrupt the state, and the state pollute the church." As an avowed Christian, Wortman believed that the church was by nature "permanent and eternal" and needed no external support to "prop" it up.[41]

John Mitchell Mason, a Presbyterian minister in New York, fired back that to keep religion out of politics was to violate the word of God. He pointed out that the Bible was "full of directions for [Christians'] behaviour as citizens." Scripture directed that the believer "in all your ways acknowledge him," and those "ways" included political affairs. Christians live under the "law of Christ" and therefore have an obligation to speak out against all the "passion and violence, the fraud and falsehood, and corruption which pervade the systems of party." Indeed, he declared, "if our religion had had more to do with our politics; if, in the pride of our citizenship, we had not forgotten our Christianity: if we had prayed more and wrangled less about the affairs of our country, it would have been infinitely better for us at this day."[42]

Wortman and Mason were Protestants and patriots engaged in a debate that would be repeated many times in American history. Each grounded his concern for the young republic's future in a vision of its past that emphasized a distinctive legacy. For Wortman, it was a secular state where popular sovereignty, minority rights, and the rule of law prevailed. As to religion, he deemed Christianity to be important in the lives of individuals and in the nation's culture, but he thought it should exert an indirect influence on public affairs by shaping the morals of citizens. Mason had a different vision, one of a Christian nation created under God's providence, a nation whose well-being depended on its adherence to God's laws. To him, only an active, direct Christian influence on public policy and officials would enable the United States to fulfill its promise as a Christian nation.

Both sides in the presidential contest of 1800 used religion for political advantage. While many of Jefferson's opponents deemed him unfit for high national office because he was an infidel or atheist, at the same time Jeffersonian Republicans made the cynical and inaccurate charge that John Adams was intent on the establishment of a national church in order to bring religious dissenters over to his side. Alexander Hamilton charged Jefferson and his supporters with hyperbolic opposition to the "honest enthusiasm of Religious Opinion," while engaging in their own "Phrenzy of Political fanaticism." Further, Jeffersonians used the rhetoric of "separation of religion and politics" as a tool to silence Congregationalist clergymen who had denounced Jefferson, thus tarnishing the image of Jefferson as the champion of religious and civil liberty.[43]

Jefferson won the election, but in supporting him, most voters did not endorse his religious views. Indeed, his Unitarian beliefs placed him in a small minority outside the mainstream of American Protestants. But though his religious beliefs did not meet with voter approval, his firm commitment to religious freedom did. In particular, the rapidly expanding Baptist denomination supported Jefferson because of their long-standing belief in the separation of church and state. Methodists and New Side Presbyterians, as well as Baptists, feared that New England Calvinists aimed at electing a president and a party that would then do what the Constitution had failed to do, namely, acknowledge the United States as a Christian nation, with "Christian" defined in Calvinist terms. Those evangelical groups were flourishing in the religious marketplace and opposed any interference.

In his postelection analysis, John Adams indicated that voter fears over religion and politics explained his defeat. He blamed the Jeffersonians for casting the election as a vote for either religious orthodoxy or religious liberty. With the factions framed in such stark terms, Adams understood that most voters opted for the latter. He imagined voters as preferring atheists and deists to an establishment designed by New England Calvinists. Ten years after his defeat, he remained sensitive about the public's perception of him as a champion of an official national religion. In 1811, when Benjamin Rush urged him to address the American people on the subjects of religion and morality, Adams declined: "I should be suspected of and charged with an hypocritical . . . attempt to promote a national establishment of Presbyterianism in America; whereas I would as soon establish the Episcopal Church, and almost as soon the Catholic Church."[44] Though a confessing Christian, Adams was not a sectarian. He regarded his religious views as private: "My opinions, indeed, on religious subjects ought not to be of any consequence to any but myself."[45]

The election of 1800 reinforced convictions to which both campaigners had long subscribed: religion and politics do not mix. They detested the nastiness of sectarian strife and the anti-intellectual, craven teachings that characterized too many religious leaders. Adams and Jefferson had been educated in the Enlightenment view that the natural and social worlds operate according to laws that can be understood if rational people apply their God-given reason. Their conception of the world and human society was informed by experience, not by fanciful notions that many religious leaders claimed to be true. Though human knowledge of the world was incomplete and often wrong, the endeavor to fathom nature's laws and harness them for human good was far preferable to the blind acceptance of such "truth" as priests and preachers foisted on their parishioners.

Years after the bitter election and long after the two contestants had buried their political hatchets, Adams and Jefferson reflected on the question of whether religious authority had any place in political affairs. Their answer was no if religion consisted of fearmongering dogmas taught by clerics instead of the noble religion revealed in nature. Perhaps remembering the sectarian attacks of 1800, Adams consigned Calvinist dogmatists to the category of "priests and kings" who rule by "fictitious miracles." He preferred the God of nature who governs the world according to his own laws rather than the fables and superstitions constructed by theologians. If religion is no better than what is often proclaimed and practiced, he wondered aloud the unthinkable: "[T]his would be the best of all possible worlds, if there were no religion in it!!!" Jefferson replied, "[I]f by religion, we are to understand *sectarian dogmas*, in which no two of them agree, then your exclamation . . . is just."[46] Like Adams, Jefferson shuddered at a world without religion, though he also shared with his friend the view that many religious leaders had reduced the Judeo-Christian faith to sectarianism and superstition. He charged them with perpetuating ignorance in the face of advancing knowledge: "The priests of the different religious sects . . . dread the advance of science as witches do the approach of daylight, and scowl on the fatal harbinger announcing the subdivision of the duperies on which they live."[47]

The concerns of Adams and Jefferson notwithstanding, religious leaders continued to exert influence in American politics. Indeed, while the two former presidents exchanged letters, moral questions in the early nineteenth century prompted concerned Protestants to mount new political crusades.

Elusive Protestant Unity: Sunday Mails, Catholic Immigration, and Sectional Division

Lyman Beecher was no supporter of religious pluralism. Rather, the Presbyterian pastor at Litchfield, Connecticut, was a staunch defender of the Standing Order, which recognized orthodox churches like Beecher's as the colony's established churches with public funds appropriated for their maintenance. But for almost thirty years following ratification of the U.S. Constitution, Connecticut Republicans had waged a determined campaign for disestablishment on the grounds that preference for one religious sect violated dissenters' rights of religious liberty. Beecher defended the Standing Order as necessary for ensuring a moral citizenry. He believed that Christianity was the fountain of moral teachings and the surest guarantee of a virtuous America. Further, he believed that religion was too important to be left to voluntary organizations that depended on their members' contributions for sustenance. As a vigorous defender of the status quo, Beecher found himself the target of anticlerical vitriol in a campaign that ended in the 1818 overthrow of the Standing Order. Beecher called it "as dark a day as ever I saw." He added, "the odium thrown upon the ministry was inconceivable. The injury done to the cause of Christ . . . was irreparable."[1]

Upon reflection, however, Beecher soon changed his opinion of disestablishment and became as vigorous a supporter of a free, competitive religious marketplace as he had been an opponent. In an astonishing turnabout, he came to interpret the end of the Standing Order as "*the best thing that ever happened to the State of Connecticut.*" What accounts for such a dramatic change of heart in so brief a time? The short answer: impressive results. Beecher explained that within months of what he called the "political revolution" that removed tax support for churches, revivals broke out and spread over the state. In his words, "[T]he Lord began to pour out his Spirit." As ministers came together for consultation and prayer in support of revival, they became united as never before. Moreover, the political revolution had cut them off from state funding and forced them to look only to God for their financial support. Ministers had previously thought that their "children would scatter like partridges if the tax law was lost." Instead, the effect was "just the reverse of the expectation." The biggest change was in the ministers' industry; they began to preach and build churches with an energy never before seen in the Standing Order. The animosity between established and dissenting congregations evaporated because all were now on the same footing. The new unity manifested itself in a concerted attack against infidels, especially through an evangelical revival that enjoyed widespread support among most denominations.[2]

In 1833, Massachusetts followed Connecticut in disestablishing religion. Now in every state all religious groups operated within the free and competitive religious marketplace. As they interacted with each other as equals, Protestants discovered, or, in some cases, rediscovered, much that they had in common. By the 1830s, Protestants put aside denominational distinctions and joined in a great evangelical movement that expressed itself in revivalism and reform. What bound them together was a commitment to four emphases: reliance on the Bible as ultimate authority, the necessity of the New Birth, activism aimed at improving themselves and society, and the centrality of Christ's redeeming grace.[3] The widespread extent and influence of the evangelical movement led historian Daniel Walker Howe to call Protestant evangelicalism the "functional equivalent of an established church." Fired by their faith that Christ could change individuals and society, evangelicals viewed the nation as a "Christian community, within which members shared moral responsibility."[4]

But alas, the formula for Protestant unity contained the seeds of disunion. In his analysis of religion in the early republic, historian Mark Noll found that by the 1830s the evangelicals' God had become "America's God," but by the 1850s that brief moment of concord was shattered on the shoals of sectionalism.[5] He maintains that while evangelicals remained steadfast in their commitment to biblical authority, they also blended into their theology strains of the secular notions of republicanism and commonsense moral reasoning. Borrowed from England's radical political culture, republicanism defined civic virtue as placing the public good over self-interest in the fight to protect freedom from the overweening power of the royal court. And commonsense moral reasoning, as defined in the Scottish Enlightenment of the eighteenth century, posited an innate moral sense within all persons that, if properly nurtured, would act as a reliable guide in determining right action. This sacred-secular amalgam produced a Protestant synthesis that led to unprecedented unity among Americans. But there was a downside to the amalgamation. Republicanism and commonsense moral reasoning injected American Protestantism with so much individualism and freedom that self-interested parties shattered church unity on the question of slavery.

Northern and Southern Christians crafted rival biblical hermeneutics that suited their respective aims.[6] Thus the questions
of slavery and sectionalism not only split the nation but dashed
the hopes of those like Lyman Beecher who had prayed for
Protestant unity.

This chapter agrees with Noll's argument but contends
that throughout the antebellum period, Protestant unity in
the public square was more illusory than real. It was one thing
to confess faith in a set of widely shared beliefs, but it was
another to translate faith into action. Social changes and
political responses to them confronted Americans with difficult and divisive choices, choices driven by self-interest or sectional allegiance as well as by religious sentiments. For example, one would think that Protestants would be solidly united
on the question of Sunday mail delivery, but in fact they were
divided on the issue. Part of the explanation is a question of
doctrinal emphasis; some stressed the commandment to keep
the Sabbath holy, while others emphasized the sacred right of
freedom of conscience. But differences also surfaced on nonreligious grounds. Some Protestant merchants deemed it a small
thing to accommodate their faith to business exigencies by
allowing their orders and invoices to move without interrup-
tion on Sundays, while others hewed to the literal meaning
of the fourth commandment. Differences on the intractable
question of slavery were even more pronounced. Again, Protestants on both sides of the question found theological and
biblical support for their respective positions. But each side
had so entwined religion and sectionalism that they split apart
over what they deemed to be "sacred" causes, including constitutional rights, free enterprise, and individual liberty. Southern and Northern churches that read the same Bible and
prayed to the same God could not transcend their respective
sectional loyalties.

———

Social Flux and Moral Decay in the New Republic

America was on the move in the opening decades of the new republic, and religious leaders eyed that movement with ambivalence. In the words of historian Robert Wiebe, the first four decades after they won independence represented for the United States an opening occasion, the beginning of its republican experiment; an opening out, the westward expansion that would continue throughout most of the nineteenth century; and an opening up, broader opportunity for individuals untrammeled by artificial constraints such as class. Population growth meant more souls to be won for God's kingdom, but it also meant that existing resources—churches and ministers—would be stretched to the breaking point. At the beginning of the War for Independence, the U.S. population was less than half that of England. But with a growth rate in the early 1800s three times greater than that of England, by 1845 there were five million more Americans than there were English.[7]

Shifting demographics were disturbing to evangelicals and republicans alike. To the former, a godly family was the cornerstone of a godly society. The family was the locus where boys and girls were nurtured in the faith, where they learned to read the Bible, where they were admonished to put biblical precepts into practice, and where sinful behavior was confronted. To republicans, the family took on added significance following independence. As more and more husbands and fathers left home to engage in the rough-and-tumble exchanges of the marketplace and the political arena, "republican" mothers and wives were left with the primary responsibility of inculcating in their children those virtues that were essential for a free and independent society.[8] Thus when tens of thousands of young men and women left home in the early 1800s, moving into the less settled West or into growing cities, evangelicals and republicans were similarly concerned.

In the Puritan imagination, the West represented the wilderness, an uncivilized, unchristian landscape, which, if left untamed, would turn all its denizens into savages. Without the restraints of tight-knit and well-ordered English communities and the admonition of God-fearing ministers and parents, those who wandered into the wilderness could easily revert to a barbarous state of nature. Similarly, cities were alluring traps for innocent young single men and women. Attracted by enticing chances for economic independence, thousands of youth succumbed to licentiousness and immorality in anonymous cities far beyond parental and pastoral supervision.[9]

American democracy in the early republic also broke down many of the surviving Old World mechanisms for ensuring social control, including that of deference to one's social superiors. Deference was a casualty of the American Revolution. By the end of the first third of the nineteenth century, white adult males enjoyed universal suffrage. Veterans of the fight for independence insisted that they were entitled to the full rights of citizens of the country they had fought to preserve. And after freedom was won, they sometimes rose up in rebellion against what they considered to be new encroachments on their natural rights. In 1786, a Revolutionary War veteran, Daniel Shays, led a group of western Massachusetts farmers in a revolt against the state government's attempts to foreclose on their farms. Facing economic difficulties in the postwar recession, the farmers could not pay their taxes—taxes they believed were levied by a legislature in which they were underrepresented. Shays's Rebellion had far-reaching implications, raising concerns among many Americans about whether domestic lawlessness might spread, and, if it did, whether the weak confederation could contain it. Even following the 1788 ratification of the

Constitution, established in part to provide the federal government with powers to ensure domestic tranquillity, rebels continued to defy authority.[10] In 1794, farmers in western Pennsylvania refused to pay federal excise taxes on distilled spirits, prompting President George Washington to send in federal troops to put down the insurrection.[11] And in 1798, German farmers in eastern Pennsylvania led by John Fries, a captain in the Continental Army, attacked tax assessors who were enforcing the federal government's first direct tax on citizens' property; this time it was John Adams who sent in the troops to stop the rebellion.[12]

European visitors noted that Americans were a people who professed a profound religious faith while at the same time acting out of material self-interest. In the early 1830s, the Frenchman Alexis de Tocqueville characterized the United States as an atomized society where individuals pursued their private interests with an "inordinate love of material gratification."[13] He maintained that Americans "universally accepted" the "doctrine of self interest." Further, he asserted, American Christianity had a worldly focus: "Not only do Americans follow their religion out of self interest, but they often place in this world the interest that one can have in following it." What Tocqueville described was the spirit of America's emerging liberal capitalist society, where the pursuit of wealth by free, enterprising individuals was challenging the republican ideals of the Revolutionary era. Under republicanism, the public was best served by virtuous citizens who put the general welfare of society ahead of private gain, while liberal capitalists thought that the public was better served by individuals pursuing private wealth in a free marketplace governed only by the laws of supply and demand. To Tocqueville, American equality produced an awesome economic machine by removing most artificial barriers to enterprise, especially that of social class. But he thought that Americans spent nearly all their energy on material gain, with little left for the refinement of manners and the creation of great works of art.[14]

Frances Trollope was another visitor who toured America and commented on the social cost of American commerce. In 1828, the English novelist and social activist arrived in the bustling western commercial port of Cincinnati, a depot for farm produce from the Northwest Territory destined for transshipment down the Ohio and the Mississippi rivers to New Orleans and world markets. The city had grown almost tenfold in the twenty years prior to her visit and had emerged as a "center of country commerce, steamboat construction, milling, manufacturing, especially pork packing." When Trollope disembarked, she counted fifteen steamboats at the wharf, the only part of Cincinnati that she found to be "noble." She was blinded in large part by what she deemed to be the "total and universal want of manners" among the people. She found them crude and barbaric at table and in conversation.[15]

While Tocqueville and Trollope judged Americans by the standards of European "polite" society and found them lacking refinement, evangelical ministers deemed their behavior to manifest a disturbing decline in morality. They pointed to the alarming increase in alcohol consumption with the accompanying high social costs of drunkenness; they denounced the lewd and licentious behavior of single men and women in cities like New York, where sexual misconduct undermined Christian family values; they decried the expansion of slavery and denounced it as a sin; and they observed how many desecrated the Sabbath by turning what should be a holy day into just another day to pursue worldly gain and pleasure.

For Protestant evangelicals, America's sins were individual transgressions, not structural faults in the liberal capitalism that was beginning to transform the country's economy and the relations between workers and their work. The root cause of sin lay more within the heart of each man and woman than within social and economic arrangements. One could be morally upright whether living under an oppressive king or in a democratic republic, and one could live according to the dictates of Holy Writ in a capitalist marketplace just as saints had obeyed scriptural precepts in the age of feudalism. Indeed, though Protestant ministers sometimes spoke out against individual politicians, they almost never denounced the polity, and while exposing individual acts of greed such as price gouging, they did not attack capitalism. A better, more moral, America would result from godlier leaders and citizens, not from overhauls of the polity and economy. Thus the focus was on redeeming individuals.

For many ministers from Federalist New England, Thomas Jefferson embodied the worst of infidel leaders. After the administrations of the godlike Washington and the upright Puritan Adams, Jefferson was a deist, which to most Protestants was tantamount to being an infidel. The problem with such a person as president, of course, was that his personal disdain for the Christian faith would find expression in public policy. During the presidential campaign of 1800, Federalist ministers had made much of his desecration of the Sabbath, describing him as a man who spent "the Sabbath in feasting, in visiting or receiving visits, in riding abroad, but never going to church." Predictably, Jefferson's disregard for the fourth commandment soon influenced public law. Just after he left office and was succeeded by his handpicked successor and fellow rationalist (if not deist) James Madison, Congress passed a law declaring that the U.S. mail would be moved seven days a week and dictating that all post offices receiving mail had to be open at least one hour a day, including Sundays. To many Protestants, the message was clear: Jeffersonians were more concerned about things of this world than they were about the Kingdom of God. In this case, they deemed it more important to facilitate commerce than to honor God's commandment.[16]

In the minds of some ministers, the root of America's moral decline was clear: Americans had abandoned their Christian heritage. In his July 4 sermon in 1812, Timothy Dwight, president of Yale College, pointed to God's providence in American history. "Look through the history of your country," he invited the students gathered in the Yale College Chapel, and "you will find scarcely less glorious and wonderful proofs of divine protection and deliverance . . . than that which was shown to the people of Israel in Egypt, in the wilderness, and in Canaan." Just as the God of Old Israel brought his chosen people out of Pharaoh's bondage to the Promised Land, so had he wrested the New Israel from King George III's oppression and delivered them into the freedom and independence of the glorious new republic. But, he warned, a people that fail to acknowledge God's providential guidance face his wrath, and though he believed that America was a Christian nation, he regretted that the state created in 1787 was non-Christian:

> We formed our Constitution without any acknowledgment of God; without any recognition of his mercies to us, as a people, of his government, or even of his existence. The [Constitutional] Convention, by which it was formed, never asked, even once, his direction, or his blessing upon their labours. Thus, we commenced our national existence under the present system, without God.[17]

Twenty years later, another minister lamented what he believed was a diabolical milestone in the separation of religion from the public square. In 1833, Massachusetts disestablished the Congregational churches, making it the last state to rid itself of a religious establishment. Many Democrats hailed the event as the long-awaited triumph of complete separation of church and state. Now all the states, as well as the federal government, made religion voluntary by removing government funding for religious institutions. To some Christian ministers, like Jasper Adams, Episcopal priest and president of Charlestown College, separation of church and state was incomprehensible. The argument "that Christianity has no connexion with our civil Constitutions of government, is one of those which admit of being tested by the absurd and dangerous consequences to which they lead." If "Christian morals, Christian sentiments, and Christian principles" were removed as the basis of educating America's youth, then no one should be surprised at the moral decay that would surely follow. Moreover, public officials must be "bound by the sanctions of Christianity" in all their conduct, both public and private, in order to provide the kind of leadership demanded by a Christian nation. As evidence of what followed from the severing of ties between church and state, Adams pointed to the move to make the Sabbath another day for commerce rather than preserving it as a holy day of worship. Behind such desecration was nothing less than infidelity, which, Adams maintained, had followed an insidious course. At first, he wrote, it proceeded with "cautious steps," and then it "put on the decorous garb of rational and philosophical enquiry," led by such luminaries as Franklin and Jefferson, until it now "assumed the attitude of open and uncompromising hostility to every form and every degree of the Christian faith."[18] Reforming the nation's morality, then, was predicated on returning the nation to its Christian foundation, and that meant making the Christian faith the center of public education, a prerequisite for public office, and the touchstone of public law. Adams stopped short of calling for a national ecclesiastical establishment; rather, he supported nonestablishment while advocating a public role for religion as the basis for public ethics.[19]

While many Protestants subscribed to Adams's diagnosis, others offered alternative views. Southern slaveholders, overwhelmingly Protestant, pointed to the growth of industrial capitalism as the root of America's moral decay. Arguing that slavery was a social order grounded in divine sanction, Southern intellectuals pointed out that the slave South provided a framework in which frail human beings could live together in safety "in a manner pleasing to God—with each given according as his work shall be, with each free to serve God in his or her proper station and thereby to prepare for salvation through Christ." By contrast they decried the triumph of capitalism as creating an un-Christian "cruel and morally irresponsible market in human labor-power." If the laws of capitalism were left to work themselves out, the result would be a society locked in a desperate class struggle between the few very rich and the many very poor.[20]

Though a minority, American Catholics tendered their analysis of the country's moral decline. Taking a conservative Christian view, most priests viewed the problem not in terms of political or social interactions, such as the relation between church and state or the struggles between capitalists and laborers, but as an individual issue. That is, they argued, the church has always had to adjust to social arrangements, from feudalism to capitalism, but its primary mission remained the same: the salvation of souls. Thus reform should not be aimed at society but at individuals. Rather than fight against structures that are of this world and therefore ephemeral, individuals should embrace the Christian "ideal of resigning oneself to God's will and to one's position in society." Schoolchildren should be taught stories of "the heroic resignation of early Christian martyrs and other saints" as exemplars of moral rectitude.[21]

———

The "Protestant Establishment"'s
Call for Revival and Reform

Pennsylvania minister Robert Baird set forth the evangelical strategy for reforming American society in his book *Religion in America* (1843). While the church operated outside the government, he believed that the religious voluntarism that prevailed in the United States was the salvation of the American polity. He declared that church and state were separate, but, he added, they were "mutual friends." The church, he contended, asks nothing from government other than "protection of the rights of conscience, and this she receives in the amplest manner." In return, government receives much from the church.

> It receives the immense moral influence of the Church—of the preaching of the Gospel, at so many thousands and tens of thousands of points, all over the land—of the Sabbath School—of the Bible class, and all the other influences of Christianity. It is in these that the laws find their surest basis, and their most effective sanction. It is just because of these influences—the Sabbath, the Church, the Bible—that a vast country of more than twenty-seven millions of people can be governed, and is governed, without the bayonet, and the cannon.[22]

Though most of the time the church's political influence was indirect—changing people rather than policies—it was, nonetheless, powerful.

To be an effective political influence, the church had to represent a sizable constituency, and that meant it had to include in its membership the great masses of Americans. In the early republic, evangelicalism became America's popular religion through what historian Nathan Hatch has characterized as the "democratization" of American Christianity, with Baptists and Methodists taking the lead. As the United States began to define itself after winning independence, Baptists and Methodists were marginal: first, in the sense of their being small, though fast-growing, sects; and second, insofar as they were located primarily along the western edge of the country. But, empowered by American egalitarianism and awakened by the religious revivals that were central to their traditions, Baptists and Methodists moved from the periphery to the center of American religion. According to one estimate, the several denominations comprised by those two churches constituted two-thirds of all Protestant ministers and church members by the middle of the nineteenth century. In 1775, 1,800 ministers served American churches; by 1845 their number had swelled to almost 40,000. At the earlier date, Congregationalists—heirs of the New England Puritan tradition—had twice the number of clergy of any other American church. By 1845, the number of Congregationalist ministers was less than one-tenth that of Methodist clergy.[23]

The astounding growth of populist denominations such as the Baptists and Methodists resulted in a significant shift in religious style, leadership, and authority. Ordinary men and women—the proverbial "common" people—began to play a much more important role by choosing the kind of religion that most appealed to them, and then insisting that those they selected as their ministers remain faithful to what the laity demanded. They preferred leaders from their own middle and working classes who were untainted by formal education; indeed, they were suspicious of those who graduated from leading colleges and paraded their theological erudition. The most profound and lasting change wrought in this mass enterprise of faith was a shift in religious authority from churches led by ministers to those where the laity exercised real power. As a result, the very operation of the religious marketplace changed. As Hatch put it: "These currents insure that churches in this land do not withhold faith from the rank and file. Instead, religious leaders have pursued people wherever they could be found; embraced them without regard to social standing; and challenged them to think, to interpret Scripture, and to organize the church for themselves. Religious populism, reflecting the passions of ordinary people and the charisma of democratic movement-builders, remains among the oldest and deepest impulses in American life."[24] The populist marketplace was a raucous one when viewed in terms of standards of decorum that had prevailed in Puritan New England or Anglican Virginia. Whether the frontier variety, such as the Cane Ridge revival in Kentucky at the beginning of the century, or the awakenings in New York's burned-over district during the 1830s, revivals were noisy affairs. Preaching was aimed at stirring individuals to change their lives by shifting their orientation from Satan to Christ, from the world to eternal life, from sin to salvation. Rather than focusing on doctrine and theology, sermons applied biblical precepts to the individual, making each person in a revival crowd believe that the preacher was speaking directly to him or her. And the competition among revival preachers was such that, to be heard, one had to be innovative, bold, and loud. At Cane Ridge, a number of orators would hold forth simultaneously throughout the encampment, with the laity free to choose among them all.[25] In addition to making joyful noises at revival services, awakeners made religion newsworthy, filling the growing number of newspapers with accounts of the revival's progress.

Evangelical revivalists and reformers during the so-called Second Great Awakening manifested an ecumenical spirit. Led by the laity, Protestant reform initiatives ignored denominational distinctions and theological disputes in an effort to organize Protestants of all sects to work for the moral reform of society. When Charles Grandison Finney, the lawyer-turned-evangelist, arrived in Rochester, New York, in 1830 to begin a series of revival services, he prepared the community for a spiritual awakening by organizing prayer groups that spanned denominational boundaries. Local realtor Bradford King expressed his impatience with "Old Church Hypocrites who think more of their particular denomination than Christ Church." Finney was pleased with the cooperation he observed among Rochester's Protestants, marveling that "Christians of every denomination generally seemed to make common cause, and went to work with a will, to pull sinners out of the fire." In both prayer meetings and formal worship services, "Christians of different denominations," Finney observed, "are seen mingled together in the sanctuary on the Sabbath, and bowing at the same altar in the social prayer meeting."[26]

Evangelicals devised two strategies for reforming individuals and thereby transforming society. First, they promoted revivals aimed at changing people's hearts through spiritual awakening. Second, they organized numerous benevolence societies aimed at promoting moral reform. The revivals that evangelicals sparked first ignited in New York's burned-over district, an area west of Albany rich in a tradition that expected periodic outbursts of God's extraordinary grace, and from there they spread to New England. In part, the awakening was inspired by the First Great Awakening of the mid-eighteenth century. Noting that much of the success of George Whitefield, the first awakening's most dynamic preacher, could be attributed to his being "an innovator," Finney sought new measures to reach mass audiences. Like Whitefield, he took his message to the people rather than waiting for the people to come to ordinary church services. He preached every day of the week, ignored denominational distinctions, and proclaimed the gospel in colorful and engaging rhetoric. Also, like Whitefield, Finney learned that novelty was important in attracting and holding crowds. He wrote in his *Lectures on Revivals of Religion* (1835) that "the object of our measures is to gain attention." Moreover, he was flexible in employing such new measures as newspaper advertising and prerevival publicity. He wrote, "[Y]ou must have something new," a sentiment echoed later in the century by the evangelist Dwight Moody, who declared bluntly, "If one method don't wake them up, let us try another."[27] In his study of the revival in Baltimore, Terry Bilhartz discovered that the revivals were hardly spontaneous eruptions from a populist base. He noted that they were "worked up" by battalions of evangelists who multiplied the opportunities in which people in the community could experience the Great Awakening. He concluded that the demand for religion intensified primarily because of a dramatic increase in the supply thereof.[28]

The revivals of the 1830s were not only evangelical; they were democratic. Indeed, as Daniel Walker Howe argued in his study of religion and politics in the antebellum North, in general, and among Whigs in particular, revivalism and democracy were closely related. Each, Howe wrote, "asserted popular claims against those of the elite, pluralism against orthodoxy, charisma against rationalism, competitiveness against authority, and innovative Americanism against European tradition."[29] As evangelicals became more engaged in politics in the early nineteenth century, they brought with them a determination to reform society; in their view, the best way to achieve that end was to change the hearts of citizens. Only then would behavior change.

The revivals were more than new measures; they offered a new message, one that appealed to a democratic society. Unlike Whitefield and the evangelists of the First Great Awakening,

Finney did not preach such Calvinist tenets as the total depravity of man and the absolute dependence of man on God, who alone could change one's heart. Finney dismissed the notion that salvation was the result of a New Birth in the sense of the convert's receiving a new heart or soul. Rather, it came through the exercise of individual choice.

> A change of heart, then, consists in changing the controling preference of the mind in regard to the end of pursuit. The selfish heart is a preference of self-interest to the glory of God and the interests of his kingdom. A new heart consists in a preference of the glory of God and the interests of his kingdom to one's own happiness. In other words, it is a change from selfishness to benevolence, from having a supreme regard to one's own interest to an absorbing and controling choice of the happiness and glory of God and his kingdom.[30]

In addition to staging revivals to win souls for God's kingdom, evangelicals promoted benevolence societies aimed at producing eternal benefits for men, women, and children. Of course, secular groups also advocated acts of benevolence, but, unlike the Enlightenment concept that "doing good" was an end in itself, the Evangelical idea was that good works should advance the "organized promotion of the Evangelical faith." Accordingly, evangelicals established a number of societies, including the American Bible Society (1816), the American Tract Society (1825), the American Missionary Society (1826), the American Sunday School Union (1817), the American Temperance Union (1826), and the American Prison Discipline Society (1825). The first four had education as their main strategy. By providing Bibles, printed moral tracts, domestic and foreign missionaries, and Sunday Schools for children, Protestants hoped to stem the rising national tide of immorality. In their various methods, each sought to promote individual morality through the spread of God's Word. Other societies, like those promoting temperance and prison reform, targeted specific social ills that plagued the nation.[31]

Through their work in revivals and benevolence societies, evangelicals hoped to reshape the nation's political culture. But on specific moral questions, they became more directly involved in politics. One notable occasion arose in 1810 when Congress passed a law requiring post offices to deliver mail on Sundays.[32] Protestants were united in their reverence for the Sabbath as a holy day set apart by divine commandment. Sabbath keeping had become a political issue in the presidential campaign of 1800 when New England Federalist clergymen made Thomas Jefferson's desecration of the Sabbath a key part of their attack on the Virginian's character. They declared that he preferred to be anywhere on Sundays but in church, singling out one occasion in 1799 when he attended a Fredericksburg reception in his honor on a Sabbath. One commentator noted, "This fact has been trumpeted from one end of the continent to the other as an irrefragable proof of his contempt for the Christian religion and his devotion to the new religion of FRANCE."[33] While one could dismiss the charge as a partisan attack in a heated political campaign, it does serve to underscore that Americans in the early republic expected their elected officials to honor the fourth commandment. At stake was more than obedience to a single dictum; honoring the Sabbath was recognition of biblical authority and the central place of Christianity in American society.

In passing the 1810 law, Congress responded to the commercial interests of businesses that were pushing westward and demanding that the federal government provide the necessary infrastructure for building an integrated, national economy. In 1790, Alexander Hamilton had proposed such an activist government to support economic development, a cry that Henry Clay would take up in the 1820s. For some evangelicals, however, the law requiring Sunday mail delivery violated a higher law. The war that ensued revisited the question of church and state that had been debated in 1787: what was the place of religion in America? On one side were those who argued that America was a Christian nation, and that its citizens must recognize God's law over all else. On the other were those who claimed that supporters of the petition to overturn the 1810 law were attempting to impose their religious views on the nation, and that the government had no voice in such religious matters.

The war comprised two battles. The first raged from 1810 to 1817 and was primarily a conflict of rival petitions. Congress received more than a hundred petitions from partisans on both sides of the question. One petition from a group of Philadelphia Protestants argued that the act would lessen regard for the Sabbath as a holy day. To these petitioners, keeping the Sabbath holy was "the command of God."[34] A New Jersey petition stated the case for repeal in language often employed by the Religious Right of the late twentieth and early twenty-first centuries: "Our Government is a Christian Government, a Government formed and established by Christians and therefore, bound by the Word of God, not at liberty to contravene His laws, nor to act irrespectively of the obligations we owe to Him." Nonetheless, Congress and the postmasters general of the period deemed the U.S. Constitution to be the supreme law of the land and dismissed the religious line of argument. They maintained that the Sunday mails were vital to the "economic lifeblood of the nation."[35]

Having lost the first battle, evangelicals regrouped in 1828 with a well-organized campaign to overturn the law. Spanning denominational boundaries, the General Union for the Promotion of the Christian Sabbath (GUPCS) represented a broad-based coalition demanding that Congress recognize its obligation to ensure that all laws conform to God's law. Led by merchant Josiah Bissel, Jr., and Lyman Beecher, the organization launched an aggressive campaign that included a series of talks railing against the nation's moral decline, printed copies of those talks, and petitions to Congress for repeal. Bissel and a group of evangelical merchants demonstrated their support of repeal by pledging to stop all commercial activity on Sunday. But the political battle again centered on the petition campaign. Between 1828 and 1831, more than nine hundred petitions reached Congress calling for repeal. The central theme was that of America as a Christian nation violating its obligations to obey divine commandments. Typical was a petition from North Carolina asserting that America was "a Christian Community, where all the chartered rights and political institutions, as well as the legislative provisions of the country, recognize the authority of the Christian religion."[36]

Seventh Day Baptists and Universalists led the religious fight against the Sabbatarians. The former took the position that Sunday was a holy day for only some Christians. Therefore, any law making Sunday a holy day was an act that violated the First Amendment by establishing a particular sect over others. Appealing to "Friends of Equal Rights," Baptists attacked "Religious zealots" who lobbied for legislation, like that proposed to terminate the Sunday mails, and who would make it "penal for others of different sentiments to follow out their own honest convictions of duty to God." They appealed to the sentiments expressed by George Washington: he who "conducts himself as a good citizen" is protected in worshiping according to the dictates of his conscience.[37]

Religious groups, however, were not the only lobbyists to influence Congress regarding the Sunday mails. More than two hundred petitions reached the lawmakers from various commercial interests who reminded congressmen of the economic costs associated with delaying such information as market fluctuations. Answering evangelicals who appealed to a higher law, one congressman insisted in a plea to his colleagues that "the first duty of the Government is to protect its citizens in their property." Other defenders of the Sunday mails act interpreted the religious campaign as the "Christian" party's plan to take control of the government and make it conform to their particular religion, a violation of the First Amendment's proscription of any establishment. Richard Johnson of Kentucky, chairman of the Senate Committee on the Post Office and Post Roads, produced in 1829 the Senate's *Report on the Subject of Mails on the Sabbath*. The report argued that Congress had no constitutional authority to stop the Sunday mails on religious grounds because such an action would establish "the principle that the Legislature was a proper tribunal to determine what are the laws of God." Such power went far beyond Congress's constitutional mandate. As Johnson pointed out, Congress was "a civil institution, wholly destitute of religious authority." In his view, if Congress became a forum for the interpretation of divine law, citizens of the United States would join 800 million others in "religious bondage." The Constitution set the United States apart by breaking with the dangerous historical precedent of allowing religion to interfere with government and vice versa. Besides, he contended, Sunday mails bring the gospel to people all over the country through tracts whose publishers were often among those petitioning Congress to stop their delivery on the Sabbath. Finally, the report affirmed the position that America is not a Christian state: "The Constitution regards the conscience of the Jew as sacred as that of the Christian, and gives no more authority to adopt a measure affecting the conscience of a solitary individual than that of a whole community." In other words, religion is a matter between the individual and God, and, therefore, the "line cannot be too strongly drawn between church and state."[38]

As did the first, the second campaign to stop Sunday postal delivery failed. However, technology soon did what moral suasion could not; the telegraph and railroads meant that commercial information could flow seven days a week without the delivery of mail on Sundays. By midcentury, individual postmasters were stopping Sunday mails, and after the Civil War Sunday mails ceased altogether.[39] The campaign illustrated the fact that evangelicals were largely a united force and were able to mobilize a nationwide effort that transcended theological and denominational differences. It also suggested that a religious attempt to establish the nation's moral obligations was sure to meet with stiff opposition from secular and material interests. As the antirepeal petitioners made clear, opposition did not mean opposition to religion; rather, it meant a rejection of that particular religious interpretation.

The failure of the campaign to stop Sunday mail delivery was due, in large part, not to evangelicals' lack of effort or organization, but to the laissez-faire attitude that prevailed in Jacksonian America. Andrew Jackson won election by declaring to farmers and workers—"ordinary" Americans—that many of their problems stemmed from public policies enacted by and for a small, privileged group of financiers and industrialists. He waged war on the national bank, high tariffs, and federally funded internal improvements that he viewed as government largesse for the wealthy few. He embraced the liberal notion that the state existed primarily to protect property, otherwise leaving individuals free to pursue their own interests according to their own ingenuity and enterprise. That same attitude extended to the relation between church and state. Jackson's comments on the subject sum up the stance of the Democratic Party. In a June 12, 1832, letter to a group of Presbyterians who had petitioned for a day of "fasting, humiliation, and prayer," he explained his rejection of the plea by articulating his aversion to "disturb[ing] the security which religion nowadays enjoys in this country in its complete separation from the political concerns of the General Government."[40] A Presbyterian and professing Christian, Jackson nonetheless thought that government had no business involving itself in religious matters.

The Supreme Court, however, acknowledged a link between religion and public affairs. In *Vidal v. Girard's Executors* (1844) Justice Joseph Story acknowledged that Christianity was part of the common law in dispute. The case arose when the relatives of a philanthropist who endowed a boys' school in Philadelphia tried to overturn the provision that no clergyman of any denomination should ever teach there. Girard denied that he intended the clause as an "insult to Christianity"; rather, he meant to protect students' "tender minds" from competing theological claims. When the case reached the U.S. Supreme Court, Daniel Webster represented the plaintiffs and gave an impassioned defense of America as a Christian nation. He declared that nothing was more certain than "this general principle, that Christianity is part of the law of the land." He asserted that "general, tolerant Christianity, is the law of the land." Writing the majority opinion for the defendant, Justice Story agreed with Webster that Christianity was part of Pennsylvania law, but he contended that that law came with "attendant personal liberties," including that of allowing charitable institutions to operate without any religious influence.[41]

Protestant Unity Shattered

While Protestants disagreed among themselves in the fight over Sunday mails, their differences were largely a matter of emphasis. They remained the overwhelming religious influence in the republic. However, two other movements threatened Protestant unity and influence. The first was the arrival in the 1840s and 1850s of more than a million Catholic immigrants, mainly from Ireland. Though they represented only about 5 percent of the U.S. population, Catholics constituted a large enough presence to spark a nativist reaction by religionists and nonreligionists alike. Anti-Catholic sentiments arrived in North America with the first Protestant settlers in the seventeenth century, but the small number of Catholics posed little direct threat to Protestant hegemony. That began to change with the arrival of large numbers of Catholics in the nineteenth century. In a series of articles published under the name "Brutus," Samuel F. B. Morse, who would win fame as the inventor of the telegraph, fanned nativist and anti-Catholic sentiments. Morse spun a conspiracy theory of a Vatican plot to take control of the United States by encouraging Catholic immigration and then mobilizing Catholic voters.[42] Morse's *Foreign Conspiracy Against the Liberties of the United States* appeared in 1835 and was followed in the same year by Lyman Beecher's history of Catholic depredations, entitled *The Papal Conspiracy Exposed.* During the next year appeared the first of several salacious works that found a ready market among Protestants who were certain that more went on behind convent walls than prayer and meditation. The most infamous was Maria Monk's *Awful Disclosures of the Hotel Dieu Nunnery,* a best seller that sold more than 300,000 copies.

Many evangelicals expressed concern about Catholic influence on American republican values and institutions. Aligned primarily with the Whigs, who were more receptive to moral legislation than was the Democratic Party, many religious groups adopted a nativist perspective toward Catholic immigrants. The editor of the Cleveland *Express* voiced the view of many in the city, where by 1860 half of the residents were foreign-born: "Roman Catholics, whose consciences are enslaved, . . . regard the King of Rome—the Pope—as the depository of all authority." Catholic attitudes and behavior reinforced the view that good Catholics could not be good republicans. Catholics objected to the use of Protestant versions of the Bible in public instruction and to evangelical restrictions of European customs relating to drinking and recreation on the Sabbath. For their part, Democrats welcomed Catholics into the party. A Michigan editor summed up their view: "We regard a man's religious belief as concerning only himself and his Maker." To Whigs, such an attitude was reprehensible; as they saw it, the Democratic Party had embraced but one more evil, adding to its immoral embrace of rum and slavery a fondness for Papistry.[43]

Far from constituting a concerted, organized threat to the United States, Catholic immigrants were divided over the relationship between Catholics and their new country. New York's Bishop John Hughes represented those who concluded that Catholics should pursue a separatist stance, removing themselves from the dominant culture. He first lobbied against the introduction of anti-Catholic books and Protestant Bibles in public schools, and when that effort failed, he demanded tax dollars to form schools that would accommodate Catholics. When that, too, failed, he became the champion of separatists by leading the development of a parochial school system.[44]

Far more menacing to Protestants were those Catholics who called on their fellow believers to catholicize America. Orestes Brownson, a layman who published *Brownson's Quarterly Review*, was the leading spokesman for this position, which to nativists seemed to be the incarnation of Morse's prophecy. Brownson argued that only the Catholic Church could serve as a mediating power between the competing interests of multiple sects and the state in a true democracy. Echoing a popular theme of the day, he agreed that it was America's manifest destiny to be the ideal Christian nation, but in his vision a strong American Catholic Church that inspired the allegiance of a majority of Americans would fulfill the country's true destiny. He contended, "The American system recognizes only the catholic religion." While in that instance he used "catholic" in its connotation of "universal," he became more partisan when he declared, "Catholics are better fitted by their religion to comprehend the real character of the American constitution." He urged Catholic immigrants to assimilate and work for the conversion of their Protestant countrymen.[45] Needless to say, Brownson's call for Catholics to become active in American politics stoked the fires of anti-Catholicism.

Anti-Catholicism became politicized in the mid-1850s with the emergence of the Know-Nothing Party. Fueled by nativist resentment of Irish immigrants, the party exploited the deep-seated and long-standing hatred of Catholics among American Protestants. Certainly not all Protestants rallied to the Know-Nothing standard, but the party did institutionalize anti-Catholic sentiment. The Know-Nothing Party itself, however, was a casualty of what came to be the most pressing issue of the day: the question of the extension of slavery beyond the South.

While the Protestant majority withstood the challenge of Catholicism, it succumbed to the second threat, that of sectionalism. Although, in Lincoln's words, Protestants in the North and South "read the same Bible," they arrived at different interpretations of how Christians should respond to the question of slavery. Southerners pointed to passages that sanctioned slavery and concluded that because the Bible was the "supreme divine authority," faithful Christians must accept the legitimacy of slavery in the United States. Radical abolitionists admitted that scripture sanctioned slavery, but their response was to abandon the Bible in order to attack what they believed was a diabolical institution. More moderate interpretations differentiated between the letter and the spirit of the Bible, pointing out that throughout scripture moral principles condemned slavery. Moreover, the presence of slavery in the biblical narrative was no justification for slavery in the United States.[46]

Protestants were divided on the question of abolitionism that surfaced in the 1830s. Some saw slavery as a sin in the eyes of God. One abolitionist in the 1830s minced no words: slavery is "a sin—always, everywhere, and only a sin." Another insisted on calling slavery "by its *right name*, Robbery." While agreeing that slavery was an evil, abolitionists were divided over the proper course of action to eradicate it. Some groups, like the Disciples of Christ, advocated a gradualist approach based on a literal interpretation of the Bible. While denouncing the cruel practices of slavery, Disciples leader Alexander Campbell declared that "the Scriptures did not condemn slaveholding as sinful," and therefore he rejected any form of church discipline against slave masters. Other gradualists maintained that only God could eliminate the sin of slavery, and he would do so in his own time. Some went so far as to admonish Christians to wait until the Second Coming, when Christ would remove all sources of humanity's "inherent imperfections." Protestants who fought for the immediate emancipation of all slaves were prepared to use any means necessary. By the 1840s, many became involved in political action, supporting Free Soil Party and Liberty Party candidates and eventually becoming Radical Republicans. They called on fellow Protestants to express their faith at the ballot box: "Vote as you Pray and Pray as you vote."[47]

Like most of the political parties of the 1840s and 1850s, evangelicals tried to ignore the divisive question of slavery. Speaking for the revivalist wing of evangelicalism, Charles Finney viewed the revival as the primary means of the nation's moral salvation, and he feared that any diversion, especially that of the antislavery campaign, would undermine that mission. Though he opposed Ohio's harshly discriminatory Black Codes and later became an ardent supporter of the Radical Republicans, Finney was unwilling to allow abolitionism to detract from the evangelical revival that he led. One critic noted, "He has long professed to be an antislavery man, but *Revivalism* is his hobby [obsession], and when mounted upon that he always forgets the slave."[48] If fighting slavery could be made an arm of the revival, Finney was for it; if not, then it should not be allowed to interfere with the revival's progress.

Though some revivalists became ardent abolitionists, generally northern Protestants were slow to embrace the antislavery movement, and, indeed, most never did. J. Miller McKim, a revivalist-turned-reformer, observed that two or three years before he joined the antislavery cause, "people's attention was directed with unusual earnestness to the subject of personal religion." Abolitionist James Birney was blunt in his criticism of Protestants in regard to slavery; he called the churches the "bulwarks of American slavery." Judge William Jay voiced a similar sentiment: "the American Church . . . [is] the great buttress of American slavery."[49]

Evangelicals' stance toward the greatest moral crusade of the day bears closer examination because it is a position that recurs in American history. Why would evangelicals sit on the sidelines or even impede the progress of a campaign to free men and women from the bondage of slavery? First, Finney's reply suggests that revivalists deemed individual salvation more important than social reform. Such a view is based on the conviction that salvation is a matter of eternal importance, while social reform has to do with ephemeral worldly concerns. Second, for evangelicals, the major focus of history is the progress of the gospel, not political and social developments. A hundred years earlier, Jonathan Edwards had traced the extraordinary saving "Work of God" through its signal moments, beginning with the outpouring of the Holy Spirit at Pentecost and advancing through the Protestant Reformation and on to the Great Awakening in America. Those were the noteworthy events of history for revivalists. Thus, in that tradition, the revival of the 1830s transcended the reform movement, even though many evangelicals participated in both. Third, evangelicals taught that God's grace liberated the souls of men and women regardless of their social condition. Christians, they pointed out, flourished during Roman opposition, and Puritans thrived even as the Stuart monarchs tried to "harry" them out of England. Similarly, benighted slaves could be liberated from sin through believing in Jesus Christ while remaining in chains.

For Southern evangelicals, theology was thoroughly enmeshed with sectional culture. In the early 1800s, some Southern evangelicals spoke out against slavery, but by the 1850s, as sectional tensions increased, they became vocal defenders of slavery as a "sacred cause."[50] They rationalized that freedom depended on order, and the slave system provided that order. Regardless of one's condition in society, he or she could find salvation and solace by submitting to God's will, a perfect will that decreed the worldly condition of both masters and servants while promising eternal life to all. Moreover, Southern evangelicals "took great comfort in the Bible's demonstrable justification of slavery." While abolitionists strained to show how slavery violated such biblical abstractions as justice and freedom, pro-slavery evangelicals readily found specific evidence that Jesus, at least implicitly, condoned the slave society of his day.[51]

The debate over slavery and its spread shattered the Protestant consensus in America. Northern and Southern Christians exchanged sectional as well as theological barbs in the religious marketplace. Protestants in the both the North and the South blurred the lines between religious and sectional loyalties. Philip Slaughter, editor of a religious periodical in the Confederacy, reminded writers that all submissions must pass one test: "loyalty to the Confederate flag." Religious publications described the Southern cause as just, holy, and righteous. Preachers and editors "pointed to a special relationship with God for the Confederacy." In language similar to that of preachers calling on people to follow Christ, religious editors urged men to support the Confederate cause. And they elided distinctions between Christianity and civic liberty, declaring that fighting for the South was fighting for both faith and freedom. Another religious editor, C. C. Gillespie, elevated the Southern cause to a pinnacle in sacred history. "It is not often," he wrote, "in the history of the world that such great criseses [*sic*], involving the very fundamental elements of truth, conscience, and manhood, are allowed by Divine Providence to occur. . . . Such was the position of the Hebrew nation in the midst of the Gentile world; such was the position of the martyr church of Christ. . . . Such is our position now."[52]

While Northern and Southern Protestants castigated one another as enemies of Christ and violators of God's laws, both groups interpreted the Civil War as the result of a nation's turning its back on God. Southerners blamed Northern commercial interests for blaspheming God by waging war against the Sabbath. South Carolina Methodist Rev. Whiteford Smith claimed that the Civil War was a war for a new national agenda. In his view, the adoption of the secular motto *E pluribus unum*, one from many, signified a union in "direct opposition to the 'order of God.'" God prevented humanity from joining together at the tower of Babel by confusing the tongues of men, and today, he added, "God obstructs us through war." Smith saw the hand of Divine Providence at work "to prevent a reconstruction of our former Union. . . . It has now been demonstrated that we are two peoples, essentially and forever separate." His aim, then, was two nations "under God."[53]

Northern Protestants also saw the war as God's judgment against a nation that had turned its back on its divine origins. Representatives of eleven Protestant denominations supported the National Reform Association's drive to amend the U.S. Constitution with an explicit statement acknowledging America to be a Christian nation under God's sovereignty. Known as the "Sovereignty of God" or "Christian" amendment, it was aimed at revoking the "un-Christian political doctrines espoused by some of the Founding Fathers," doctrines—such as popular sovereignty—that had led to anarchy, revolution, and secession. Connecticut Congregational pastor Horace Bushnell reminded Americans that any polity, including the United States, is "a grand providential order," declarations to the contrary notwithstanding. The amendment failed in large part because of widespread sentiments among Christians that the founders had been right in separating church and state, and the proposed amendment threatened the guarantee of religious liberty for all. Nonetheless, religious sentiment found expression in other ways. For the first time, the phrase "In God We Trust" was engraved on coins, and the Christian observance of Thanksgiving became a national holiday.[54]

On the question of sectionalism and the expansion of slavery, American Christians broke fellowship with each other in the name of regional interests. Beginning with Presbyterians in 1838 and followed by Methodists in 1844 and Baptists in 1845, evangelical churches divided over the sectional conflict, setting the stage for the spectacle of Christians killing Christians in the Civil War. And each piously declared that its way was the righteous cause that God would bless. Southern Baptists, for example, emphasized their loyalty to the South rather than their commitment to Christian unity. In public, at least, they rarely "wavered in their certainty that God was on the side of the Confederacy." Commingling secular notions of states' rights and property rights, they accused Northerners, again including Northern Baptists, of subverting Southern constitutional rights.[55] Northerners, including Baptists, accused Southerners of placing the interest of the "Slave Power" above that of the Kingdom of God. Abraham Lincoln voiced skepticism that either side enjoyed the moral ground that each claimed, or that either merited divine favor for its cause. In his second inaugural address (1865), he wrote, "Both read the same Bible and pray to the same God, and each invokes his aid against the other. It may seem strange that any men should dare to ask a just God's assistance in wringing their bread from the sweat of other men's faces, but let us judge not that we be not judged."[56]

If the United States enjoyed a de facto Protestant establishment at the beginning of the new republic, at the end of the Civil War that establishment lay shattered. Moreover, the commingling of Protestantism with secular notions of individualism, pluralism, and sectionalism further weakened any religious voice raised in judgment of national morality. In the fifty years following the Civil War, a new gospel based on the accumulation of wealth offered a compelling message to industrial America.

The "Gospel of Wealth" and the "Social Gospel": Industrialization and the Rise of Corporate America

In the fifty years following the Civil War, industrialization transformed the United States' economy, society, and culture. The increase in productivity was astounding, vaulting the country from a fourth-rate economy to the world's leading industrial power by World War I, with a GNP that surpassed that of Britain, Germany, and France combined. Not only was productive capacity increased; industrialization changed the way that Americans did business, giving rise to big business in the form of large corporations and trusts that mobilized huge amounts of capital and employed thousands of workers. At the same time, the workplace changed for millions of wage earners; in fact, the census of 1890 indicated that the nation's workforce had shifted from being predominantly agricultural to predominantly industrial. Moreover, industrialization was accompanied by urbanization, with cities acting as magnets for capital and labor. By 1920, for the first time, more Americans lived in cities than in the countryside. Millions of immigrants from southern and eastern Europe and from East Asia arrived to work in the nation's factories, mills, refineries, and expanding transportation networks. And with them came religious and cultural baggage that would challenge the dominant Anglo-Saxon, Protestant culture.

Mark Twain labeled the period the Gilded Age.[1] On the surface, it was a time of dazzling brilliance, manifested by the glittering wealth of those industrial magnates who made fortunes from steel, oil, railroads, finance, and shipping. These captains of industry were heralded for their enterprise and ingenuity in exploiting the great opportunities offered by a free market that rewarded their entrepreneurial ventures. Anyone, it was said, could succeed if government continued its laissez-faire stance toward the marketplace and allowed the laws of supply and demand to operate freely. Andrew Carnegie epitomized the rags-to-riches possibilities, arriving in the United States the child of poor Scottish immigrants and rising to become the wealthiest man in America.

But, as Twain pointed out, the Gilded Age's golden surface masked a dark and miserable underside of social inequities, wrenching poverty, and political corruption. While the nouveaux riches flaunted their wealth in lavish living at palatial homes located at Newport, Rhode Island, and other spots far removed from filthy, overcrowded cities, their workers were packed into cheaply built tenements designed for a fraction of the number actually living in them. Further, the government was hardly laissez-faire at all, favoring bosses over workers. Though industrialists used such devices as interlocking directorates and trusts to reduce competition, courts interpreted antitrust legislation to undermine the power of labor organizations while virtually ignoring the industrial monopolies crafted by men like John D. Rockefeller. Immigrants turned to local "bosses," like New York mayor William Marcy Tweed, whose extralegal interventions on behalf of poor workers came at the price of their unquestioning electoral support in maintaining them in power.

The Gilded Age altered America's predominantly Protestant religious marketplace. Immigration swelled the ranks of Catholics, so that by one estimate, at century's end the number of Catholics in the United States outnumbered the combined membership of the top five Protestant denominations. Though a much smaller number, Jewish immigrants also made their presence known in American cultural and intellectual life. Further, new homegrown religions such as Jehovah's Witnesses (1872), Christian Science (1879), and Pentecostalism (1906) added to the nation's religious pluralism. A growing challenge to religious leaders of all stripes was that posed by the therapeutic promise of a consumer culture that offered a sort of secular salvation, promising that consumption could satisfy one's need for self-actualization. That same culture, however, offered new means for evangelicals and other proselytizing sects to convey their messages to large numbers of prospective members. Supported by such commercial allies as department store entrepreneur John Wanamaker, evangelist Dwight Moody proved the power of merchandising in promoting religious revival.

Americans viewed the Gilded Age through a gospel lens—indeed, three different gospel lenses. First, some offered a triumphant, market-affirming view through the gospel of wealth, popularized by Andrew Carnegie. This perspective, shared by many Christian ministers and laypersons alike, saw the free marketplace and the wealth it made possible as an expression of Christianity itself. Indeed, one enthusiast who praised the new corporate order portrayed Jesus as the prototypical corporate magnate. The gospel of wealth called for a continuation of the laissez-faire approach to government, positing that market-driven individuals, not political action, would continue to bring good things to the truly deserving. A second gospel voice was that of evangelists proclaiming the old-fashioned gospel calling on individuals to repent of their sins and follow Christ as their personal savior. Shoe-salesman-turned-revivalist Dwight L. Moody was the best-known representative of this Bible-based message that paid far more attention to sinful individuals than to an unjust society. Christ was the answer to the problems of the Gilded Age as he had been in all ages. Relying on God's grace, revivalists engaged in politics only in narrowly defined moral issues, such as the ongoing fight for temperance laws and for a ban on Sunday mails. The third gospel, the social gospel, offered a harsh critique of the Gilded Age, castigating its leaders as robber barons whose quest for personal wealth and power knew no moral boundaries. They criticized a society that allowed a few individuals to enjoy a disproportionate share of the nation's bounty while relegating the masses to lives of want and misery. Baptist minister Walter Rauschenbusch and other social gospelers believed that societies as well as individuals should conform to Christian principles. Accordingly, they became social activists in seeking remedies for problems of poverty, workplace injustice, and government corruption. Many joined forces with the Progressive movement, which sought political remedies to reform society, beginning with local communities. More radical social gospelers advocated the jettisoning of liberal capitalism altogether in favor of Christian socialism.

This chapter explores these diverse critiques of the Gilded Age and their corresponding solutions. It examines the shifting boundaries between religious and material interests, especially the tension between biblical commandments to serve God and one's neighbors and market demands to maximize profits. It concludes that while the old-fashioned gospel reigned supreme during revivals and the social gospel represented the nation's conscience, the gospel of wealth became America's gospel during market hours and in corporate boardrooms.

The Gospel of Wealth

The Puritan architects of the "City upon a Hill" warned against a preoccupation with the accumulation of wealth and the love

77

of riches. One was to pursue his or her vocational calling with industry and was to practice frugality in husbanding one's resources. While personal wealth could be an indication of God's favor, it was also fraught with moral snares, including pride, worldliness, and covetousness. Good Puritans needed to be reminded that theirs was a spiritual, not a material, "errand into the wilderness."[2]

In 1776, Americans reflected on the relation between individual wealth and republican virtue. Though the wealthy no longer bore much of the old Puritan stigma, how one gained wealth was a matter of concern. For Thomas Jefferson, there was a moral hierarchy of vocations, with agriculture being the most moral and manufacturing the least. Farmers were independent producers who worked with their hands and relied only on their own labor and God's bounty for their livelihoods. While others, like Alexander Hamilton, hoped that the United States would follow Britain and become a great manufacturing nation, Jefferson warned that industrialization brought more liabilities than benefits. He asserted that manufacturing would debase workers by making them permanent wage earners dependent upon industrialists for their livelihoods. As a republican, he believed that political independence rested on economic independence; if an individual depended on another for his daily bread, he might vote in his employer's interest rather than voicing his own preference.[3]

Jefferson also identified industrialization with another evil: cities. Factories were located predominantly in cities that could supply their workforce as well as provide access to shipping and marketing services. Cities disrupted the family that had, from early English settlement, served as the model of civic life. New England Puritans had conceived of the nation as the family writ large, a close-knit community of Christians devoted to each other and to God, living together under godly rulers. Cities siphoned off from the countryside surplus laborers, including young sons and daughters, and poured them into overcrowded, anonymous neighborhoods that promoted licentiousness. Recognizing parental fears, early New England industrialists had provided closely supervised dormitories for young female textile workers who moved to the mill towns on the Merrimack. The weekly regimen included Bible study and church services. However, evils of the city overcame virtue. First, the girls grew rebellious when mill owners reduced their wages while increasing production. When the owners replaced the striking girls with poor Irish immigrants, the limits of paternalism became clear; the factory existed for the benefit of the industrialists, not the workers. Second, industrialists realized that they could play one group of marginalized Americans off against another for their economic benefit. Religion and morality did not matter. Irish Catholics, if desperate enough, would work under conditions rejected by New England Protestants.[4]

The Gilded Age brought to fruition all the evils that Puritans and Jeffersonians feared: unrestrained greed, massive wealth, unequal distribution of riches, vicious cities, and corrupt politics. Mark Twain satirized the age in *The Gilded Age: A Tale of Today* (1873), ridiculing swaggering industrialists and venal congressmen who combined their wealth and power for personal gain, often at the expense of the public. Speaking through the fast-talking, ever-scheming Colonel Sellers, Twain gave voice to the "get rich quick" mentality that fired the imagination of aspiring capitalists all over the country. Sellers regaled the young and impressionable Washington Hawkins with a string of schemes all designed to net millions in a short time. Sellers had "made and lost two or three moderate fortunes" but at the moment was in a state of poverty. The colonel had the younger man salivating with the following "sure-fire" plan:

> I have a small idea that may develop into something for us both, all in good time. Keep your money close and add to it. I'll make it breed. I've been experimenting (to pass away the time,) on a little preparation for curing sore eyes—a kind of concoction nine-tenths water and the other tenth drugs that don't cost more than a dollar a barrel. . . . I'm progressing, and before many weeks I wager the country will ring with the fame of Eschol Sellers' Infallible Imperial Oriental Optic Liniment and Salvation for Sore Eyes—the Medical Wonder of the Age!

He reckoned that the medicine would sell in two sizes, for fifty cents and one dollar, respectively, and the bigger size would cost only seven cents to produce. He told Washington that they would sell ten thousand bottles in their native Missouri alone, and by the third year one million bottles in the United States. But the real money would come from Asia, because "in the Oriental countries people swarm like the sands of the desert."[5]

In addition to showing how capitalist schemes redefined the American Dream, Twain also suggested that profitable enterprises depended upon the purchase of political influence. One of Sellers's projects was the "Columbus River Slack-Water Navigation Company"; Sellers had encouraged an honest but naive engineer by the name of Brierly to invest in and manage this enterprise. On a visit to the company headquarters on Wall Street, Brierly discovered that the business did not operate as he had expected. After being congratulated by the president of the company, who acknowledged the "gratifying progress" that the engineer had made on the project, Brierly learned that instead of receiving additional capital for his productivity, he was personally liable for thousands, including funds due workers whose wages were in arrears. The president explained that the funds Congress had appropriated to initiate the project had been spent, not on operations as Brierly had thought, but on bribes to congressmen. Each member of the House Committee demanded $10,000; $20,000 went to the chairmen of a couple of other key committees, and $10,000 to a "female lobbyist." The president explained that he had to pay additional funds to "a high moral Congressman or Senator here and there," adding that "the high moral ones cost more, because they give tone to a measure."[6]

Indeed, in Twain's Gilded Age, morality and religion were instruments employed to win appropriations. Capitalists who visited Washington in pursuit of funds for various projects learned that their support of Sunday schools and attendance at temperance meetings brought a "great moral influence" to a cause, resulting in "the weightiest of friends flock[ing] to its standard." Of course, businessmen plied congressmen with food and drink to ensure favorable treatment. The president of the Columbus River scheme advised Brierly to "write up our little internal improvement for a religious paper of enormous circulation." He said that wrapping the scheme in a shroud of piety would go a long way toward getting religious folks to buy bonds. He explained, "Your religious paper is by far the best vehicle for a thing of this kind, because they'll 'lead' your article and put it right in the midst of the reading matter; and if it's got a few Scripture quotations in it, and some temperance platitudes and a bit of gush here and there about Sunday Schools, and a sentimental snuffle now and then about 'God's precious ones, the honest hard-handed poor,' it works the nation like a charm, my dear sir, and never a man suspects that it is an advertisement." The president recommended placing the article in metropolitan religious newspapers "that know how to serve God and make money at the same time."[7] Clearly, Twain saw a cozy link between American Christianity and American capitalism of the day.

Unlike Twain, Jefferson, and the Puritans, Andrew Carnegie regarded the amassing of great wealth as a virtue. Raised a Presbyterian but in maturity a skeptic and agnostic, Carnegie embraced the tenets of social Darwinism. Instead of subscribing to the Bible as his moral guide, particularly such doctrines as original sin and eternal damnation, he believed that human societies, like nature itself, were subject to the operation of evolutionary laws by which some—the fittest—bore the responsibility and privilege of using their superior talents to lead society. The result would be social progress and economic prosperity.[8] Carnegie published his thoughts on social Darwinism in the *Gospel of Wealth* (1889), an essay on the new economic relations brought about by industrialization that lauded the changes as progress. He acknowledged that the new industrial order created a social caste system with a few very rich people at the top of society and masses of underpaid workers at the bottom. However, he viewed the new arrangement as an advancement of human progress, far better than the universal squalor that prevailed throughout much of history. Besides, the benefits were great. He claimed that the "law of competition" was responsible for the nation's "wonderful material development, which brings improved conditions in its train." Carnegie, sounding like a preacher but citing a different text, called on men and women to conform to the new gospel: "But, whether the law be benign or not, we must say of it, . . . It is here; we cannot evade it; no substitutes for it have been found; and while the law may be sometimes hard for the individual, it is best for the race, because it insures the survival of the fittest in every department."[9] He extolled industrial capitalism under laissez-faire government as conformity with the natural order; with the fittest in charge, all of society benefits, albeit with evident inequalities.

Some Christians developed their own versions of the gospel of wealth. In 1894, Randolf Rock of the United Brethren Church argued that material wealth, manifested primarily through imposing church buildings, could lend new churches the prestige they needed to succeed in the competitive religious marketplace. Appealing to "the law of Christian and business economics," Rock preached a message of "success" and "victory" that would be readily displayed in a church whose grandeur would set it apart from others in the community. Recognizing that in the Gilded Age, wealth and the appearance of wealth were the marks of progress, he declared, "A good church house in a community is a great promoter of evangelistic success."[10] His message was clear: churches would do well to emulate successful corporations.

In a more explicit endorsement of the gospel of wealth, other Christians maintained that individuals should as a matter of Christian duty pursue the accumulation of wealth. Russell Conwell, a Philadelphia Baptist minister, unapologetically urged Christians to become rich; his popular lecture, "Acres of Diamonds," was delivered more than five thousand times between 1900 and 1925. In a reversal of the Puritan attitude toward wealth, Conwell declared, "I say that you ought to get rich, and it is your duty to get rich." He explained the link between money and piety to those who argued that Christianity was primarily about spiritual matters:

> Of course there are some things higher than money. Oh yes, I know by the grave that has left me standing alone that there are some things in this world that are higher and sweeter and purer than money. Well do I know there are some things higher and grander than gold. Love is the grandest thing on God's earth, but fortunate the lover who has plenty of money. Money is power,

money is force, money will do good as well as harm. In the hands of good men and women it could accomplish, and it has accomplished, good.[11]

Perhaps the most enthusiastic Christian promoter of the gospel of wealth was advertising executive Bruce Barton, who depicted Jesus as a first-century Andrew Carnegie. The son of a Congregational minister, in 1925 Barton published *The Man Nobody Knows*, an account of Jesus recast in the Gilded Age. While some criticized the power and wealth of corporations in early twentieth-century America, Barton praised corporations and those who built and ran them. He claimed that Jesus began his public ministry as an obscure man who rose to eminence because of "his wonderful power to pick men." In a success tale rivaling Horatio Alger's popular rags-to-riches stories of the day and Andrew Carnegie's biography, Barton portrayed the gospel as Jesus' phenomenal rise:

> a poor boy, growing up in a peasant family, working in a carpenter shop; gradually feeling his powers expanding, beginning to have an influence over his neighbors, recruiting a few followers, suffering disappointments and reverses, finally death. Yet building so solidly and well that death was only the beginning of his influence! Stripped of all dogma this is the grandest achievement story of all![12]

While some endorsed the gospel of wealth as an expression of Christianity, others pointed out that it inspired a new morality that challenged religious faith. The Gilded Age promoted a consumer culture that turned the Protestant work ethic on its head. The Puritan ethic extolled self-denial; one should work hard and save his or her money. One should avoid temptations of ephemeral earthly treasures and, instead, rely on God to provide eternal heavenly treasures. But by the end of the nineteenth century Americans found desirable therapeutic value in consumer goods that they could acquire. The most successful industrialists displayed their "conspicuous consumption" in huge country homes like Cornelius Vanderbilt's 250-room Biltmore estate situated on 125,000 acres in North Carolina's Blue Ridge Mountains. Their parties were widely reported in accounts that portrayed the good life in material terms: expensive gowns, sumptuous feasts, and diamond favors. Advertisers began to peddle wares more as means of self-improvement than as mundane practical commodities. Soap was no longer just a cleansing product used in personal hygiene; it enhanced sexual attraction. In 1911, Woodbury Soap launched its "The skin you love to touch" campaign in the *Ladies' Home Journal*, perhaps the first time sex appeal found expression in advertising. The consumer culture promised beauty and happiness and fulfillment in the expanding marketplace, and it required only a purchase.

Proponents of the gospel of wealth were not political activists; they did not have to be in an age of laissez-faire government. Some championed the idea that the free market was a natural institution ordained by God and, if allowed to operate according to its own laws, would benefit all of society. Others, like John D. Rockefeller, believed that the fittest should override market forces when these forces hindered production. Unlike Carnegie, Rockefeller thought that competition was harmful to maximizing production and profits, and therefore he championed in the oil industry the formation of collectivities such as trusts that would set prices and run small producers out of business. Of course, he did not grant to workers the same right to form collectivities that would promote their own interests.[13] When Progressive reformers insisted on government regulation, industrial insiders dominated the regulatory agencies as "experts" who alone had sufficient knowledge to set sensible guidelines.[14]

The gospel of wealth's greatest political influence came through indirect means. Colleges and universities both reflect and shape cultural values, and in the Gilded Age those values underwent a profound shift. Protestants had long held that moral instruction in schools and colleges was essential to a moral society and a virtuous citizenry. Before the 1870s, most American colleges were Protestant establishments where compulsory chapel services were common and Protestant values were evident at every turn. Fifty years later, in large part because of the demands of industry, universities were institutions devoted primarily to serving industry and the nation. Moreover, Protestantism was but one of several forces shaping American higher education, sharing the stage with economic, technical, and professional interests. According to historian George Marsden, by the 1920s commitments to scientific and professional ideals in higher education rendered Christianity "at best superfluous and at worst unscientific and unprofessional." He noted that in "academic life, as in so many other parts of modern life, religion would increasingly be confined to private spheres."[15]

Marsden's observation of religion's relegation to the private sphere bears closer scrutiny. To many Protestants, especially evangelicals, such a shift represented a disturbing change in American public life. They had long conceived of the United States as a "Christian nation" where Christian principles formed the bedrock of the culture. Now, a hundred years after the Revolution, Americans seemed to be following unscriptural and even antiscriptural tenets in their daily lives. Though many Christians viewed industrial capitalism as part of the natural and even divine order, they were at the same time disturbed by its preoccupation with the material over the spiritual and its focus on worldly pleasures rather than on heavenly treasures. Industry imposed on life an artificiality that ignored natural rhythms. Control over time itself seemed to pass from God's hands to those of industrialists who beckoned millions to work by the factory whistle, not by the sun's movement. Worst of all, Americans now measured success increasingly by the acquisition of individual wealth rather than by the old Protestant-Republican notion of service dedicated to the public good. Thus while Christian teachings and values continued to find expression in homes and churches, they did not provide the moral compass for making and spending wealth in the Gilded Age.

The "Old-Fashioned" Gospel

Many Protestants rejected the gospel of wealth as a distortion of the New Testament gospel. To them, faith was rooted in the revealed Word of God, not in theories of social Darwinism. Moreover, one's well-being rested on spiritual faith that transcended time, not on fleeting pleasures derived from consumer goods. Thus these evangelicals determined to preach the "old-fashioned" gospel, the timeless Word of God, to a society that had become too enamored, they feared, with things of the world.

Dwight Moody, Billy Sunday, and other evangelists in the Gilded Age came out of America's revivalist heritage that for 150 years had made the saving of individual souls the "one thing needful." Believing that God periodically dispensed grace through extraordinary outpourings, these awakeners viewed themselves God's instruments in a long history of providential soul winning. Further, the revivalists rejected the claims of postmillennialists who stressed the immanence of God at work through individuals whose good works would reform society during the thousand years before the return of Christ. Instead, they emphasized God's transcendence and the belief that he alone could redeem individuals and restore America to its Christian heritage.

The best-known evangelist, Dwight L. Moody, warned Americans against the "false gods" of wealth, fashion, and pleasure. He argued that the "world" offered only ephemeral and therefore empty promise: "This world that so many think is heaven, is the home of sin, a hospital of sorrow, a place that has nothing to satisfy the soul."[16] He singled out the love of money as the most prevalent in the Gilded Age:

> With many it is the god of money. We haven't got through worshiping the golden calf yet. If a man will sell his principles for gold, isn't he making it a god? If he trusts in his wealth to keep him from want and to supply his needs, are not riches his god? Many a man says, "Give me money, and I will give you heaven. What care I for all the glories and treasures of heaven? Give me treasures here! I don't care for heaven! I want to be a successful businessman."[17]

Moody reminded his readers and listeners that, like Job, modern pursuers of wealth will discover the emptiness of riches.

Moody was the most dynamic evangelist of his day, attracting huge crowds in Britain and America. In a sense, he was a product of the Gilded Age, a rags-to-riches Horatio Alger figure who rose from being an obscure, though successful, shoe salesman in Chicago to becoming the best-known religious figure in the Atlantic world. Moreover, his early success depended in large part on newspaper publicity from British and American dailies eager for any story that would increase circulation. When his performances matched the advance publicity, Moody became a hot commodity that newspapermen loved. While recognizing that publicity was effective in generating crowds, Moody was uncomfortable with it and constantly warned his audiences that Christ, not Dwight Moody, should be the focus of attention. He told a New York crowd in 1876, "The papers in Philadelphia puffed us up . . . and big crowds came." But, he added, there was no revival until the people realized the work was God's.[18]

While denouncing the priorities of some businessmen, Moody embraced modern means of promotion with an old-fashioned message. A self-educated man with little knowledge of or interest in theological studies, he preached the same message George Whitefield had popularized 150 years earlier: the necessity of a spiritual New Birth. Moody had undergone a profound conversion under the ministrations of the YMCA, a "leading evangelistic agency" of the day. He regarded his being born-again as a life-changing experience, often saying, "I was born of the flesh in 1837. I was born of the Spirit in 1856."[19] For him, his conversion defined his mission: to preach a message of the salvation of souls to people at home and afar. He established himself as the leading evangelist of the age in his two-year tour of Britain in 1873–1875 when he attracted huge audiences by "preaching a simple old-time gospel of salvation through re-birth in Christ" and charming them with "sentimental stories and the conventional moralism of middle-class Victorian Professionalism."[20] By the time he returned to the United States, his name was a household word and his arrival was eagerly awaited by thousands who wished to see and hear the sensation that had captivated British crowds. For the next twenty years, Dwight Moody and his song leader Ira Sankey preached revival services throughout the United States. Cities, the dens of Gilded Age iniquity, proved to be especially fertile ground, supplying plenty of sinners as well as large-circulation newspapers to "puff" the services. New York, Philadelphia, and Chicago all hosted Moody revivals.

Moody was an innovator in mass evangelism. He employed such techniques as house-to-house canvassing of residents before launching a crusade, organization of local churches to promote his services, and enlistment of financial support from sympathetic businessmen. In Philadelphia, department store magnate John Wanamaker actively supported Moody's crusade there, while in Chicago inventor and corporate leader Cyrus McCormick helped him finance the Bible institute that would carry Moody's name. In addition to preaching, Moody was an educator determined to prepare a cadre of lay evangelists to preach the gospel throughout the world. In the late 1870s and early 1880s, he founded Bible-training centers for women and men who would be the vanguard of what he envisioned as God's army. Then in 1886, when the Haymarket Riot rocked Chicago and raised the specter of anarchy, Moody responded by organizing a training center for lay evangelists. He explained his motives: "Either the people are to be evangelized or the leaven of communism and infidelity will assume such enormous proportions that it will break out in a reign of terror such as the country has never known." He added, "It don't [sic] take a prophet or a son of a prophet to see these things." He set about training a cadre of "men who know the Word" to go out into the shops and businesses and "meet these bareheaded infidels and skeptics." He expressed his conviction that if the world is to be reached for Christ, the mission must be undertaken by thousands of ordinary people rather than a few professional evangelists.[21] At educational conferences begun in his home in Northfield, Moody taught the gospel in fundamentalist strains. From that beginning, the Moody Bible Institute and Moody Press emerged as the central institutions for proclaiming the preached and printed Word of God.

For Moody, evangelism, not politics, would restore America to its Christian heritage and moral roots. The Word of God, not Progressive legislation, held the key to reformation. In that sense, he and his supporters embraced a laissez-faire philosophy based on their conviction that if left free to preach the gospel of Jesus Christ, they would be able to redeem Americans, and, in turn, America.

If Moody was the best-known revivalist of the Gilded Age, Billy Sunday was the most colorful. A professional baseball player who became an evangelist in the 1890s, he unashamedly preached an old message to a modern age. He summed up his views in a sermon entitled "Old Time Religion":

> I believe the Bible is the word of God from cover to cover. I believe that the man who magnifies the word of God in his preaching is the man whom God will honor. Why do such names stand out on the pages of history as Wesley, Whitefield, Finney and Martin Luther? Because of their fearless denunciation of all sin, and because they preach Jesus Christ without fear or favor.[22]

Rather than relying on politicians and government, Sunday placed his faith in a "good old-time kind of revival" to reform America. That kind of revival, he claimed, would cause people to pay their debts, stop drinking, love their neighbors, and raise their children to be moral beings.

Moody and Sunday were not the only spokesmen for evangelicals; others offered an even deeper spiritual experience than that of a new birth. Like Moody, they responded to the spiritual crisis of the day, not by tackling social ills, but by offering individuals a more intimate relationship with God. A splinter group of Methodists founded the Holiness movement, "a cross-Atlantic spiritual revival movement" whose followers believed the Holy Spirit would "fill a person with direct, ecstatic power."[23] This filling of the Holy Spirit constituted a second, more intense spiritual rebirth. The Holiness quest for a greater spiritual intensity led directly to modern Pentecostalism, which emerged at the turn of the century. In comparison to Moody's evangelical crusades, the Pentecostal revival that broke out in 1906 on Azusa Street in Los Angeles constituted a new and competitive strain of American revivalism. Characterized by "a dramatic experience of the Holy Spirit, miraculous powers and expectations, and a holy life," Pentecostals embraced an ecstatic style of worship that sometimes included speaking in tongues in an echo of the first Pentecost.[24]

Moody's and Sunday's revivals and the Holiness and Pentecostal movements attracted mainly white Protestants. However, revivals had a prominent place in nonwhite religious traditions and during the Gilded Age found new expression for groups excluded from the glittering success of material culture. The quest for direct, intense relations with God was a central part of both West African and Native American religions. Each followed worship practices aimed at uniting the human and divine spirits. According to historian of black religious experience Albert Raboteau, the eighteenth-century Great Awakening was "the dawning of the new day" in the conversion of slaves to Christianity. Responding to the demonstrative emotional release of the revivals, blacks were "lifted to new heights of religious excitement" in the preaching and praying of evangelists like George Whitefield and Gilbert Tennent. Moreover, with its emphasis on religious experience, the awakening permitted slaves who had undergone a New Birth to exhort others to a similar experience of grace.[25] From there, black evangelicals began to preach their own African American message, an amalgam of West African spiritualism and New Testament Christianity that sometimes alarmed whites who feared that their construction of such concepts as redemption could put the wrong ideas into slaves' heads.

———

After the Civil War, revivalism became a mainstay in black Christianity throughout the South. William Wells Brown was a black man of letters, a Boston author and reformer who traveled in the South in 1879–1880 to promote, among other things, an educated ministry. He commented on how religion—revival religion—constituted the center of black social life. Brown remarked that after his love for cabbage and bacon, "the next dearest thing to a colored man, in the South, is his religion." He explained that for most black evangelicals, religion was a "thing" to be got, "as if they were going to market for it," and the preferred market was the revival service, with all its shouting and movement and excitement. Caught up in the need for moral reform of individuals and institutions, Brown lamented the black revivals' emphasis on otherworldly concerns. He quoted one lay revivalist, who told his audience, "I hope to live to see you show that you've got the Witness, for where the grace of God is, there will be shouting, and the sooner you comes to that point the better it will be for you in the world to come."[26] With white "Redeemers" regaining control of the post-Reconstruction South and stripping blacks of their civil rights, the call of black revivalists to place their hope in the other world did not seem misplaced to many in their audiences.

Native Americans were another group on the margins of society who sought solace in a revival of traditional religion. In their long struggle with white invaders, American Indians had periodically responded to the call of their own religious leaders to resist assimilation into white culture, including that of Christianity, and return to the faith of their fathers and mothers. Facing white reform movements centered on eradicating native culture on white-mandated reservations, some leaders sought to revive such faiths as the Ghost Dance religion. Originating with a Paiute shaman, the Ghost Dance was a peaceful

movement with big promises: to bring back the bison and remove the white invaders. As interpreted and publicized by the
white sensational press, however, the Ghost Dance was an omi-
nous call for Indians to rise up against whites. Thus when a
group of Lakota Sioux gathered at Wounded Knee in South
Dakota in late 1890 to participate in the Ghost Dance, the U.S.
cavalry units tracking them expected violence—tragically, a
self-fulfilling expectation.[27]

African Americans and Native Americans had no voice in
America's religious marketplace in the late 1800s, and therefore
the most publicized revival was that of the dominant white
evangelical culture. However, there were similarities that
spanned racial boundaries. Like the African and Native revivals, the white evangelical revival focused on spiritual matters,
giving it an otherworldly emphasis. Unlike Charles Finney, revivalists of the Gilded Age rejected the postmillennialist notions suggesting that Christians could have a hand in reforming
the world before Christ's return following a thousand years
of preparation. Salvation was a matter of accepting Christ's
forgiveness for sins of this world with full expectation of living
with Christ in the next.

The Social Gospel and Progressive Politics

Religion often is a conservative force in society, calling on men
and women to return to traditional mores. But it can also be
a force urging radical change, envisioning a future social order
based on spiritual ideals heretofore unattained. The social gospel qualified as a radical expression of Christianity, imagining
the United States as a redeemed nation dedicated to a just society for all its citizens rather than a land of opportunity for a
few rich individuals.

———

Participants in the social gospel movement were an ecumenical lot consisting of liberal Protestants, socially active Catholics, and Reform Jews. Like the revivalists, they were appalled at the godlessness and immorality in society, but they differed from the awakeners in their interpretation of America's religious heritage and in their moral vision. They rejected the claim that America was ever a Christian nation because God "was not the God of one nation." Indeed, as one of them expressed it: the gospels are about Christ's "crossing the racial boundary lines and outgrowing nationalistic religion."[28] In fact, the primary focus of the social gospel movement was not saving individual souls but redeeming a lost and sick society. To its devotees, America had sold its soul to the oppression and greed and materialism of the Gilded Age. Industrial capitalists had cornered the nation's resources and had relegated millions to the hell of wage dependency. While some of the robber barons, like John D. Rockefeller, professed to be devout followers of Christ, in the view of the social gospelers they had perverted Christ's teachings. Jesus had taught that the greatest good came from serving others. As Charles Brown told the National Council of Congregational Churches in 1904, "Jesus would found the social order on the basis of human brotherhood in the service of one another," not as capitalists had done, on the basis of maximum profits for themselves.[29] Jesus' virtues of service and self-sacrifice were those embodied in the republican ideals of the American Revolution; thus capitalist virtues of competition and personal aggrandizement were eroding the nation's founding culture.

The social gospel emerged from the religious marketplace as a cooperative effort among social activists, predominantly Protestant, but including Catholics and Jews as well. They also made common cause with reformers who took a more secular approach in addressing the nation's ills. Like social workers such as Jane Addams and Mary Eliza McDowell and social scientists like Richard Ely, social gospel advocates focused on society as the root of immorality and injustice. Some of them developed their social consciences while living in the squalor of working-class urban neighborhoods. Walter Rauschenbusch, a Baptist pastor and theologian of the social gospel, saw the underside of the Gilded Age firsthand from his pastorate in New York's Hell's Kitchen. Situated west of Ninth Avenue and between Thirty-sixth and Fifty-ninth Streets, Hell's Kitchen epitomized the sordid life of poor immigrant workers living in overcrowded tenements located in the shadows of the slaughterhouses, breweries, and factories where they worked. Children grew up as urchins in streets that proved to be recruiting and training grounds for the criminal gangs that preyed on residents, exacerbating the fear and misery of the area. While the Vanderbilt brothers Cornelius II and George Washington commissioned Richard Morris Hunt to build palatial summer homes—respectively, the 70-room mansion dubbed the Breakers at Newport and the 250-room Biltmore located in Asheville, North Carolina—siblings in Hell's Kitchen sometimes shared one room with their entire family. It was from that perspective that Rauschenbusch viewed America's Gilded Age.

Cities were the scene and symbol of moral decline in America. It was there that social inequality and political corruption were most evident. A *New York Times* article dated May 8, 1892, focusing on family life in the city attributed the alarming spread of immorality to the "hiving of humans like bees" in overcrowded neighborhoods. Quoting Jacob Riis, author of *How the Other Half Lives* (1890), the article called tenements "nurseries of death, pauperism, and crime," plagues that "touch family life with deadly moral contagion." Riis discovered that most of the criminals in New York were people "who have either lost connection with home life, or never had any, or whose homes have ceased to be sufficiently separate, decent, and desirable to afford what are regarded as ordinary wholesome influences of home and family."[30] If the family broke down, American society itself was in jeopardy.

To Rauschenbusch, the root of the social decay lay not in individual weakness but in America's collective sins. He believed that the country's greatest transgression was social sin, that is, iniquity committed by the "principalities and powers" ruling the nation. And given the nature of the sin, salvation, he thought, must be directed toward the collectivity, not just individuals. In short, America must come under the "law of Christ." While admiring the productivity of capitalism, stating that the "effectiveness of the capitalistic method" in the production of wealth is not questioned, he blamed capitalism for the "production of human wreckage." In a scathing indictment of capitalism, he wrote, "Its one-sided control of economic power tempts to exploitation and oppression; it directs the productive process of society primarily toward the creation of private profit rather than the service of human needs; it demands autocratic management and strengthens the autocratic principle in all social affairs; it has impressed a materialistic spirit on our whole civilization."[31]

Rauschenbusch's solution was radical: to replace capitalism and its competitive principle with socialism and its cooperative ethos. He argued that organizations and societies formed on "the cooperative principle are not primarily for profit but for the satisfaction of human wants, and the aim is to distribute ownership, control, and economic benefits to a large number of co-operators."[32] The hoped-for result would be the elimination of the great gulfs that existed between life at the Breakers or the Biltmore and life in Hell's Kitchen.

Such a vision was a Christian vision, but certainly not one shared by all or even a majority of Americans. Even fellow laborer in the social gospel movement Washington Gladden viewed capitalism almost as a part of the divine plan. According to historian Robert Wiebe, Gladden "stood in awe of the traditional economic laws . . . and predicted disaster if the government interfered further in society's operations."[33]

And yet Gladden joined Rauschenbusch as well as Josiah Strong and Lyman Abbott in advocating association as the organizing principle of American society. Rauschenbusch argued that "new forms of association must be created. Our disorganized competitive life must pass into an organic cooperative life." Gladden agreed, arguing that interdependency and cooperation should replace the individualism that stood at the heart of capitalist culture. "To live is not to separate ourselves from our fellows," he wrote, "but to unite with them in multiform ministries of giving and receiving. We are parts of a whole."[34]

Ironically, Rauschenbusch and Gladden were calling for a shift that some of the industrialists they criticized had already embraced. When John D. Rockefeller surveyed the oil-refining industry in 1870, he concluded that the industry would benefit far more from cooperation than from competition. He estimated that 90 percent of the refineries operated in the red because of industrywide overcapacity and cutthroat price wars. His solution was a giant cartel that would bring discipline and order to the industry by regulating capacity and stabilizing prices. The result was the Standard Oil Company, a vertically organized behemoth that controlled oil from the wellhead to the final consumer. Buying out small competitors or forcing them out of business by charging exorbitant freight rates for oil, Rockefeller succeeded in realizing his dream of association. Of course, it came at a very high price to his competitors. One congressional committee investigating Standard Oil's monopolistic tactics called Rockefeller's cartel " 'the most gigantic and daring conspiracy' ever to threaten a free nation."[35] Though

Rockefeller evoked association as the principle for bringing order to the oil industry, his primary motivation was individual profit. When workers associated together for higher wages and better working conditions, industrialists, with government backing, denounced the unions for restraining trade—that is, for impeding the efforts of individuals to make money without interference from dangerous associations of "selfish" workers.

While Rockefeller and others stamped out competition through their own version of association, leaders of the social gospel movement joined with social scientists and social workers in replacing American individualism with what economist Richard Ely called "social solidarity." Believing that all social and economic relations are the results of specific historical moments rather than systems derived from natural or divine order, Ely called on Americans of the late nineteenth century to reorient their society toward interdependence and away from individualism. "Social solidarity," he wrote, "means that our true welfare is not an individual matter purely, but likewise a social affair." Countering the premises of a society that extols individual profit making, Ely declared, "[O]ur weal is common weal; we thrive only in a commonwealth; our exaltation is the exaltation of our fellow men, their elevation is our enlargement."[36]

Though the social gospel failed to change America's political and economic structures, it did contribute to significant social and cultural shifts. It appealed to large numbers of women who founded and ran settlement houses and served as social workers in poor urban neighborhoods. Typical was Mary Eliza McDowell, a social settlement worker who spent most of her career in Jane Addams's shadow. As a young girl, she, along with her father, joined a Methodist Church, where she developed a deep love and appreciation for "common people" who attended, admiring in particular their egalitarian perspective. For McDowell, religion "became real" when she became engaged in the needs of people rather than merely splitting theological hairs. As she involved herself in the social gospel and public service, her Victorian values of faith, industry, and frugality began to change. When Pullman workers went on strike in 1894, McDowell at first could not understand why "wage-earners who had work" refused to do their jobs. As she sought to fathom that question, the Methodist pastor at Pullman helped her look beyond the individual strikers and see that the strike was "only typical of a great world unrest which must be understood." That set her on a course of learning about the "drab parts of industrial life" and immersing herself in efforts to alleviate suffering and fight for justice.[37]

The fundamental split among Protestants centered on the diagnosis of and remedy for the ills that beset industrial America. Evangelical revivalists concentrated on individuals and sought their salvation through preaching the gospel. To them, the primary problem was not the social or economic system; it was what it has always been: sinners disobeying God's commandments rather than submitting to his will. To be sure, revivalists were active in seeking political solutions for such problems as alcoholism and desecration of the Sabbath, but they were concerned more about things of the spirit than things of this world. While activists in the social gospel movement took the opposite approach, focusing on social sins and problems of this world, they were divided over the question of priority. Should the emphasis be on working toward a new social and economic order or striving for a new kind of person? Washington Gladden thought it folly to change the system without changing the people operating within it. "It is idle to imagine that changes in our governmental machinery, or in the organization of our industries will bring us peace," he wrote. He located the root problem deeper, "in our primary conceptions. What we have got to have . . . is a different kind of men and women." Rauschenbusch agreed that a "regenerated personality" was necessary if Americans were to restore the republican and Christian ideals of virtuous men and women serving the public good, rather than greedy, rapacious people working to amass private fortunes. Theodore Roosevelt agreed that the reform of individuals must take priority, recognizing that such reform was a long process: "It is only by a slow and patient inward transformation . . . that men are really helped upward in their struggle for a higher and fuller life."[38] As president, however, he did not wait for that "inward transformation"; instead he worked toward erecting a big and powerful government that would check the selfish aims of big business and big labor.

With the social gospel, American religion shifted its emphasis from republican to democratic values. As Mark Noll argues in his study of the period between the American Revolution and the Civil War, evangelical Christianity constituted a uniquely American religion. Evangelicalism shaped and was shaped by republican and Scottish commonsense values about virtue and the public good.[39] Large-scale industrialization challenged that amalgamation as well as the homogeneity of American religion. To social gospelers, if Christians were to have an impact in public affairs, they must engage in the rough-and-tumble business of democracy, which meant mobilizing like-minded people to participate in elections, organize and fund lobbying efforts to sway politicians, and attempt to influence public opinion by exposing the "sins" of the Gilded Age. Oberlin College in Ohio emerged as a center for Christian democracy as social gospelers and social scientists were frequent guests on campus advocating Christian activism in politics. Professor Simon MacLennan summarized the thinking at Oberlin when he remarked, "[T]he religion of Christ was really democracy," adding that "all religion as well as all government should be by the people and for the people."[40] Social gospelers and social scientists joined the "growing clamor for more government" that characterized the reform movement of the 1880s and 1890s. Powerful corporations that acted like the "selfish individuals" who controlled them were preying upon workers, competitors, and customers with impunity in the prevailing laissez-faire political climate. Economist Simon Patten voiced the sentiments of many social gospelers in calling for an activist state. He argued that the nation needed "a new society and a state whose power will be superior to that of any combination of selfish individuals and whose duties will be commensurate with human wants." If government is of and by the people, it should interfere when its interference would likely promote "better health, better education, better morals, [and] greater comfort of the community."[41]

In marshaling popular support for their political agendas, activists sometimes borrowed from evangelical experiences. Particularly in the Midwest and South, reformers organized camp meetings similar to those that Baptists and Methodists had long used to bring revival to rural communities. Populist leaders included prayers and songs to prepare their audiences for lectures and political speeches.[42] And politicians sounded very much like evangelists, with cadences and anecdotes and appeals that echoed those emanating from pulpits.

In terms of concrete political results, the impact of the social gospel movement was modest at best. According to Robert Wiebe, the social gospel sought to effect social change through "transcendental means." But such an approach had limited appeal, and it operated on the "periphery" of reform. Part of the problem was the lack of institutional development. For the most part the movement was the work of individuals like Rauschenbusch and Gladden. Not until 1908 did the social gospel find institutional expression in a coalition of thirty-one denominations called the Federal Council of Churches (FCC). Its primary role was to offer Christian commentary on political, social, and economic issues, but it could point to no significant legislation that bore its imprint. Social gospel leaders urged all Christians to stand united against the tide of materialism that was sweeping American culture. But its message was ignored by many conservatives, who thought that the FCC was too liberal in its pronouncements and had become so consumed with social issues that it had abandoned its distinctive Christian role of proclaiming the gospel to lost sinners.[43] Indeed, one could argue that it was the gospel of wealth, far more than the social gospel, that proved to have an enduring influence on American culture.

Faith and Science:
The Modernist-Fundamentalist Controversy

Industrialization and its accompanying problems did not cause lasting fissures within America's religious marketplace. Differences in how to respond to the Gilded Age were primarily a matter of emphasis and strategy. Conservative evangelicals preferred to pursue moral reform by praying down and preaching up a revival, believing that redeemed individuals would make virtuous voters and officeholders. Those in the social gospel movement took a more direct approach by lobbying for political reform that would curb the power of corporations, eradicate corruption in government, and ameliorate the miserable living conditions in urban centers. Christians who embraced the gospel of wealth reconciled competing demands of their faith with those of the market. What did split Protestants into two irreconcilable camps and created a divide that persists to the present were radical notions imported during the Gilded Age, ideas that shook the very foundations of religious faith.

Arriving with the immigrants who threatened America's dominant Protestant culture were new ideas about human origins, biblical authority, and the question of sin. Charles Darwin raised doubts about biblical accounts of creation in his hypotheses about the origins and development of life, including those of human life. In Darwin's theory, life in all its variety unfolds according to impersonal laws rather than through specific acts of a personal God. Indeed, to many, science, not the

Bible, offered the more convincing explanation of how the universe operated. Further, many moderns agreed with Karl Marx that the driving engine of social and historical change was economic conflict, not the hand of Providence. And Sigmund Freud called into question the concept of sin, arguing instead that unresolved issues from the individual's early development account for personality disorders and unsocial behavior. A final threat to faith came from the new higher criticism emanating from German universities that examined the Bible as literature and raised serious questions about its authorship and even the truth of its claims.

Protestant responses to these modern ideas fell along a continuum ranging from rejection of and hostility to modernity at one end to acceptance of and affinity with modernity at the other. In the early twentieth century, those taking the former stance became known as fundamentalists while those assuming the latter were labeled modernists. Fundamentalists came to see the Christian faith in opposition to modern ideas and emphasized God's transcendent judgment of a world that had wandered away from the Bible's revelation of divine authority. They stressed scripture as the inerrant Word of God whose commandments must be revered and accepted as divinely inspired. The world would be redeemed, they thought, only when Christ returns to begin his millennial reign on earth. In their version of the gospel, fundamentalists saw little reason for direct political action except to insist on the guarantee of religious freedom. Modernists, on the other hand, saw Christian faith and modern ideas as compatible. These world-affirming Christians believed that they must live in the world, and they stressed God's immanence as enabling them to work toward bringing about his Kingdom. Modernists, therefore, were often political activists working for candidates and legislation that promoted a more rational, moral, and tolerant world. However, the modernist-fundamentalist struggle exerted its most profound political influence primarily in its shaping of political culture, rather than in its direct impact on electoral politics. It was a battle over the underlying beliefs and authority that are foundational to American culture and politics.

The Great Protestant Schism

It has been argued that fundamentalism has been the norm most of the time for most religions.[1] In that generic sense, it is the response of particular sects to threats from other sects or from secular forces that question its core tenets. The group under attack reasserts its claim that it is defined by a set of changeless beliefs grounded in an authoritative text that transcends the ebb and flow of time. The movement under discussion here is historical fundamentalism, that is, a specific reaction by American Protestants to modern ideas and practices that called into question what it means to profess oneself a Christian. By the early 1900s, some Protestants had taken a liberal attitude toward modernity and reconciled tensions between faith and modern ideas. For example, where liberals saw conflicts between the findings of science and the teachings of the Bible, they resolved them through a naturalistic interpretation of scripture. They contended that the Bible is not a science book, that it contains a prescientific understanding of the physical world, and that its truths must be separated from the dated context in which they are embedded. In other words, the Bible is not to be taken literally; it must be interpreted in the light of modern knowledge and with the aid of modern scholarship.

Fundamentalists viewed such liberal manipulation of the Bible as an attack on faith itself. If the Bible is human interpretation based on modern knowledge instead of God's holy and unchanging Word, then faith rests on shifting sand. Furthermore, can those who subscribe to such a view be considered Christians? Is Christianity a faith whose adherents can choose to believe what they wish and reject the rest? Fundamentalists in the early twentieth century thought it necessary to define the faith by identifying fundamental beliefs that distinguished a Christian. The intellectual underpinning for fundamentalism was formalized in the publication of *The Fundamentals: A Foundation of Truth*, a series of ninety-four essays written by sixty-four British and American conservative Protestant theologians, and published between 1910 and 1915 with the help of a $250,000 grant from Lyman Stewart, head of the Union Oil Company of California. At the same time these essays appeared, the General Assembly of the Presbyterian Church distilled the main tenets into what was known as the five fundamentals: (1) inerrancy of the scriptures, (2) the virgin birth and the deity of Jesus, (3) the doctrine of substitutionary atonement through God's grace and human faith, (4) the bodily resurrection of Jesus, and (5) the authenticity of Christ's miracles.[2]

The debate between modernists and fundamentalists began when some Protestant leaders challenged *The Fundamentals* as the basis of Christian identity. Harry Emerson Fosdick, a liberal Baptist minister in New York, picked up the fundamentalist gauntlet in 1922 by preaching a sermon entitled "Shall the Fundamentalists Win?" He portrayed liberals as "sincere evangelical Christians who were striving to reconcile the new knowledge of history, science, and religion with the old faith." Fundamentalists, on the other hand, were, he argued, "intolerant conservatives determined 'to shut the doors of Christian fellowship' against all who would modify any traditional doctrines." Fosdick thought it too bad that fundamentalists had drawn the battle line at specific doctrines such as the virgin birth of Christ, inerrancy of scripture, substitutionary atonement, and the literal second coming of Christ. As he saw it, these were "opinions" that invited different "points of view" from Christians of goodwill, not benchmarks for determining who was and who was not a "true" Christian. He recognized, for example, that many "devout Christians" held the virgin birth to be a historical event because they thought that there was no way for the Son of God to become flesh except by a "special biological miracle." Yet other, equally devout Christians believed that the virgin birth was not a historical event but an interpretation crafted by people who could not explain the incarnation of such a divine Master without phrasing it "in terms of a biological miracle that our modern minds cannot use." Fosdick called on fundamentalists to be tolerant of diverse views and end their "narrow-minded bickering."[3]

Clarence Edward Macartney, pastor of the Arch Street Presbyterian Church in Philadelphia, was quick to answer Fosdick's sermon with one of his own, entitled "Shall Unbelief Win?" The titles of the two sermons suggest that each side viewed the struggle as a mighty contest or even a war with dire consequences if the wrong side prevailed. Macartney argued that Fosdick's "naturalistic" perspectives were irreconcilable with evangelical Christianity. Refuting Fosdick's sermon point by point, he claimed that the virgin birth of Christ, "far from being myth or rubbish, was historical fact because the Bible proclaimed it so, and the Bible "was the inspired and authoritative Word of God." He accused liberals like Fosdick of slowly "secularizing the Church" with their modernist and rationalist ideas. If fundamentalists tolerated it, liberalism would replace biblical faith with a "Christianity of opinions and principles and good purposes, but a Christianity without worship, without God, and without Jesus Christ."[4]

With those two sermons, and others like them, the contest between modernists and fundamentalists was joined, with lines quickly hardening and blurring other positions along the theological spectrum. A number of so-called moderate stances emerged that tried to reconcile differences between the extremes of the fundamentalist and modernist sides, but their voices were muted in the contentious struggle.[5] Some Protestants, for example, agreed with the modernist interest in engaging the world and trying to reconcile Christian faith and modern ideas, but disagreed with modernists who stressed God's immanence at the expense of his transcendence. In the view of these "Christian realists," modernists ran the risk of becoming so identified with the secular world that they would lose their prophetic biblical voice. However, as they stressed God's transcendence, these realists soon came under attack by modernists who claimed that they were fundamentalists dressed in wolves' skins. In the highly charged debate between fundamentalists and modernists, all commentators were soon drawn into the conflict as partisans.[6]

Of the challenges to American Protestantism, none was more divisive than that of higher criticism, a movement emanating from German biblical scholars that subjected the Bible to historical analysis of its text, context, authorship, editorship, and literary tropes. Indeed, twenty-seven of the ninety-four essays published in *The Fundamentals* were devoted to refuting the claims of higher criticism.[7] The debate had profound importance for American culture as well as for the Christian faith. From earliest settlement the Bible had been central to the development of American culture. It was the most widely owned, read, and quoted book throughout the colonies, and in the Puritan colonies it was cited as the authority for the criminal code. Politicians quoted the Bible frequently, and in some instances memorably, as when Abraham Lincoln referred to a "house divided" against itself. For most Americans, the Bible was the literal Word of God. As one Methodist minister put it in 1851, "The Bible is a plain book, addressed to the common sense of man." A central Protestant tenet was the belief that no one, including priests, stood between God's Word and the believer. Moreover, the Bible was deemed to be a "holy" book, divinely inspired and utterly true in every word. In one critic's caricature of that view, written in 1883, "A book let down out of the skies, immaculate, infallible oracular—this is the traditional view of the Bible."[8]

The historical-critical analysis of the Bible turned that traditional view on its head. The process was evolutionary, beginning in the mid-nineteenth century in such German universities as that of Tübingen, entering American seminaries and colleges in the last quarter of the century, and finding expression in congregations in the early twentieth. By 1911, Congregationalist minister Lyman Abbott could pronounce that the transformation in the popular conception of the Bible was so great that it could be said that a "genuinely new book" had found its way into American churches. Higher criticism challenged traditional views of the entire Bible from Genesis to Revelation. Genesis was not, as the King James Version proclaimed, the work of Moses. Rather, according to the Wellhausen theory—named for its German originator, Julius Wellhausen—it was actually written by a number of authors who drew upon several sources. In the ironical depiction of one Presbyterian, M. B. Lambdin, "The Pentateuch is thus not Mosaic; but a mosaic." Similarly, higher criticism called into question the history of the New Testament, from the life and miracles of Jesus to the allegory of the book of Revelation. Like the Pentateuch, the Gospels were shown to have been based on several, contradictory sources that resulted in various accounts of the life of Jesus. After subjecting the New Testament to historical analysis, critics concluded that it was a work of dogma, not history. To them, what traditionalists regarded as reliable history was myth or legend.[9]

Higher criticism split American Protestants at the most fundamental level: the authority of their faith, the Word of God. The resulting controversy started with a basic difference in assumptions regarding scripture. Traditionalists took an a priori view of the Bible by assuming it was the Word of God. Liberals took a different point of departure, as explained by Lyman Abbott:

> The literary method takes up the Bible without any pre-conceptions whatever. It takes it up exactly as it would take up any other collection of literature, to see what kind of a book, or what kind of a collection it is. . . . It assumes nothing. It leaves the conclusion of the questions, whether the Bible came from God, how far and to what extent it came from God, all to be determined by examination of the book itself.[10]

Each side in the controversy attacked the other's position and defended its own with an intensity that deepened the gulf between them. Liberal biblical scholars insisted that their view of the Bible in no way undermined its truths; rather, they claimed, literary and historical analyses helped uncover God's message. Any interpretation that did not consider the historical context of the events described could not be regarded as accurate. For instance, the Flood, viewed from the perspective of local observers, appeared to be universal. And the account of Jonah's being swallowed by the big fish, when read anew, is to be taken not as history but as a parable uncovering profound truth. Liberals insisted that their views led to a more enlightened reading of the Bible, "whose claim to Divine authorship was not diminished."[11]

Needless to say, conservatives did not share that view. They believed that liberals advanced an unorthodox, heretical perspective on the Bible. Princeton Theological Seminary Professor Charles Hodge's definition of orthodoxy was centered on his view of scripture: "That the Scriptures of the Old and New Testaments are the Word of God, written under the inspiration of the Holy Spirit, and therefore infallible, and of divine authority in all things pertaining to faith and practice, and consequently free from all error, whether of doctrines, fact, or precept."[12] From his perspective, the text itself was holy.

Debaters on both sides found a usable past in the nation's history to explain their differences. Fundamentalists portrayed themselves as descendants of Bible-believing Puritans and orthodox evangelicals, while representing modernists as descendants of the secular Enlightenment. Fundamentalists called themselves torchbearers of "Christian" America, casting modernists as deists. They characterized higher criticism as nothing more than warmed-over rationalism, the same anti-Christian worldview perpetuated by Enlightenment thinkers. They accused liberal Christian scholars of beginning their examination of the Bible with a set of a priori rationalist assumptions negating miracles and divine inspiration; it was thus no surprise that they found neither in scripture. In that regard, they were no different from Voltaire and Thomas Paine, who dismissed much of the Bible as unscientific superstition and hearsay. One conservative critic charged liberals with being "engaged in the business of threshing old straw, straw that has been threshed a thousand times and that yielded only chaff at the first threshing." Conservatives concluded that modern liberals were nothing more than deists parading as Christians.[13]

Conservative Christians viewed their battle with liberals over the inspiration and truth of the Bible as the greatest struggle since the Reformation. The very authority of their faith and the power of the church were at stake. Therefore, they felt compelled to contest every liberal assertion regarding biblical facts, regardless of how minute or insignificant it might seem to outsiders. Liberals pointed out that the church had a long history of resisting new scientific discoveries that contradicted scripture, citing specifically Galileo's trial by the Inquisition for reinterpreting the Bible in light of Copernicus's heliocentric model of the universe. Noting that, over time, most Christians had reconciled Copernicus's theory with biblical teachings, liberals thought that conservatives should make similar efforts to reconcile modern science with scripture. But conservatives resisted, making the argument that if one part of the Bible were found to be in error, then the whole would be endangered. A New York Lutheran pastor, Junius Remensnyder, laid out that view in response to Lyman Abbott's assault on inerrancy, an assault in which Abbott dismissed such stories as Jonah and the fish as allegorical, not scientific fact. Remensnyder insisted that the Jonah story is of the same order as the New Testament miracles, and that it belonged to the "domain of the supernatural." As such, it must be accepted or rejected according to faith that the Bible is indeed the inspired Word of God. If Christians reject the Jonah story, then they call into question all similar stories, including those of miracles attributed to Jesus. "We must accept or reject them as a whole," he declared."[14]

The fight over the Bible was primarily one between Christians rather than between believers and nonbelievers, or Christians and secularists. It was a debate, however, that soon spread far beyond the religious marketplace, and into the political and cultural arenas of communities across the country. The Bible had long enjoyed a privileged place in American education, so any questions about its authority and interpretation were sure to have implications for what was taught and how it was taught in public schools. The growing acceptance of science in American culture raised the question of the place of the Bible in education and led to contentious discussions within local school boards and state education commissions, as well as in the media.

Natural Selection versus Providential Design

Protestants read Charles Darwin through two different lenses. Princeton theology professor Charles Hodge read Darwin's *On the Origin of Species* (1859) with admiration for the writer's intellect and fear for the book's implications. Writing in 1874, Hodge focused on Darwin's thesis that the vast variety of plant and animal life "evolved by the agency of the blind, unconscious laws of nature." Hodge considered the great flaw in Darwin's work to be the "exclusion of design in the origin of species"; by design, he meant "the intelligent and voluntary selection of an end, and the intelligent and voluntary choice, application, and control of means appropriate to the accomplishment of that end." He found it inconceivable that anyone who observed nature closely and had ever heard of God could conclude that life is the result of chance and not design. What made Darwin's theories particularly disturbing to Hodge was that the denial of intelligent design led to the denial of God as designer. He dismissed Darwin's view that the Creator eons ago called matter into existence and then stepped aside and left the unfolding of the universe to chance. Such a view, Hodge argued, was tantamount to consigning God to nonexistence. Hodge reasoned that even though Darwin maintained a belief, albeit flawed, in the Creator, his views were atheistic and therefore were likely to promote atheism.[15]

In 1892, Lyman Abbott, pastor of the Plymouth Congregational Church in Brooklyn, read Darwin's theory from a perspective opposite that of Hodge. A leading spokesman for a modern, rational perspective in American Christianity, Abbott embraced the idea of evolution. Citing the authority of science, he noted that "all scientific men to-day are evolutionists." He said that they agreed substantially with the notion that all life evolves from lower to higher forms under the direction of laws "which either now are or may yet be understood." Abbott declared that evolution was a truth that extended even to religious life, which "proceeds by regular and orderly sequence from simple and lower forms to more complex and higher forms, in institutions, in thought, in practical conduct, and in spiritual experience." From that premise, he concluded that Christianity was a stage in the manifestation of God, "historically made in and through Jesus Christ, which has produced the changes in the moral life of man whose aggregate result is seen in the complex life of Christendom." Moreover, Christianity has been not a fixed entity but a life that has evolved through "continuous, progressive change." In other words, Christianity "has exemplified the law of evolution." Progress in Christianity has not always been harmonious and uninterrupted; rather, it has been filled with a kind of warfare between contending factions including those that cling to pagan beliefs and practices. Abbott asserted that the Bible reflected the "errors and partialisms" of Christianity. Moreover, he insisted that the Bible does not claim to be the "absolute Word of God"; instead, it declares that the "Word of God was with God and was God" long before the world came into being. The Bible, then, is the "Word of God, *as perceived and understood by holy men of old.*" It is their interpretation and is imbued with their partial understanding of truth.[16]

In interpreting Darwin's science, American Protestants confronted one of the fundamental boundaries that had divided them since the eighteenth century: the role of reason in the Christian faith. The Enlightenment had sparked debate among American Protestants over revelation versus reason as the path to truth. Hodge could have been describing Thomas Jefferson when he charged that Darwinism pushed the Creator to the sidelines of the creation process. As a deist, Jefferson believed that God was creator in the sense of beginning the process—a cosmic Watchmaker who wound the clock—but he also thought that matter behaved according to natural laws discernible by human reason. And Abbott could have had the Sage of Monticello in mind when he talked about the Bible as a book of partial truths and errors. For Jefferson, reason, not revelation, was the surer guide to truth. In his well-known edition of the Bible prepared while he was president, all biblical claims that could not be confirmed by modern science were removed, leaving little more than the moral teachings of Jesus.

Hodge was much more comfortable with Jonathan Edwards's views of faith and reason. While Edwards incorporated much of the Enlightenment in his worldview, he expressed grave concern about deism and its threat to the Christian faith. Edwards described deists as those who

> [w]holly cast off the Christian religion, and are professed infidels. They are not like the Heretics, Arians, Socinians, and others, who own the Scriptures to be the word of God, and hold the Christian religion to be the true religion, but only deny these and these fundamental doctrines of the Christian religion: they deny the whole Christian religion. Indeed they own the being of a God; but they deny that Christ was the son of God, and say he was a mere cheat; and so they say all the prophets and apostles were; and they deny the whole Scripture. They deny that any of it is the word of God.

They deny revealed religion, or any word of God at all;
and say that God has given mankind no other light to
walk by but their own reason.[17]

For Edwards, reason was a God-given faculty intended to aid
men and women in understanding God's revealed truth, but
he also placed great importance on what he called "holy af-
fections" in the drama of salvation. Redemption came through
the indwelling Christ, not at the end of deductive reasoning.

While Edwards viewed scientific knowledge as secondary
and limited, Benjamin Franklin saw it as the means for men
and women not only to understand the created order but to
shape it to their ends. He delighted in the "rapid Progress *true*
Science now makes." In what reads like a secular millennial
vision, he imagined a world transformed by science:

It is impossible to imagine the Height to which may be
carried, in a thousand years, the Power of Man over
Matter. We may perhaps learn to deprive large Masses
of their Gravity, and give them absolute Levity, for the
sake of easy Transport. Agriculture may diminish its
Labor and double its Produce; all Diseases may by sure
means be prevented or cured, not excepting even that
of Old Age, and our Lives lengthened at pleasure even
beyond the antediluvian Standard.[18]

Read Edwards and science threatened revealed truth. Read
Franklin and science ushers in the millennial age.

During the first half of the nineteenth century, science and
religion flourished alongside each other in the United States in
a relationship that was harmonious, not contentious. Science
was visible to most Americans in the amazing inventions that
produced a transportation and communication revolution.
Steamboats on inland waterways overcame the one-way mo-

tion of currents and moved people and cargo upriver as well as down. Steamships revolutionized ocean travel as well, making transatlantic crossings faster and more reliable. By midcentury, thousands of miles of railroad tracks linked the various regions of the country and, shortly after the Civil War, spanned the nation from the Pacific to the Atlantic. Parallel to railroad beds, telegraph lines enabled Americans to send messages that connected families and friends as well as businesses and customers. In 1865, the first Atlantic cable linked the United States with Europe, thus making the world smaller and distant lands more accessible.

The period from the second half of the nineteenth century through the first quarter of the twentieth introduced a new discursive style into American culture. Science offered novel methodologies and coined a vocabulary for explaining religious authority and discussing the natural and social world. Most disturbing for many Christians was criticism of the Bible itself. If Holy Scripture was not the immutable, indisputable Word of God that provides a bedrock for faith, then all the doctrines and teaching resting on it became less certain as well. American Protestants divided over how to respond to the new criticism and to the findings of science. Some had little trouble assimilating the new knowledge and making it compatible with their faith. Others saw the new teachings as deeply disturbing, and they set about to discredit them first through argumentation both within and without the church and then in the political arena.

The political battle between modernists and fundamentalists was primarily a cultural war fought out in local school boards, state legislatures, and university faculties across the country. Until the 1870s, Protestants exercised "cultural hegemony" in higher education: Christians dominated boards of directors, Christian principles were openly professed in chapel services, and Christian morality was taught as the foundation of American republicanism. Most colleges embraced a "nonsectarian Protestantism," and many maintained divinity schools for the purpose of educating ministers. But to the chagrin of many who had taken comfort in the status quo, by the 1920s that hegemony had been destroyed by two forces. First, secular interests, especially those of science and industry, insisted on modernizing American universities to meet the demands of a public life that had undergone significant change over the past fifty years. Second, modernists prevailed over fundamentalists in their attitude toward modernity, with the former reconciling the basic principles of Christianity with those of a scientific, liberal, capitalist society. Thus universities were transformed from "broadly Christian institution(s)" into establishments whose commitment to scientific and professional ideals eclipsed their Christian origins. In light of this new orientation, "academic expressions of Christianity seemed at best superfluous and at worst unscientific and unprofessional." Though most administrators associated with higher education were still Christian, "in academic life, as in so many other parts of modern life, religion would increasingly be confined to private spheres."[19] Rather than integrating Christianity into the new scientific and professional ethos, many people compartmentalized their lives, professing their religious faith in their churches and homes on the Sabbath while functioning the rest of the week in a world that operated by non-Christian standards and goals.

The shift in higher education had profound moral implications that extended to political culture. Protestants had long argued that moral instruction was the heart of public education, and that morality was rooted in religion. Further, they argued that Christian moral education was essential to a republic based on virtuous citizens. They believed in the constancy of human nature and in the timeless authority of scripture; the Bible's code of ethics was as relevant in the nineteenth century as it had been when God presented Moses with the Ten Commandments. As modernists and secularists made their presence felt in universities, one of the most notable changes was the replacement of the Christian view of morality with that of social scientists. At Syracuse University, a Methodist institution, Professor Edwin Earp taught that "sociology showed that moral beliefs were evolutionary products of experience and it was therefore unscientific and absurd to surmise that God ever turned stone mason and chiseled commandments on a rock." At the University of Chicago, as well as at Syracuse and elsewhere, moral codes were reduced to merely "mores," and traditional institutions, including that of marriage, were not "sacred." Catholic universities also made accommodations to modernity. At Notre Dame, physics professor John Zahn published *Evolution and Dogma* (1896), "detailing the compatibility of biological evolution, church teaching, and Scripture."[20]

The result of the transformation in higher education has been that Christianity became but one of several forces that shaped curricula and instruction. Universities no longer were extensions of churches; they now served all of society, and in the late nineteenth and early twentieth centuries, that meant a fast-growing industrial state. Industrialists like John D. Rockefeller, Andrew Carnegie, Leland Stanford, and Cornelius Vanderbilt founded universities dedicated to Christian principles but also to those of capitalism and science. Historian George Marsden characterizes the transformation of American universities as the "disestablishment of religion." Though built on Protestant evangelical foundations, by the 1920s many American universities had become "conspicuously inhospitable" to their evangelical heritage.[21]

While modernists and secularists were redefining American universities, fundamentalists were organizing Bible colleges. Many of the new schools grew out of the Holiness movement, an outgrowth of Methodism in the late nineteenth century. At its heart was an emphasis on the Holy Spirit, which offered Christians the opportunity to deepen their faith and live a godly life in an ungodly world. Further, believers held that the present age was the age of the Holy Spirit, the long-awaited day when God's spirit would move among people as it had on the day of Pentecost. Supporting this view were men like C. I. Scofield, minister and Bible publisher and commentator, who found in the Bible proof of what they called dispensationalism. By that, they meant that God dispensed his grace in different, but predictable, ways, sometimes employing what revivalists called "ordinary" means such as preaching, praying, and church services, and at other times pouring out his grace in "extraordinary" effusions. Underlying dispensationalism were two fundamental beliefs. First, the Bible was accurate and reliable as to facts as well as truth. And, second, history unfolded according to supernatural power, not according to mechanistic natural laws. Scofield found seven dispensations in the Bible: the age of Innocence that ended with the Fall; the age of Conscience that ended with the Flood; the age of Human Government that for Jews ended in the Captivity and for Gentiles continues as long as people look to man and not to God; the age of Promise from Abraham to Moses; the age of Law from Moses to the death of Christ; the age of Grace from the cross to the Second Coming; and the age of the Kingdom or the millennial reign of Christ.[22]

The growing distance between modernists and fundamentalists can be gauged by differences between American universities and Bible colleges. In the former, the focus was on the natural and humanist world where human reasoning and imagination reigned supreme, and science was the primary authority for ascertaining facts. Religion, including Christianity, was understood as a cultural construction that changed its shape in relation to human learning and to accommodate the modern age. In Bible schools, the focus was on the supernatural and the authoritative text was the Bible, a body of facts that explained history and science. Changes in religion unfolded according to a divine plan that believers could discover in scripture. By the 1920s, these two worlds offered little opportunity for discussion and exchange.

The rift between modernists and fundamentalists revealed a deeper divide that had long separated American Protestants. At the center were long-standing disputes over such basic questions as the relation between faith and reason, the nature and interpretation of the Bible, the church's stance toward secular society, and the question of morality and history. Shortly after the Civil War, Oliver Wendell Holmes, Jr., a liberal transcendentalist, predicted that Protestantism could not long remain unified, that it would splinter in its impending clash with modernity. He thought that evangelicals were too committed to and too vested in what he called evangelical "idolatry and bibliolatry." Holmes believed that a literal interpretation of the Bible could not stand up to science and its discoveries of the world, and without an inerrant Bible, evangelicals had little that distinguished them. "The truth is staring the Christian world in the face," he wrote in 1869, "that the stories of the old Hebrew books cannot be taken as literal statements of fact." For their part, evangelicals did not bury their heads in the sand amid the changes whirling around them. They knew that science discovered facts at odds with those claimed by scripture, but they were not perturbed. Protestants were accustomed to attacks from powerful forces; indeed, their movement was born when "papal bugles" sounded all around them. Now, in the

modern age, science and its "infidel bugles" were heard on all
sides, but, in the words of Professor Roswell Hitchcock pronounced at the Evangelical Alliance in 1873, "we are not
alarmed." Evangelicals compared the new threat of skepticism,
deism, and atheism to that of the eighteenth-century Enlightenment. They had beaten back that assault with revivals that
appealed to the masses, and they were confident that once again
their message would prevail. The "popular heart," that of ordinary men and women, would not be turned aside by "modern
skepticism, rationalism, the claims of the Papacy, and every
other false system."[23]

Taking the Debate into the Political Arena

William Jennings Bryan confounds the view that religious fundamentalism and political conservatism are inextricably linked.
Three times the Democratic Party's presidential nominee,
Bryan was a Progressive who fought against monopolies and
the power of big business, championed the rights of working
people, and opposed America's imperialist designs. Born in Illinois in 1860, he embodied midwestern populist values in his
political life, believing that eastern financiers and industrialists
were wringing hard-earned money from workers and farmers.
He advocated government regulation of the trusts, and he supported legislation that helped his constituents. His "Cross of
Gold" speech in favor of inflationary silver coinage underscored his determination to fight for debtors who needed a
plentiful money supply, in opposition to powerful creditors
who wanted the gold standard to preserve their wealth. Indeed,
some have argued that Bryan's view of big government as a
means of protecting the many against the few came to fruition
in Franklin Roosevelt's New Deal.[24]

In light of Bryan's liberal political views, his position at the Scopes trial at Dayton, Tennessee, in 1925 seems incongruous. He went to Dayton at the invitation of fundamentalist leader William Bell Riley, and, as a representative of the World Christian Fundamentals Association, he became the fundamentalist champion of the Bible as the inerrant, inspired Word of God. Bryan declared that he was "more interested in religion than in government" and thought that the most important things in life lay outside the realm of government. He believed that religion and the Bible were essential for a moral society and a peaceful world, and he peppered his political speeches with biblical references supporting his fight for justice, morality, and peace. One possible way to reconcile Bryan's political liberalism with his religious conservatism centers on his concerns over the social implications of Darwin's theories. It was social Darwinism that, according to this interpretation, bothered Bryan because it ran counter to his belief in the common man and woman. If science were allowed to define a society based on the "survival of the fittest," then all his battles against the wealthy and powerful were for naught. Such a view explains his attacks on evolution as yet another chapter in his defense of democracy. However, it goes only so far. Bryan went to Dayton not to make another political speech on behalf of democracy but to defend the Bible as the inspired Word of God. As he saw it, Americans and America depended on God's Word.[25]

Until 1925, religious debates over evolution occurred primarily within colleges, universities, Bible schools, churches, and church conferences. In the summer of that year, however, it took center stage in a dramatic court case in sleepy Dayton, Tennessee, that attracted such national figures as Bryan and Chicago defense attorney Clarence Darrow. More than one hundred reporters, many of whom represented the nation's largest newspapers, gave the trial front-page coverage, and radio broadcasters heightened national interest by providing live reports.

The case itself was straightforward, and the outcome was never in doubt. The state of Tennessee had passed a law in the spring banning the teaching of Darwinism in public schools. A Dayton biology teacher, John Scopes, challenged the law by teaching evolution, and, after being charged with violating the law, he was brought to trial in July. The American Civil Liberties Union supported Scopes and supplied him with three top attorneys, the best known of whom was Clarence Darrow, who had served as defense counsel in the kidnapping and murder trial of Nathan Leopold and Richard Loeb. That case established Darrow's reputation as a fierce defender of civil liberties in large part because of his twelve-hour summation that included an oratorical tour de force against the death penalty.[26] William Jennings Bryan saw the setting and the case as an ideal opportunity for him to deal a fatal blow to rationalists who threatened biblical truths and the American way.

With such high-powered figures involved, the case soon became a much-publicized debate over the central arguments in the modernist-fundamentalist struggle. Fundamentalists contended that the trial was about the unchanging truth of the Bible. For modernists, it was not about biblical truth at all, but rather about different perceptions of the truth. They argued that fundamentalists were unable to adjust to the social changes that had transformed America into a modern, scientific, urban, pluralistic, industrial nation. More than one commentator noted that sleepy, rural Dayton was the perfect stage for Bryan's defense of a way of life that had passed. Whether seen as a clash of worldviews or as a debate on biblical truth, the trial riveted the nation's attention, especially when Bryan himself took the witness stand and was examined by Darrow, arguably one of the finest trial lawyers of the day. Under a blistering and relentless attack on Bryan's claims, Darrow exposed Bryan's ignorance concerning other world religions and critical accounts of the origins of the Bible. The most dramatic moment came when Darrow forced Bryan to defend his literal interpretation of biblical passages that ran counter to the claims of scientific knowledge. Bryan pleaded ignorance on questions regarding how Eve could have been created from Adam's rib, what would happen if the earth stopped rotating and the sun stood still, and when exactly Noah's great flood occurred. When asked what he thought about calculating the time of the flood through biblical evidence, Bryan replied, "I do not think about things I don't think about." And when Darrow then asked whether he thought about things he did think about, Bryan answered, "Well, sometimes."[27]

The fundamentalists won the verdict at the Dayton courthouse, but they lost the verdict in the court of public opinion. The jury found Scopes guilty of violating the law, and he was ordered to pay a one-hundred-dollar fine. But public opinion poured derision on the fundamentalists, sapping the movement of much of its influence in national life. No one was more acerbic than newspaper columnist and social critic H. L. Mencken in ridiculing fundamentalists as backward, ignorant, and superstitious rubes. Before the trial he had taken the position that the case was more about democracy than about evolution. The people of Tennessee had the unquestioned right to decide what was taught in their public schools, he asserted, arguing that "a democracy had every right to make itself look as foolish as it could." His remarks drew quick response from scientists, who retorted that science and its conclusions depended on evidence, not on votes or court cases. During the trial, Mencken accused Bryan of trying to become "Pope" to America's "peasants." And he concluded after the trial that Bryan had in fact become a rural saint, adding that the "gaping primates of the upland valleys" would ensure his sacred place in Tennessee hagiography. Writing of the late politician two weeks after the trial ended, Mencken indicated that Bryan had perpetuated superstition: "If the village barber saved any of his hair, then it is curing gall-stones down there today."[28]

The verdict was headline news in the *New York Times*. The story line was that of a titanic "battle on evolution" and a personal duel between Clarence Darrow and William Jennings Bryan. The *Times* declared Darrow the winner in his questioning of Bryan the day before "to the delight of hundreds." The abrupt settlement between the lawyers that ended the trial prematurely denied Bryan the chance to put Darrow on the stand for a grilling of his own. In a tone suited to a report on extraterrestrial creatures, the *Times* noted that each day of the trial had begun with prayer, that the judge had declared that the "Word of God was given to man that man may use it as a waybill to the other world," and that he had ended with a prayer to "God that he had decided right."[29] Such open expression of faith in an industrial, scientific age underscored the chasm between modernists and fundamentalists.

In many respects, the Scopes trial was a sideshow in the larger culture war, and its impact on American politics was minimal. However, the debate between modernists and fundamentalists had profound implications because of its influence on political culture. It was a battle for what historian Mark Noll calls the "control of public discourse," the way that Americans conceive of themselves, their religious heritage, their providential mission, and their moral values.[30] Each side believed that it represented what George Marsden calls "the normative American creed."[31] Fundamentalists like Billy Sunday considered that creed to be evangelical and revivalist. He castigated as liars those who said that revivals were "abnormal," and he called for a "good old-time . . . revival" in the tradition of

Whitefield and Finney. That, he suggested, was the normative creed for Americans.

Not all fundamentalists engaged in the heated political discussions of the day. Indeed some, notably those in the Holiness movement, believed that Christians had far more important concerns than those of politics. They believed that theology, not politics, was at the center of what was wrong with America. Americans, in their view, had strayed from their heritage of relying solely on God for salvation and had embraced such heresies as Pelagianism and Arminianism that emphasized the role of humans and free will. In a dramatic example of the effort to shift the focus of Christian hope back to divine election and away from political elections, a tract printed by the Moody Bible Institute appeared as a ballot in an "important election." The ballot asked, "Will You Be Saved?" with two columns, one with the heading "Yes" and the other "No." The ballot was partially marked, indicating that God had already voted "Yes" and that Satan had voted "No." The issue must be decided by the individual whose "Yes" vote witnessed to God's transforming grace.[32]

For some, the bitter battle between fundamentalists and modernists raised anew questions about the wisdom of sectarian influence in politics. Moreover, some Americans wondered whether Christianity had become so divisive that it no longer served as the foundation of public morality, an unthinkable prospect for most of the nation's founders. John Adams had talked about a "very extensive Connection" between religion and "the great Interest of the Public." Christian benevolence, he argued, demanded that Christians promote and support political systems and regulations advancing the pursuit of happiness of the multitudes. Moreover, Christian morality encouraged the "Benevolence, Charity, Capacity and Industry" that, when exerted in public as well as private life, instilled freedom and virtue in order to rid society of "Misery, Want and Contempt."[33] But in the late 1920s, many agreed with journalist and secular Jew Walter Lippmann, who was convinced that "anti-intellectual popular fundamentalism and extremism had irremediably discredited traditional Protestantism among thinking people in the community." He regarded fundamentalism as backward-looking and narrow, hardly the basis for morality in the modern world. Further, he thought that the modernist-fundamentalist division among Christians had forever destroyed the United States' moral consensus. Lippmann advocated a new consensus based on a new humanism: "When men can no longer be theists, they must, if they are civilized, become humanists."[34]

Religious and Political Liberalism:
The Rise of Big Government
from the New Deal to the Cold War

Oak Ridge, Tennessee, is situated only about sixty miles from Dayton, but in 1942 the two towns were located in different universes. Like Dayton, the area between Black Oak Ridge to the north and Clinch River to the south, what was to become the new city of Oak Ridge, was farmland dotted by small rural communities such as Scarborough, Wheat, Robertsville, and Elza. But within months after the Japanese bombed Pearl Harbor and the United States declared war on the Axis powers, the federal government purchased the land, relocated the residents, and built three laboratories to develop and produce weapons-grade uranium-235 for an atomic bomb. Tens of thousands of scientists, engineers, and workers flooded into the region; working around the clock for a little more than three years, they succeeded in producing the uranium for the first atomic bomb test at Los Alamos, New Mexico, and the devastating bomb that hit Hiroshima, Japan, on August 6, 1945. What had been a sleepy stretch of Tennessee had become the launching pad for the nuclear age.

While the Bible was the ultimate authority at Dayton in 1925, science reigned supreme at Oak Ridge in 1942. Learning that Hitler's Germany was engaged in similar research for the purpose of producing an atomic bomb, the Roosevelt administration vowed to win the race of scientists and therefore launched the ultrasecret Manhattan Project. Physicists such as

Albert Einstein, Leo Szilard, Edward Teller, Enrico Fermi, and Robert Oppenheimer had developed theories suggesting that splitting the nuclei of uranium atoms would release enormous amounts of energy. Oak Ridge was more than an important part of the Manhattan Project; it had significant implications for the role of religion in American politics during and after World War II. First, in mobilizing to win the war, Americans looked to science and industry to provide the weapons for defeating the Axis powers. That is not to say that religious faith ceased to be important; indeed, soldiers, sailors, and marines in combat zones and civilians back home sought divine guidance and protection through prayer and worship. But public policy directing the war effort relied primarily on scientists and engineers, not ministers, priests, and rabbis, to win the war. With the atomic bomb's success in bringing the war against Japan to an end, Americans increasingly believed that science and scientists could solve all sorts of problems, from fighting disease to making daily life easier and more convenient.

Second, Oak Ridge was a creation of the federal government, which had mushroomed in size and scope during the Depression and World War II. Increasingly Americans turned to the federal government instead of religious institutions for such basic services as medical care, social security, housing, and education. In 1925, the federal government was not a major visible presence in rural eastern Tennessee; by 1945 that had changed dramatically. The Tennessee Valley Authority (TVA), with headquarters in Knoxville, was part of Roosevelt's New Deal to help Americans recover from the Depression. It transformed the lives of eastern Tennessee residents with dams that generated affordable hydroelectric power, stimulated regional economic development, and provided reliable flood control. The Oak Ridge project, located near Knoxville in large part because of the TVA, endured after the war as a major center

developing and producing fissionable materials for national security and peaceful purposes.

The growth and reach of Big Government and the revolutionary advances in science were but two of the cataclysmic
social changes that faced American religion in the period from
the Great Depression to the Cold War. The result was what
Princeton sociologist Robert Wuthnow called the "restructuring of American religion."[1] Confronted with new secular forces
that threatened to silence the voice of religion in the national
political discourse, religious groups were forced to forge new
organizational alignments and adopt new strategies. Denominations lost influence as religious groups formed new coalitions
constructed primarily along ideological rather than theological
lines. Religious conservatives and religious liberals offered
competing moral visions for America: the former calling for
reaffirmation of the nation's Christian, or at least Judeo-Christian, heritage; the latter more willing to embrace secular instruments to advance their vision of a just society in a rapidly
changing age. This chapter examines, first, what some have
called the secularization of America, a claim that the modern
liberal-capitalist state and scientific knowledge relegated religion to the margins of culture. The chapter then explores more
specifically how various religious groups engaged the liberal
state, and ends with an examination of conflicting religious
visions for world peace and domestic morality.

Social Change and the Secularization of America

From the onset of the Depression, at the beginning of the
1930s, to 1960, the United States underwent seismic social
changes with profound moral implications. First, the population grew by about 40 percent, with the increases trending

sharply higher after World War II. In addition to more people, there was a population shift following the war with millions moving to the suburbs, which resulted in a more segregated society, in terms of both race and class. Second, science produced technological wonders that placed theretofore unimaginable powers in human hands. On August 6, 1945, the United States forever changed the face of warfare when it dropped an atomic bomb on Hiroshima. Within a decade, the world faced the prospect of nuclear annihilation as the Soviet Union and the United States threatened each other and all human life with their respective arsenals that grew larger and deadlier each year. But science also turned atomic energy to the benefit of people in medical diagnosis and treatment. Moreover, by the end of the period, Americans were poised to explore the "new frontier" of space, a venture that produced promising new technologies with applications on earth. As a result of scientific wonders, Americans developed a deep faith in the power of science to solve all sorts of personal and social problems, a disturbing notion for some religionists. Third, the U.S. government exploded in both size and reach. From 1930 to 1960, the federal government's outlays in consumption, expenditures, and investment burgeoned tenfold in constant dollars.[2] Further, citizens increasingly looked to the federal government and the welfare state that the New Deal helped create for a wide range of vital services, including employment, unemployment relief, health care, education, and old-age assistance. Finally, the United States emerged from World War II as a superpower in global affairs. Unlike the aftermath of previous wars when the country retreated to an isolationist position, the post–World War II era thrust the United States into the role of leader of the free world, providing Americans with enormous global influence for good or ill.

[margin note: Onset of the Depression]

[margin note: grew]

In response to those social changes, lawmakers, judges, and presidents formulated new public policies, and religious groups were divided in their assessment of those policies. Generally, the point of contention between religious conservatives and religious liberals was that the former wanted less government intrusion into individuals' lives, and the latter wanted more. Liberals applauded such New Deal programs as Social Security and the National Labor Relations Act, designed, respectively, to help the elderly and workers. But many wanted to see services expanded to include all Americans regardless of race or creed, and they wished to see public assistance extended to address other social problems such as the lack of medical insurance for the poor. Conservatives, on the other hand, viewed much of the New Deal as "creeping socialism" that threatened the moral fabric of society by making individuals dependent on the state for basic services. Other government programs had unintended consequences that further divided religious liberals and conservatives. For example, as millions of soldiers, sailors, and marines returned to civilian life after World War II, they benefited from the G.I. Bill, which enabled many to get a college education. While liberals and conservatives applauded the act as providing a much-deserved benefit to veterans, some religious conservatives became disturbed over the secularization of higher education that the bill helped fuel. Accompanying the billions of federal dollars pouring into colleges and universities were regulations including those prohibiting sectarian discrimination on the part of recipient institutions. Some critics declared that the result was the establishment of secular humanism in higher education and discrimination against Christianity.

Some sociologists employ secularization theory to explain the fate of religion in post–World War II America. According to that perspective, secularization is one dimension in the modernization of society, a process that includes rationalization, industrialization, bureaucratization, and urbanization. By all accounts, they argued, the United States had become thoroughly modernized and secularized by the 1950s. Secularization was evident in the way that Americans thought and behaved and in the institutions that they built. Large numbers of Americans replaced supernatural explanations for the way the world works with techno-rational explanations. And while religion continued to matter, the theorists contended, it moved from the public to the private sphere where its influence was much more circumscribed. Finally, secularization attained institutional expression through autonomous secular organizations, both private and public, which assumed many of the functions formerly performed by religion.[3]

While few could argue with the growing influence of secular ideas and institutions in the United States, not all were ready to consign religion to the dustbins of history. Indeed, at the same time sociologists were pronouncing America a secularized society, the number of Americans attending churches and synagogues reached historic highs. How could one call the United States a secular nation when the vast majority of its population professed a belief in God and God's providence and were enrolled in congregations for worship? Further, the 1950s saw yet another revival on a national scale. Billy Graham was the evangelist, and he exploited new "secular" methods of communication to reach tens of millions through his televised "crusades." Some sociologists elucidate the paradox of religious growth in an increasingly secular society through the theory of religious economy. While acknowledging growing secular trends, they explain religious vitality by pointing to America's competitive religious marketplace. Because no sect has a monopoly, all religious groups are free to seek new members, and they freely spend their resources to do so. Further, by making demands on their members to spread the gospel, churches create battalions of "salespersons" who become recruiters. And, through energetic and innovative efforts, churches find new ways to promote themselves. Moreover, new sects and cults spring up to meet spiritual needs and tastes unsatisfied by existing religious groups. Just as entrepreneurs in the marketplace of goods find imaginative ways to increase market share, entrepreneurs in the marketplace of religion discover new avenues for extending religious influence.[4]

While competition was essential for the growth and invigoration of American religion, cooperation was necessary for it to speak with authority and confidence on public issues. Protestants had long envisioned a time when Christians would offer the world a united vision, but that goal proved elusive because of differences rooted in history, culture, and theology. In the United States, for example, the rift between fundamentalists and modernists had widened to the point that there was little chance of a union of all Protestants. What evolved instead were two unions, one composed of liberals and the other of conservatives. In the postwar period, each coalition claimed to represent America's moral conscience and to reflect its religious heritage. And each engaged in political action to advance specific public policy issues that they identified as most critical to the nation's morality.

The history of the liberal and conservative coalitions underscores the ideological rift that prevented religious Americans from speaking with a single voice. In April 1942, a group of 147 fundamentalist Protestants met in St. Louis to discuss ways that conservative denominations and churches could work together to revive "the fortunes of evangelical Christianity in America." Working in the shadows of the great events of the day, the group, soon to be organized as the National Association of Evangelicals (NAE), recognized that with the nation recovering from depression and fighting a world war, "American energies were being directed to the war effort, not matters of religious endeavor." Furthermore, the group acknowledged that few Americans expected anything positive from fundamentalists because "the Scopes Trial of 1925 and the resultant loss of fundamentalist influence in the mainline denominations had led many to believe that conservative Christians had vanished from the scene, never to be heard from again." These conservatives considered themselves outsiders, having suffered "public defeats" in the 1920s and remaining outside the "cultural mainstream" during the 1930s and early 1940s. From the ashes of their apparent demise, however, they determined to rise through new organizations and strategies.[5]

Some of the NAE organizers took a militant view of the group's mission. They envisioned a great conservative army that would engage in warfare against liberals and secularists. Liberal Christians formed their own coalition in 1950 by organizing the National Council of Churches (NCC), which recognized the diversity of America's religious marketplace and embraced an ecumenical approach in applying the principles of their faith to the problems confronting the nation. They stressed religious toleration and interfaith cooperation, while downplaying theological differences among member groups, in order to advance the Kingdom of God on earth by working for social justice and world peace. Moreover, the NCC applauded the liberal, humanitarian programs of secular institutions, especially those of the federal government and the United Nations, as important allies in reaching their goals of justice and peace.[6]

The split between religious conservatives and religious liberals is explained in large part by their opposing perspectives on secular ideas and institutions. Stressing God's immanence and focusing on matters of this world, liberals found much common ground between the sacred and the secular. On the other hand, many conservative religionists viewed secular interests with suspicion and contended that America had indeed fallen victim to secularization. They pointed to the 1930s and 1940s as the dawning era of a new "religion" that they called "secular humanism." Secular humanism, as they saw it, was a coherent religion in which humans replace God as the central authority underlying faith and practice. Moreover, they argued that the U.S. Supreme Court's endorsement of the Jeffersonian "wall of separation," which excluded Christianity from public schools, resulted in the establishment of secular humanism, in violation of the First Amendment.

Liberal Politics and Liberal Faith

Liberal religionists were much more receptive than were conservatives to the big social programs initiated by Franklin Roosevelt in the New Deal and Harry Truman in the Fair Deal. Though rooted in the Bible, liberal theology easily accommodated new ideas, including those of secular origin. Theological liberalism rested on the premise that the world has changed dramatically since the days of the New Testament, and that it is incumbent upon Christians to make the gospel comprehensible in the modern age. Speaking for liberals, Harry Emerson Fosdick, pastor of the nondenominational Riverside Church in New York, argued that while the Christian faith contains "abiding experiences" that transcend time, it must express that faith within "changing categories" to accommodate modernity. Liberals also embraced a biblical hermeneutics receptive to the claims of science. Rather than interpreting the Bible as the infallible revelation of God, they pointed out that biblical authors were limited by their own cultural and historical circumstances, and that their writings must not be accepted as "absolute authority." The "essence of Christianity," not the words of the

Bible, was authoritative. Moreover, that essence was revealed in a number of ways; God's beauty was expressed in nature as well as through scripture. Thus liberals blurred the lines between the sacred and secular, as well as between faith and science. Liberals emphasized the presence of God within the world as opposed to his transcendence. In the view of liberals, God worked primarily through individuals and groups of all sorts, not just through those who called themselves Christians. Hence liberal Protestants were ecumenical and saw Catholics and Jews as fellow laborers in working for justice and peace on earth. Liberals saw sin not as some "fundamental flaw in the universe," but as an imperfection or maladjustment that could be eradicated through education, prayer, reflection, and good works. Further, there was a close affinity between liberal theology and the so-called secular orientation of American universities. Liberal education sought to understand people and the world they created and occupied, and was thus consistent in its aims with those of liberal religion. Finally, liberal theology was optimistic. Liberals believed that through working together in an enlightened way, men and women under God's guidance could inaugurate an era of moral reformation, of social justice, and of world peace—in other words, they could usher in the Kingdom of God on earth.[7]

As the Great Depression worsened in the early 1930s, liberal Protestants and Catholics alike denounced unregulated capitalism as an immoral and failed system. In a social creed declared on Labor Day, 1931, the Federal Council of Churches called for the subordination of the "profit motive" for a system of social planning that would result in "a wider and fairer distribution of wealth." It also called for a more activist federal government that would provide social insurance "against sickness, accident, want in old age, and unemployment."[8] When the New Deal failed to bring a more equitable distribution of wealth, the National Catholic Welfare Conference issued a call for "a Christian Social Order" in America. Though endorsing capitalism as the best means of producing wealth, the conference advocated worker participation in profits and management, and a wider "distribution of ownership of productive machinery." Like the Protestants, liberal Catholics called for a welfare state that would provide "decent housing" and "security against illness and dependent old age."[9]

For many religious liberals, liberal politics provided a vehicle to reach their goal of realizing God's earthly kingdom. Certainly there were many religious people who were sharp critics of the New Deal and of the welfare state that it helped create, and there were many others who criticized American foreign policy; nonetheless, social activists applauded many of the Democratic Party's initiatives of the 1930s and 1940s. Liberal religionists supported FDR's efforts to save, yet reform, American capitalism. They endorsed a well-regulated market economy, one that rewarded individual enterprise while at the same time holding persons accountable for their actions. They by and large embraced Roosevelt's welfare state, designed to relieve human suffering from market dislocations and to offer a modicum of social security. They backed the war to defeat fascism and the Cold War against totalitarian communism. And they welcomed the United Nations as a global peacekeeper. They also cheered the Supreme Court's decision to erect a "wall of separation" between church and state, believing that religion was a private matter to be pursued by individuals without state support or interference. Clearly, there was a close affinity between the aims of liberal Christians and the political establishment. Indeed, it might be said that liberal Judeo-Christian religion acted as a religious establishment for liberal politicians.

Conservatives, on the other hand, longed for a return to a time when their religious perspectives found voice in national politics. Calvin Coolidge's presidency (1923–1929) had been such a time. Born into a New England Congregationalist family, he became in his public life, in the words of one biographer, a "Puritan in Babylon." In his autobiography, Coolidge ascribed his lack of faithfulness as a church member to the work of Satan, a spiritual force for evil that inhabited the president's world. Despite his Puritan self-doubt, Coolidge remained steady in the conviction that America was a Christian nation with moral values grounded in religious faith. He believed that hardworking, property-owning, law-abiding, and God-fearing citizens—not government programs dependent upon high taxes—were the best hope for social justice. Pursuing that belief, his administration became an exemplar of the laissez-faire philosophy of government.[10]

Though some conservative Christians accused New Deal Democrats of abandoning America's Christian heritage, Franklin Roosevelt himself publicly expressed his religious belief and called on the nation to renew its faith in God as well as in democratic principles. An Episcopalian, Roosevelt on several occasions linked the fortunes of society with its piety. In his 1939 State of the Union message, delivered in a world threatened by Hitler's Nazi Party and Stalin's communist regime, he reminded the nation of its cherished legacy of religious freedom:

> Where freedom of religion has been attacked, the attack has come from sources opposed to democracy. Where democracy has been overthrown, the spirit of free worship has disappeared. And where religion and democracy have vanished, good faith and reason in international affairs have given way to strident ambition and brute force.

He called upon the nation to reaffirm its commitment to religious faith as the basis of freedom and democracy, warning that any society that relegates religion and democracy "to the background can find no place within it for the ideals of the Prince of Peace." He declared that the United States "rejects such an ordering, and retains its ancient faith."[11]

President Harry Truman was a religious liberal in the sense that he considered morality more important than theology and believed that religious faith was primarily a matter between God and the individual, not a matter of public policy. Though the Baptists with whom he was affiliated preached against such personal sins as drinking and cursing, Truman drank whiskey, played cards, and spiced his language with profanity. Further, while Baptists in the South opposed equal rights for blacks, Truman in 1948 desegregated the U.S. armed forces by executive order. He placed more stock in right behavior than in right theology. Early in his life he expressed his views: "I am by religion like everything else," he wrote in 1911. "I think there is more in acting than in talking. I had an uncle who said when one of his neighbors got religion strong on Sunday, he was going to lock his smokehouse on Monday. I think he was right from the little I have observed." Holding that religion was a private matter, he expressed his opinion that "people's religious beliefs are their own affair, and when I don't agree with 'em I just don't discuss religion. It has caused more wars and feuds than money, and that seems a shame too." He had little use for people who "publicly parade their religious beliefs. . . . I've always believed that religion is something to live by and not to talk about."[12]

During Truman's administration, the U.S. Supreme Court agreed with the president that religion was a private matter that should be left to the individual without governmental assistance or interference. In *Everson v. Board of Education* (1947), the court in a 5–4 decision declared that the New Jersey legislature, in providing state funding for bus transportation for parochial school students, had not violated the establishment clause of the First Amendment. What is significant about the decision is that both sides relied on Thomas Jefferson's and James Madison's separationist interpretation of the relation between church and state. Writing for the majority, Justice Hugo Black invoked Jefferson's "wall of separation" metaphor to set the boundary between church and state. "Neither a state nor the Federal Government," he wrote, "can pass laws which aid one religion, aid all religions, or prefer one religion over another." While arguing that the Court could not approve of the "slightest breach" of that wall, Black concluded that New Jersey's law represented no breach at all. In his view the law was neutral in respect to religion, neither favoring nor disadvantaging anyone because of religious convictions. Justice Wiley B. Rutledge dissented and, like Black, based his opinion on Jeffersonian and Madisonian arguments. He wrote, "Neither so high nor so impregnable today as yesterday is the wall raised between church and state by Virginia's great statute of religious freedom and the First Amendment, now made applicable to all the states by the Fourteenth." As he saw it, the New Jersey law breached the wall of separation, which, in his mind, represented the second such breach by the Court. Rutledge feared that there would be subsequent, wider breaches until "the most solid freedom steadily gives way before continuing corrosive decision."[13]

In subsequent cases in the late 1940s to the early 1970s, the Court advanced a separationist doctrine in deciding the place of religion in public institutions, especially public schools. In *McCollum v. Board of Education* (1948), a majority held that an Illinois school district's policy of allowing religious groups to use classrooms during the school day to teach religion was unconstitutional, even though student attendance was voluntary. Writing for the majority, Justice Black argued that the practice amounted to the use of public funds for the "dissemination of religious doctrines." Moreover, it constituted "invaluable aid" to religious groups through its "compulsory public school machinery," which helped provide students for their religious classes. In *Engel v. Vitale* (1962), the Court ruled unconstitutional a New York program prescribing "daily classroom invocation of God's blessings." Again Justice Black wrote for the majority, and he declared that it is "no part of the business of government to compose official prayers." The Court further removed religion from public schools in *School District of Abington Township v. Schempp* (1963). In addition to prohibiting prayer, this decision proscribed "all public school exercises that were exclusively religious." In 1971, the Court adopted three criteria to be applied in all cases to determine whether a law is in violation of the establishment clause. As set forth in *Lemon v. Kurtzman* (1971), the Court gleaned three tests derived from cases heard since *Everson:* "First, the statute must have a secular legislative purpose; second, its principal or primary effect must be one that neither advances nor inhibits religion; finally, the statute must not foster 'an excessive government entanglement with religion.' "[14]

Though generally supportive of the prevailing political culture, liberal Christians hardly represented a united voice concerning the country's purpose and mission. Some liberal theologians believed that liberals had so embraced secular culture that they had lost their distinctive Christian message. Further, some critics like Reinhold Niebuhr pointed out that events such as the Great Depression, two world wars, and the Cold War made a mockery of the liberal faith in progress. He and other Christian realists reminded men and women that sin had hardly been stamped out, and the transcendent God was the world's only sure hope against destruction. At the same time, however, Christian realists, like their fellow liberals, were social activists and worked hard for social justice and world peace. Indeed, they were active supporters of the United Nations.[15]

In post–World War II America, religious fundamentalists found little favor in mainstream culture and in the national political arena. However, this does not mean that they were without influence. Viewing themselves as "religious outsiders" to the liberal establishment, conservative evangelicals created their own sphere of influence where they preached a populist message inspired by an earlier and simpler time, a time before secular influences pushed religion out of the public sphere. That populist message informed Charles Fuller's *Old Fashioned Revival Hour*, which during the Depression and World War II became one of the nation's most popular programs. A Holiness minister trained at the Bible Institute of Los Angeles, Fuller resigned his pastorate in 1933 and started the Gospel Broadcasting Association, which he led until his death in 1968. He tried to interest the networks in carrying his broadcast, which originated from Hollywood's KNX. When CBS purchased KNX in 1936, the network dropped Fuller's program because it no longer wished to carry "paid-for religious programs." For the next three decades, Fuller battled fruitlessly for a spot on one of the large networks, whose heads, according to one historian, "were turned by the powerful religious radio commission of the more theologically liberal Federal Council of Churches." Fuller found a receptive outlet in 1937 with the fledgling Mutual Broadcasting System, and the show enjoyed spectacular success. By 1939, the *Old Fashioned Revival Hour* aired on 152 stations, reaching every state and across southern Canada. The broadcast made Fuller a popular evangelist who attracted forty thousand people to an evangelistic meeting at Soldier Field in Chicago and filled New York's Carnegie Hall. By the end of the 1930s, his program reached more than ten million listeners, topping the audiences of such popular shows as *Amos 'n' Andy* and *The Bob Hope Show.*[16]

By making his show nondenominational and noncontroversial, Fuller was able to unite a broad spectrum of fundamentalists and conservative Protestants. He told his listeners, "We are allied with no denomination," adding by way of explanation, "We are fundamental, premillennial and our desire is to bring up no controversial questions, but only to preach and teach the Word of God." Fuller also appealed to his audiences through savvy marketing. He offered free Bibles to children who memorized twenty-five specific Bible verses. And he incorporated topical references into his programs, capturing the immense interest generated by such exploits as Admiral Byrd's Antarctica expedition.[17]

Combining evangelicalism and patriotism during World War II, Fuller took his program to new heights of popularity. Targeting troops overseas as well as families back home, the broadcast by 1944 ran on 575 stations and shortwave bands around the world, reaching an audience estimated at twenty million. The program commingled the sacred and the secular, interweaving foreign and domestic news with such revival hymns as "Jesus Saves."[18] Fuller sought to make his broadcasts reflect an idealized American family culture by "making each broadcast just as spiritual and 'homey,' as comforting and cheery as possible."[19]

Fuller's popular show complemented the more intellectual efforts of the National Association of Evangelicals to preach and teach conservative Protestantism to Americans. Rather than trying to shape the national culture through political activism, fundamentalists opted to unite and broaden their base by employing modern communications to disseminate their traditional message. As author Harner Vance acknowledged in *Moody's Bible Institute Monthly* in 1963, fundamentalists were religious outsiders in America, and that was an acceptable designation. In words that applied to the 1940s and 1950s as well, he wrote, "In this era of the Insider it may shock us for a moment to remember that the greatest Outsider of all time is Jesus Christ. . . . If we follow Him we shall be outsiders too." Some fundamentalists—like Carl McIntire, who founded the militant American Council of Christian Churches in 1940—fostered what one historian has called an "aggressive and judgmental separatism." And when J. Franklyn Norris, fundamentalist pastor at Fort Worth, was shunned by the Baptist General Convention of Texas for behavior fostering discord rather than harmony among Texas Baptists, he wrote a friend, saying, "There are a few that think I am dying to get in, that I need to get in. . . . My work has prospered more by being 'out,' more people have turned in sympathy toward my work than if I were in."[20] Though not all conservative Christians shared the views of fundamentalist extremists that made them religious outsiders, many did think that America's traditional Christian values were in jeopardy, and that McIntire and Norris were unafraid to take on the liberal establishment.

Envisioning World Peace

Liberal and conservative religionists also put forth different views of the United States' role in the postwar world. The latter believed that the United States had a divine mission to spread Christianity and democracy to the rest of the world, a mission that took on added urgency with the spread of communism and its atheistic stance. Billy Graham's popularity is explained in part by William Randolph Hearst's decision to endorse and publicize Graham's anticommunist message. A newspaper proprietor and staunch crusader against communism, Hearst welcomed a conservative religious voice in the fight against godless Marxist-Leninist views. Graham and other evangelicals in the 1950s appealed to tens of thousands who found the promises of modernity to be empty. Graham staged revival crusades and called on Americans to return the nation to its Christian roots and reaffirm their commitment to traditional moral values.[21]

Conservative denominations such as the Southern Baptist Convention accelerated their foreign missions efforts after World War II. They almost doubled the number of missionaries they sent into foreign countries to preach the gospel during the first decade following the end of the war. Excluded from communist countries, such as the People's Republic of China, evangelical missionaries concentrated on developing nations. For 150 years, American Protestants had engaged in foreign missions, but the Cold War lent an added element. Not only were missionaries carrying the gospel to benighted men and women; they were spreading democratic ideals.

Religious liberals had a different vision of world missions. In contrast to the practice of of American churches sending missionaries to the rest of the world, they preferred a program of cooperating with religious leaders of other nations. The former strategy smacked of religious imperialism, they thought. Consequently, in 1948 liberal American Protestants met with Protestants from around the world in Amsterdam to organize the World Council of Churches (WCC). Like the National Council of Churches, the WCC was an ecumenical body with a shared vision for advancing the gospel of Christ around the world while respecting the distinctive traditions of the member groups. Its mission was a Christian version of that of the United Nations: Christians from all nations uniting for the purpose of promoting international justice and peace by preaching a common gospel. Expressing their unity, delegates avowed: "Christ has made us his own, and he is not divided. In seeking him we find one another. Here at Amsterdam we have committed ourselves afresh to him, and have covenanted with one another in constituting the World Council of Churches. We intend to stay together."[22] Most conservative denominations refused to join the World Council of Churches, charging it with being too pluralistic and tolerant, charges similar to the suspicions they voiced concerning the National Council of Churches. Southern Baptists, the largest Protestant group, instead opted to pursue international cooperation with fellow denominationalists solely through the Baptist World Alliance (BWA). While the WCC emphasized issues of world peace and human rights, the BWA focused on evangelism.[23]

In contrast to its isolationism in other postwar periods, after World War II the United States could not disengage from world affairs, nor could Americans ignore international developments in debates over the nation's culture. While the country refused to join the League of Nations after World War I, it was a charter member of the United Nations, whose headquarters were located in New York City. At the same time, as one of two superpowers emerging from the war, the United States was also a charter member of the North Atlantic Treaty Organization (NATO) as it confronted the Soviet bloc in the Cold War. For many Americans, world events were freighted with religious significance that bore upon American identity and values.

Religious conservatives and liberals alike endorsed the United Nations' fight for religious liberty. Both the liberal National Council of Churches and the conservative National Association of Evangelicals applauded the organization's commitment to promoting freedom of conscience and human rights around the world. The charter stated that all persons in signatory countries had the right to join whatever religious group they chose, and, as important, to leave any religious group they wished to leave. Though they disagreed on many other matters, and though they did not always agree on the exact meaning of the First Amendment, liberals and conservatives cherished religious liberty and wished to see it extended to people everywhere. Beyond its commitment to religious freedom, however, the United Nations came under attack from many religious conservatives. Premillennialist evangelists such as Carl McIntire, Billy James Hargis, and Bob Jones were leading critics of the United Nations because they viewed it as a prelude to one-world government.[24]

In addition to supporting the United Nations' fight for religious liberty, religious conservatives and liberals were united on the question of U.S. recognition of the state of Israel, founded in 1948. Of course religion did not drive American policy in the Middle East; access to and development of oil reserves as well as checking Soviet designs in the region were major considerations. However, Israel evoked support from across the entire religious spectrum. The Jewish lobby used its considerable political assets to influence politicians on behalf of Israel, mobilizing a bloc of votes, campaign contributions, and media coverage. In addition, both liberal and conservative Christians backed Israel, with the former voicing admiration for Israel's social values and the latter for Israel's military successes that seemed to fulfill biblical prophecy. Though the influence of religious lobbies on Middle East policy was and is limited when compared to that of powerful, well-connected secular lobbies, the degree of religious unity remains nonetheless noteworthy.[25]

The Cold War raised a number of issues that divided rather than united American religion. For many Christians, the global confrontation of the United States and the Soviet Union and the prospects of nuclear war presented the church with awesome responsibility and enormous challenge. After World War

II ended in 1945, the *Christian Century* proclaimed the church's mission in the new era: "to face man with his present inescapable choice between life and death and to bring him to a decision in favor of the unsearchable riches of life in a world whose energies all derive from God." Behind that statement was the bold claim that "there is simply no alternative to the Christian faith except destruction." But in order to save the world from itself by Christianizing it, Christians had to set aside their differences and unite. Catholics and Protestants, the Eastern and the Western churches, as well as the myriad Protestant denominations must dedicate themselves to this single mission. The editors called for the suspension of "every large denominational project . . . until there is evolved an ecumenical plan which will eliminate competition on the community level, insure maximum cooperation among the churches of the nation and strengthen the world witness of the Christian faith."[26] In short, the competitive religious marketplace must be transformed into a co-op where pooled resources are dedicated to a common cause.

Though some American Christians called for a united effort in pursuit of a single mission and condemned sectarian divisiveness, unity during the Cold War remained as elusive as it had been before. Jesuit theologian John Courtney Murray thought that pluralism was inevitable in democracies; nonetheless, he condemned it as being "against the will of God." Writing during the Second World War, German theologian Dietrich Bonhoeffer had expressed similar sentiments, adding that Americans were less capable than any other people in the world of realizing the "visible unity of the Church of God."[27] How could American Christians unite when America's religious marketplace offered so many choices and American culture made individual choice a sacred right?

No moral question exposed religious divisions more than that of America's dropping the atomic bomb on Japanese civilians. Some secular as well as religious commentators tried to place the debate within the larger framework of the morality of war itself. In late August, just after the bombs were dropped on Hiroshima and Nagasaki, the Gallup Poll found that 85 percent of Americans approved of the use of the bomb on the two population centers as a means of ending the war. Over the next two years, however, criticism increased, with just over half those polled by Gallup in October 1947 believing it was a "good thing" and almost 40 percent considering it a "bad thing."[28] As the debate intensified, it triggered a broader discussion of American morals and values, and religious groups weighed in with various assessments.

Supporters of the decision to drop the atomic bomb often defended it in providential language. Echoing sentiments expressed by the founders in 1776, they saw the hand of God behind all of history, and they deemed that the Almighty had once more favored the United States. President Truman put it this way: "We thank God that it [i.e., the bomb] has come to us, instead of to our enemies; and we pray that He may guide us to use it in His ways and for His purpose." Letters to newspaper and magazine editors echoed that sentiment. One soldier from Camp Shelby, Mississippi, in a letter to *Life* magazine, wrote, "Thank God for the atomic bomb, which has proved so essential and valuable already." In a symposium addressing the "moral meaning of the atomic bomb" organized by the Episcopal Church, Arthur Compton, a leading Protestant layman, declared, "Atomic power is ours, and who can deny that it was God's will that we should have it?"[29]

It was not the use of the atomic bomb as a military tool but its deployment against civilians that caused most anguish. When General Curtis LeMay introduced "large-scale terror bombing" of Japanese cities in March 1945, Americans learned that almost 200,000 people died from the incendiary bombs. In one night raid alone, more than 100,000 died. Religious commentators were relatively silent; when they did speak, it was with ambivalence. While consistently deploring the practice, the *Christian Century* added that it was just part of the "hell of war." The editors hoped that the awful act would hasten the conclusion of the war and prevent killing on an even greater scale. But the Federal Council of Churches condemned atomic bombs as part of its condemnation of "total war," which included the killing of civilians as a means of defeating the enemy. In a 1944 report, the FCC denounced the "massacre of civilian populations" by Axis and Allied powers alike, and questioned whether Christians could acquiesce "in the view that modern war may properly, even in cases of extreme peril to nation, church, or culture, become total war." Pope Pius XII weighed in as well, questioning whether modern warfare could be regarded as "an apt and proportionate means of solving international conflicts." Despite such criticism, most Americans accepted both the Tokyo raids and the dropping of the atomic bombs as essential to the war's progress. The *Chicago Sun* on August 9, 1945, declared, "There is no scale of values which makes a TNT explosion right and a uranium explosion wrong." As horrible as they both are, they are means of ending the war. The *Christian Century* agreed with the *Chicago Sun*, but condemned both conventional and atomic bombing of civilians as immoral: "In the regime of war—that is, in the regime ruled by military necessity—the bombing of cities, whether by an atomic bomb or by B-20s, is on the same plane as the killing of an enemy soldier with a rifle. . . . War has no moral character. When a nation commits its destiny to the arbitrament of sheer might, it abandons all moral constraints." Thus the editors shifted the focus of debate from the atomic bomb to modern warfare itself. The question was not whether America should have dropped the bomb, but whether it should commit itself to the modern notion of total war.[30]

In March 1946, the Federal Council of Churches' Calhoun Commission issued its report, "Atomic Warfare and the Christian Faith." Consisting of twenty-two members—including Richard Niebuhr and Roland Bainton of Yale, and Reinhold Niebuhr of Union Theological Seminary, and chaired by Robert Calhoun of Yale—the group was dominated by Protestants from the modernist, liberal wing. The commission's condemnation of America's dropping of the bomb was unanimous: "We would begin with an act of contrition. As American Christians, we are deeply penitent for the irresponsible use already made of the atomic bomb. We are agreed that, whatever . . . one's judgment of the ethics of war in principle, the surprise bombings of Hiroshima and Nagasaki are morally indefensible." Conceding that the bomb probably shortened the war, the commission concluded that "the moral cost was too high. . . . We have sinned grievously against the laws of God and the people of Japan." Catholic and Jewish leaders joined the liberal Protestants in condemning the bomb's use. The Catholic *Commonweal* in August 1945 declared that "the name Hiroshima, the name Nagasaki, are names for American guilt and shame."[31]

A. J. Muste, a Dutch-born pacifist, used even stronger language in condemning the United States' use of the atomic bomb as an unjustifiable act of terror. In his book *Not by Might* (1947), he argued that "if Dachau was a crime, . . . Hiroshima is a crime." While condemning war itself, he considered America's act the "ultimate, atomic atrocity." For Muste, Truman's decision to drop the bomb and Americans' overall approval of the act came, not from fear, but from sin, and therefore the only way to prevent similar future acts was for the nation to

undergo "moral conversion and spiritual rebirth." Nuclear ho-
locaust would be prevented not by political means but by spiritual renewal. "People who know no peace in their own spirits,"
he wrote, "do not really want peace in the outward order and
their fitful and distracted efforts to achieve it will be constantly
thwarted. . . . The reordering of our lives and of society, the
establishment of control over atomic energy, must begin with
the individual spirit."[32]

While agreeing that Americans needed to experience spiritual conversion, fundamentalist and conservative Protestants
thought the answer was revival, not moral outrage over the
bomb. Theologically conservative Protestants generally agreed
with the "necessary evil" argument that justified the dropping
of the bomb on civilians as a means of shortening the war.
Fundamentalists read the event as a sign that human civilization was on the brink of destruction, and "that God would
soon bring history to an end." The answer was to pray and
work for revival, an outpouring of God's grace that had always
come when spiritual light was most clouded. The figure who
emerged to lead a postwar revival was Billy Graham, a full-time
evangelist for the Youth for Christ organization, founded in
1945. Graham preached a double-edged message, with one side
directed toward "godless" communism and the other toward
sinful America. Making America sound more like "Babylon
than Israel," Graham linked the threat of nuclear annihilation
and the judgment of God for sin. He singled out atheism and
materialism as sins undermining America's traditional Christian values, and called on individuals to accept Christ as their
personal savior.[33]

By the time Graham emerged as a national religious figure
in the 1950s, religious liberals exercised greatly diminished influence in the public square. Some broke from their ranks because they worried that liberals had ignored God's transcen-

dence, and had become too closely tied to modernity and its confidence in human progress. Reinhold Niebuhr was the best-known defector, and he reminded liberals that sin was hardly in retreat, as world events attested, and that human responses were woefully inadequate to counter the evil it caused. In addition to internal divisions, liberals saw their authority weaken in relation to that of the secular institutions they endorsed: science and higher education, the free, regulated market, the welfare state, and the United Nations. People who had once placed their hope in the church looked increasingly outside the church for help. Some went so far as to question the relevance of the church in modern society.

With Dwight Eisenhower in the White House and Republicans enjoying a majority in Congress, conservative Protestants in the 1950s found political allies in their fight to reclaim America as a Christian nation. Like members of the National Reform Association after the Civil War, a group of conservatives after World War II petitioned Congress to give official recognition to the country's Christian heritage. They pointed out that the founders, lured astray by the false doctrines of the Enlightenment, had failed to acknowledge God's Providence when they framed the Constitution. Moreover, in the past several decades, with liberals as the dominant spokespersons for religion in the public square, the transcendent, providential God that had always guided the United States was hardly mentioned. Further, the Supreme Court had officially driven prayer from public schools. Most important, the country was at war, a Cold War against a godless enemy. Indeed, many understood the confrontation between the world's two superpowers in terms of a larger apocalyptic battle between Judeo-Christianity and atheism. Thus they sought legislation that would do what the Constitution had failed to do: declare that America is a Christian nation and acknowledge God's providence in American history and culture. In 1954, Congress added the words "under God" to the Pledge of Allegiance. The following year, President Eisenhower, acting under Public Law 140, ordered that the words "In God We Trust" be stamped on all coins and currency. Then, in 1956, Congress officially designated those words as the national motto, supplanting "E pluribus unum," the motto selected by Jefferson, Franklin, and Adams. Symbolically, the faith of America's fathers now took on a decidedly Christian character as opposed to that of the Enlightenment.

By the end of the 1950s, religious liberals were in retreat. Conservatives charged liberals with being either soft on communism or even sympathetic with the godless ideology; by contrast, conservatives called on the country to return to traditional family values. Perhaps the biggest blow to liberals' political fortunes, however, came when they shrank from leading the fight for social justice for all Americans, including black Americans. Liberals had consistently stated social justice to be one of its cherished goals, yet after the Supreme Court declared school segregation unconstitutional in *Brown v. Board of Education* in 1954, religious as well as political liberals—rather than being the "headlights" for civil rights, as Martin Luther King, Jr., had hoped they would be—were little more than the "taillights" in the country's greatest struggle for social justice.

In 1960, American voters elected a liberal Catholic to the highest office in the land, reflecting a significant shift in American culture since 1930. After more than three centuries of anti-Catholicism, dating to the earliest English settlement, Catholics finally enjoyed acceptance in the nation's religious marketplace. Though constituting the largest single religious group in the country, Catholics were still outnumbered by Protestants almost two to one. But there was a qualitative difference in the religious marketplace that translated into the historic election of John Kennedy. Theretofore, voters had imposed an unofficial religious test on presidential aspirants, demanding that they represent the Protestant heritage and values. But by 1960 there was a new, broader religious test, one that required office-seekers only to embrace what might be called the religion of America, a civil religion with roots in the nation's beginnings.[34]

Responding to attacks on his religious views by both Protestants and Catholics, Kennedy invoked America's civil religion in his oft-quoted speech before the Houston, Texas, Ministerial Association on September 12, 1960. He began by suggesting that religion was a red herring in the campaign, one fabricated by those who rejected the core value of religious freedom for all Americans. Moreover, he said, the real issues that demanded attention were not religious at all, but such concerns as "too many slums, . . . too few schools, and too late to the moon and outer space." Problems of war and hunger and ignorance, he insisted, knew no religious boundaries. He called on voters to embrace the principles of toleration and religious freedom that Baptists in Virginia had fought for in 1776, principles that later became the foundation of America's commitment to religious liberty. If he were denied the presidency because of his Catholic faith, then in another time the same religious intolerance might work against a Baptist or a Quaker or a Unitarian or a Jew. Kennedy concluded by calling on religious and lay leaders, including "Catholics, Protestants, and Jews," to set aside the bigotry that they had too often employed in the past to emphasize distinctions among Americans and promote instead the American ideal of brotherhood.[35]

Five years earlier, sociologist Will Herberg had published a book entitled *Protestant-Catholic-Jew*, which supported Kennedy's vision of an America in which religious differences had no bearing on the nation's civil life. Herberg declared that while Americans were divided by the "professed" religions of

Protestantism and Catholicism and Judaism, they were united by their common "operative" religion, the "American Way of Life." That civil religion "involved a faith in democracy, individualism, optimism, idealism, humanitarianism, nationalism, and tolerance of other Americans." To illustrate his point, Herberg suggested that while almost all Americans clung to the professed Christian belief that one should love one's neighbor as oneself, for many Americans, such love did not find expression in their "operative" religion. During the Cold War, the American way of life disapproved of Americans who expressed love for communists in general and Soviets in particular. While professing trust in God to direct their lives, Americans, in practice, placed their trust in such human means as education, technology, economics, and government to solve the problems facing them.[36]

Herberg and others suggested that America's religion was influenced by both traditional religious and secular humanitarian ideals. While most Americans considered themselves Protestant or Catholic or Jewish, a growing number might be regarded as "secular and humanistic," a designation that historian Martin Marty applied to those who subscribed to the "religion of democracy." John Courtney Murray thought that secularists were prominent enough as a group to be added to Protestants, Catholics, and Jews as the fourth faith in America.[37] Whether secularism in 1960 constituted a religion is debatable, but what is more certain is that the United States maintained its dual sacred-secular culture in a tension that strained relations within the religious marketplace.

Civil Rights as a Religious Movement: Politics in the Streets

V oices long silent in the religious marketplace demanded to be heard in the 1960s. And when once again they were denied a fair hearing by the religious establishment, they took their message directly to the country and sought a hearing in the court of public opinion. Blacks, students, women, Native Americans, and the poor denounced the cultural and political elite dominated by white, middle- and upper-class, Protestant males. These protesters charged the white Anglo-Saxon Protestant (WASP) establishment with perpetuating a morally bankrupt society that promoted greed, war, racism, and sexism. The new voices offered alternative interpretations of the gospel that were more inclusive and emphasized justice for all. When the political establishment ignored them, they defied the power structure through direct political action by protesting in America's streets, challenging the two major political parties, and grabbing headlines. What resulted was a grassroots movement that found its greatest power, not in legislative assemblies and courtrooms, but in a determined, persistent, and effective "politics out-of-doors," in which an oppressed people broke unjust laws in the name of a higher law.[1]

Southern blacks had long epitomized the religious outsider. In the South, de jure segregation had defined race relations from the end of Reconstruction, relegating African Americans to separate but unequal schools, housing, public services, and public accommodations. Moreover, blacks lived under laws not of their making; white rulers had disenfranchised them, thus negating the Fifteenth Amendment. Denied economic opportunity, blacks eked out livings in the lowest-paying, most menial jobs, and millions lost their places as agricultural laborers when mechanization made them redundant. White terrorist groups like the Ku Klux Klan enforced strict segregation through criminal acts such as lynching and firebombings, perpetrated with impunity and, in some cases, with the active participation of law enforcement officers. Just as they were political, social, and economic outsiders, southern black Christians were religious outsiders with no effective voice in America's religious marketplace.[2]

The civil rights movement of the 1950s and 1960s was a social and political movement, but it was also a religious one. Martin Luther King, Jr., was a Baptist preacher, and many other leaders, including Ralph Abernathy, Andrew Young, and Jesse Jackson, were ordained ministers as well. King's organization bore a distinctive religious title: the Southern Christian Leadership Conference. Civil rights meetings and rallies often took place in black churches, which had long constituted the one organization that blacks controlled, a community's social and political center as well as its religious heart. Blacks envisioned the struggle for equal rights to be a Christian mission akin to that of the Apostle Paul to spread the gospel to the gentile world. "Just as the prophets of the eighth century, B.C. left their villages and carried their 'thus saith the Lord' far beyond the boundaries of their home towns," King wrote from the Birmingham jail in 1963, "and just as the Apostle Paul left his village of Tarsus and carried the gospel of Jesus Christ to the far corners of the Greco-Roman world, so am I compelled to carry the gospel of freedom beyond my own home town. Like Paul, I must constantly respond to the Macedonian call for aid."[3]

King's strategy was one of nonviolent resistance to the white power structure, a strategy successfully employed by Mohandas Gandhi in India's fight for independence from British colonial rule. To his black brothers and sisters, King preached the gospel of freedom as the true gospel, a message that transcended religious and national boundaries, applying to Hindus and Muslims in India as well as to Christians and Jews in the United States. Like Frederick Douglass before him, King rejected the white gospel of racial injustice that taught blacks to stay in their assigned places and work hard for their white bosses. At the same time, King had a religious message for whites. The civil rights movement, he insisted, was not only about salvation for blacks; it was for the "salvation of our nation and the salvation of mankind." His words echoed those of America's founders in 1776, who claimed that the revolt against oppressive British rule was a fight for the rights of mankind. King rejected the role of "outsiders" for blacks, arguing that "anyone who lives inside the United States can never be considered an outsider anywhere within its bounds."[4] Employing language from America's civil religion, he reminded all Americans that the national creed called for freedom and justice and tolerance for all. Thus King transformed black Americans into insiders with a mission to carry the gospel of freedom to whites who, in violation of the nation's great founding principles, considered blacks to be outsiders.

In the tradition of white religious leaders who called upon the nation to return to its religious heritage and moral values, King based his call for civil rights for all Americans on his view of that heritage and those values. He pointed out that black Americans had been denied their "constitutional and

God-given rights" for more than 340 years. And, like leaders of the American Revolution denouncing tyrannical imperial laws, King differentiated between "just" and "unjust" laws. The former he defined as a law that "squares with the moral law or the law of God," while the latter was "out of harmony with the moral law." He considered segregation to be immoral because "any law that degrades human personality is unjust." Segregation gives whites a sense of superiority and gives blacks a sense of inferiority; as such, it violates the ideal of the Declaration of Independence and the moral law. Like the Revolutionary leaders, King called on Americans to reject immoral laws and claim anew those natural rights that God has given to all people.[5]

Black Churches as Outsiders in the Religious Marketplace

The Christianity to which slaves were introduced defined them as outsiders. Wary of the effect the gospel might have on slaves, slaveholders stressed those themes that promoted obedience and subservience. Accordingly, the emphasis was on salvation, not from the injustices of this world, but from malign spiritual forces. In this world, slaves must accept their lot as the will of God, who made some to rule and others to serve, some to be rich and others to be poor. The very structure of worship services reinforced slaves' outsider status. Relegated to the balcony or to the back of the congregation, they were separated from white Christians. And, often, they were subjected to sermons directed solely at them and aimed at putting the full weight of faith behind a selective moral code: one that made stealing master's chickens a sin, while overlooking master's stealing their God-given natural rights, rights that slaveholders had boldly claimed in the Declaration of Independence.

Slaves who became Christians differentiated between the Christianity of the Bible and that of their masters, and they constructed their own version suited to their condition. Slave codes forbade teaching slaves to read, with good reason. Reading was a means of knowledge, and knowledge, including that of the Christian gospel, was power. Nevertheless, a few slaves learned to read, and some of them became exhorters or preachers to their fellow slaves. Their version of the gospel was different indeed from that of their masters. To be sure, some preached messages similar to those heard at the white church: prepare for eternal life and accept one's lot in this life. But others preached a different gospel, one of hope for freedom and justice in this world, a gospel that had a dual message aimed at eternal salvation and earthly deliverance from bondage. When southern whites learned of the 1741 slave uprising in New York, some saw at its roots a distorted Christianity whereby "African-Americans gave their own revolutionary meanings, . . . spreading stubborn rumors that baptism meant freedom." As one Anglican priest put it, "the Negroes have this notion, that when they are baptized, they are immediately free from their masters."[6] Such dangerous notions set slave Christianity and slaveholder Christianity at odds.

The origin of black churches in America is rooted in race, that is, in the experiences of African Americans in a society where race determines one's place. The nation's founding documents affirm as a natural, God-given right the "pursuit of happiness," Jefferson's gloss on John Locke's insistence upon the undisturbed right to own property, including the possession of slaves. And in the United States slavery was race-based, confined to persons of African descent. Even for free blacks, the United States was not the Promised Land where "all men are created equal"; rather, it was a place that consigned African Americans to lives of servility and separation. It was within that segregated world of the late eighteenth century that free blacks organized their own churches, a pattern that southern blacks would follow after the Civil War. The history of the black church in America is one of blacks creating a religion of their own, and it cannot be told apart from the experience of slavery. Uprooted from their West African homes, slaves as captives aboard slave ships and, later, as forced laborers on plantations, turned to their native religion for comfort, healing, and revenge. Nature-worship was at the center of West African spiritualism, marked by belief in invisible surrounding forces, both good and bad, whose influences individuals could direct through incantations and prayers. When their masters introduced them to Christianity, slaves did not discard their own religious heritage; rather, they combined the two into something unique: African American Christianity. Like the conjurers and medicine men of their native land, black preachers rose up as spiritual leaders, and under their direction blacks created the "first African-American institution, the Negro Church." In its origins it was neither Christian nor organized; it was an amalgamation of heathen and Christian elements expressed in songs and tropes of the slaves' own making. The overwhelming majority of black churches both during and after slavery were Baptist and Methodist. Apart from the fact that many of their masters were members of those two churches, slaves found the Baptist polity particularly adaptive to lives confined to plantations. Local, democratic, and congregational, the Baptist polity enabled slaves on particular plantations to gather churches that fit their needs and tastes. Moreover, Baptist and Methodist churches gave prominence to feeling and fervor, characteristics of West African worship expressed through song and dance and in the "call and response" practice, whereby congregations participated fully in the worship ritual.[7]

To speak of "the" black church is, of course, misleading. While sharing common race experiences, black men and women stretched across a broad spectrum of congregations based on such variables as region, North or South, and location, urban or rural. Though he rarely attended church as an adult, W.E.B. DuBois was intrigued by the power of religion among blacks in the South and, consequently, wrote extensively on black churches. He observed that worship among southern blacks in the late nineteenth and early twentieth centuries centered on three characteristics of slave religion: "the Preacher, the Music, and the Frenzy." The preacher was many things: orator, politician, leader, boss, idealist, and intrigant, a figure whom DuBois called the "most unique personality developed by the Negro on American soil." The music of southern black Christianity perhaps best reflected the soul of the people. Its rhythmic melodies and minor cadences originated in the forests of West Africa, but its adaptations underscored both the pathos and the hope of an oppressed people who longed for deliverance. The "Frenzy" had its origins in shouting that was such an integral part of West African religion. In America, the frenzy arose from an intense experience whereby the worshiper was transported by the Spirit of God, "making him mad with supernatural joy." Pervasive in black churches, the frenzy was sometimes manifested as a "silent rapt countenance or a low murmur and moan" and sometimes as the "mad abandon of physical fervor" resulting in dancing, shrieking, and shouting. Northern urban churches, particularly those of the more cultured and aristocratic blacks, expressed a very different kind of worship experience, one that focused more on this world and less on the world to come. Of the spectrum of black churches, DuBois wrote, "Their churches are differentiating,—now into groups of cold, fashionable devotees, in no way distinguishable from similar white groups save in color of skin; now into large social and business institutions catering to the desire for information and amusement of their members."[8]

Excluded as blacks were from participation in the public institutions of American life, the black church was the only community organization that they owned and controlled. For whites, the free and unrestricted ownership of private property was a defining element of the American Dream, but for most African Americans for most of American history, it was a dream barely imaginable. Though many, if not most, members of a congregation could not afford to own their own homes, blacks took pride of ownership in their self-supporting churches. More than offering the rare experience of owning something, the black church provided opportunities for members to be "somebody." In their survey of black churches in the 1930s, Benjamin Mays and Joseph Nicholson encountered countless instances of the church's stimulating "the pride and preserv[ing] the self-respect of many Negroes who would have been entirely beaten by life." In the church, a truck driver could become chairman of the board of deacons, a hotel worker could become superintendent of the Sunday school, and a housemaid could become head of the missionary society. Though they received little or no recognition in their menial jobs, at church they could give full expression to their talents.[9]

Like DuBois, Mays and Nicholson found worship in black churches to be filled with emotion. While others explain such emotionalism as a part of blacks' nature or their West African heritage, Mays and Nicholson are more convinced that environmental conditions in segregated America explain it. As African Americans moved about in society, they knew that in many places they were "not wanted"; even "in most white churches of the United States [they were] not desired." By contrast, black churches offered their members and guests the "freedom to relax," to give release to their hopes and fears and frustrations that had little vent in white America. A sign tacked onto one church in a southern city in the 1930s said it all: "We offer riches to the poorest, friendliness to the friendless, comfort to the sorrowing—a welcome to all, step in." Inside the churches, blacks found more than the freedom to worship without restraint and without the disapproving and threatening eye of the white majority; they also found information and assistance for daily life. Black churches in segregated America acted as community centers where lectures, concerts, recitals, debates, and plays were staged, and they were places where men and women could learn about educational and job opportunities.[10]

Just as African Americans had no voice in the white-dominated religious marketplace, they were not full participants in the rituals of the nation's civil religion. Indeed, blacks lived a double life. As Americans, they lived within a great modern, democratic society with a noble national creed—the belief that all persons were entitled to the inalienable rights of life, liberty, equality, and self-determination. But as blacks in a segregated land, they were systematically denied those rights and relegated to the lowest civil, political, and economic status. Evocations of America as a Promised Land reminded blacks of promises denied, and citations of America's scriptures—the Declaration of Independence, the Constitution, and the Bill of Rights—of contradiction and hypocrisy. After World War II when black soldiers returned from defending rights and principles denied by their own nation to their people, African Americans accused white Americans of sins against the civil religion and demanded retribution.

African Americans were virtually invisible in the marketplace of religion. In one analysis of black Protestants at the end of the Depression in 1939, 90 percent worshiped in "separate

Negro denominations." Of the remaining tenth, 90 percent were part of segregated congregations. Thus only about 1 percent "actually gathered together with whites to worship." Moreover, white Protestants regarded blacks as unequal beings in the sight of God, and as a people whose segregated worship was divinely ordained. Considering segregation within the American Protestant churches to be an irrefutable fact, one black leader wrote, "Of all the groups devoted to social uplift, I have least hope in the white Christian ministers." Frank Loescher surveyed racial attitudes and practices of American white Protestant churches and concluded, "Protestantism, by its policies and practices, far from helping to integrate the Negro in American life, is actually contributing to the segregation of Negro Americans."[11] Writing in 1963, Martin Luther King, Jr., expressed a similar sentiment toward white clergymen in the South. He had thought that Christian ties would bind blacks and whites in a common struggle for justice, but he was disappointed to find that, for most white ministers, race transcended religion. Some were outright opponents of the civil rights movement, while others "remained silent behind the anesthetizing security of stained-glass windows."[12]

While all white southern denominations were segregated and kept black Protestants from having a voice in the religious marketplace, Southern Baptists were particularly notorious. Though they professed to be a People of the Book, Southern Baptists in their treatment of their black neighbors were far more obedient to the strictures of white southern culture than to the commandments of Christ. After examining three studies of Southern Baptist sentiments regarding race, one commentator concluded, "It is enough to say that Southern Baptists defended Negro degradation in the mid-twentieth century as fervently as they had Negro slavery in the mid-nineteenth." To be sure, there were a few Southern Baptists who spoke out for

racial justice as an expression of Christian love. Most notable
was Clarence Jordan of Georgia, who preached a message of
reconciliation and inclusion.[13] The Southern Baptists were not
alone in perpetuating racial segregation. One group of progressive southern Presbyterians convened in 1929 and voted in favor
of "interracial good will and understanding—*after carefully seg-
regating the Negro delegates.*"[14]

Northern white Protestants were little better, often making
overtures toward improving race relations without taking substantive steps. The Northern Baptist Convention of 1929, for
example, announced that its Committee for Interracial Relationships had nothing to report because for the last several years
it "has had no appropriation for its work." That same year, an
Episcopal priest in Brooklyn informed black worshipers in his
congregation that "they were not welcome." And when another
Episcopal minister in New York insisted on permitting blacks
to worship, his vestry voted to have the church "closed" for
repairs and locked.[15]

Black Churches and the Civil Rights Movement

Many black activists considered the civil rights movement to
be a religious movement. In language that echoed and restated
sentiments expressed in the social gospel movement, Andrew
Young asserted, "Ours was an evangelical freedom movement
that identified salvation with not just one's personal relationship with God, but a new relationship between people black
and white." On a more personal level and in a more direct
way, Ethel Gray, a Mississippi civil rights activist, captured the
religious dimension of the civil rights movement: "We stood
up. Me and God stood up."[16]

To call the civil rights movement a religious one is to beg the question: in what sense was it religious? The most enduring popular images of the era would lead one to conclude that it emanated from within black churches and was led by black ministers. We see the photographs and videos of Martin Luther King, Jr., Ralph Abernathy, and other members of the clergy bravely walking at the head of freedom marches in Montgomery and Selma. An Atlanta newspaper correspondent asked, in regard to black churches, "Have they not provided the meeting-places, theme-song, and leaders for the center of the non-violent protest?" And while blasting white churches for "doing nothing at all" to address racial injustice, Ralph McGill, editor of the *Atlanta Constitution*, added that the charge did not apply to black churches. "When one views the churches and Christianity without regard for color," he declared, "it becomes strikingly clear that Christianity and the churches have never been more relevant (taken as a whole)—or less on the sidelines."[17]

When viewed from within the civil rights movement, however, the role of the black church looks quite different from the familiar public images. Many activists in the voter registration drives recall the reluctance of ministers to open their churches or even lend their support to such activity. According to two local activists in Mississippi, "the preachers . . . didn't have nothing to do with it [the early civil rights movement]." They added, "[U]ntil things got when they could tell they wasn't gon' kill 'em, and then they went to comin' in." Another civil rights worker recalled, "We got turned down a lot of time from the black minister. . . . He mostly was afraid because they [whites] whooped a few of 'em and bombed a few churches. The preacher did'nt [*sic*] want his church burned down, and them old members was right along in his corner." The ministers' fears were hardly groundless; in the early summer of 1964 alone, more than forty black churches were burned in Mississippi.[18]

To gauge the importance of black Christianity in the fight for civil rights, one must recognize that its influence goes beyond the institutional church and its clergy. When asked how they were able to continue the struggle in the face of hatred and violence, many activists cited their personal faith as providing the courage to carry on. Since the days of slavery, African American Christianity had opened believers to a world of spirits that provided weapons "to protect themselves or to attack others," a sacred realm that civil rights activists of the 1960s drew upon to withstand racist sheriffs, hate-filled Klansmen, and deadly assassins.[19]

Among the most powerful religious vehicles of the movement were the freedom songs that arose from evangelical, revivalistic black churches. Music had always played a central role in black worship, expressing deeply held beliefs, otherworldly hopes, and inspirational sentiments for the day. When white Christians attend black worship services, they often comment on the power of the music and the "mystical, ecstatic experience" that transports the singers to the very throne of God. During the 1960s and the civil rights movement, that same music helped topple a hundred years of segregation. Andrew Young explained the influence of the freedom songs. Through music, he wrote, "Black people otherwise cowed, discouraged, and faced with innumerable and insuperable obstacles, could transcend all those difficulties and forge a new determination, a new faith and strength, when fortified with song. The music was not a political or economic gift to the people from the authorities, nor could it be taken away by them—music was the gift of the people to themselves, a bottomless reservoir of spiritual power." The whole world heard blacks sing freedom songs, such as the adaptation of the gospel song "I'll Overcome Someday" or the arrangement of the church tune blacks had sung for decades "Don't You Let Nobody Turn You 'Round."

But perhaps the real importance of sacred music to the movement manifested itself outside the public's view. Like the New Testament account of Paul and Silas, who sang when imprisoned, civil rights workers broke into song when imprisoned in jails from Jackson, Mississippi, to Birmingham, Alabama. They found comfort and encouragement in such old favorites as the hymn "Leaning on the Everlasting Arms."[20]

Many of the activists in the movement came from outside the southern black evangelical church, but nevertheless they recognized the importance of religion in inspiring and encouraging African Americans. Radicals in the Student Non-Violent Coordinating Committee (SNCC), Jewish radicals, and students from the free-speech movement had little personal connection with the faith of their fellow workers in voter registration drives and freedom marches. Yet they drew on "what moved the people: prayer, song, and testimony." One nonreligious activist recalled, "The religious, the spiritual was like an explosion to me, an emotional explosion. I didn't have that available to me [before]. It just lit up my mind. The music and the religion provided a contact between our logic and our feelings. . . . And gave the logic of what we were doing emotional and human power to make us go forward."[21]

While high-profile ministers like Martin Luther King, Jr., captured the headlines, some determined women conducted their own "private guerilla warfare" against southern segregation. One such woman was Mary Fair Burks, a longtime member of the Dexter Avenue Baptist Church in Montgomery where King was pastor. She was moved more by action than by words, and when King first came to Dexter Avenue, she thought he might be too studious. She liked King's predecessor, the iconoclast Vernon Johns, who often preached in patched pants and thundered a social gospel message that railed against American greed, materialism, and injustice. He urged his congregation to find fulfillment in simple living and high thinking, a philosophy that Burks found more appealing than did many others in the church. Burks did what she could to challenge white supremacy: entering white-only restrooms, sitting at "forbidden" lunch counters. After being arrested in one such incident, she helped organize the Women's Political Council, which she served as president for many years. The council was a vehicle by which Burks and other black women could combine their deep religious faith and political activism through grassroots organization. The women went door-to-door handing out leaflets, encouraging other women to participate, and they solicited funds from sympathizers all over the country. Though their activism made them targets for black ministers and laity who did not want to incur the wrath of the white establishment, the women found solace in their faith and, through their courage and example, inspired others to join the movement. Jo Ann Gibson Robinson recalls what happened inside the Dexter Avenue Baptist Church after she and others were arrested. Supporters had gathered for a mass demonstration, and Robinson felt that "certainly the Spirit from above must have been among the crowd, for people were mentally, spiritually, psychologically serene inside. Even I, always demanding proof for statements, felt a special peace within myself. A quiet calm seemed to invade and relax me. At the very beginning of the movement, I had put myself in the hands of the unseen power from above, and since then there had been no turning back."[22]

In addition to providing solace and stiffening resolve, black Protestantism also contained a radical religious vision for embattled civil rights activists. Accompanying the radicalization of the movement during the 1964 Freedom Summer was a radical theological message. One SNCC idealist wrote that racial prejudice was a "judgment on the lie we have been living. . . . For though the days of lynching may be over, the lynching of personhood continues. It is a spiritual issue."[23] That sentiment had deep roots in black radical theology that extended from Reconstruction. Bishop Henry Turner of the AME Church emphasized blackness and black Christianity as essential for saving not only blacks in the segregated South but America itself. Largely unsuccessful in promoting his views even among blacks, Turner preached a message of resistance, a message that he thought had been sanctified by the preacher-led slave revolts in the antebellum South. The idea that civil rights activists of the 1960s adopted was Turner's assertion that black Christianity was fundamentally incompatible with the "dominant values of white racist society."[24] With that statement, Turner, and later the civil rights activists, dared indict America's religious heritage and moral values. They confronted all Americans with the charge that if America was once a Christian nation, then it was a racist Christian nation that had made a mockery of the gospel and had violated the sacred beliefs of the civil religion, including its commitment to freedom, equality, and justice. Denied a voice within the religious marketplace, blacks in the mid-1960s condemned that marketplace as racist, unchristian, and un-American.

The civil rights movement and the role of religion within it underwent a profound change during the mid-1960s. Prior to that time, it had been confined primarily to the South and had been by and large nonviolent. When King and the SCLC went north, they met an entrenched white power that enforced de facto segregation with a determination that matched the de jure segregation of the South. As Northern cities erupted into riots and violence in the summer of 1965, southern civil rights leaders saw their dreams of a nonviolent movement go up in smoke. Black youths rejected the old authoritarian figures in their communities, including the elders of black churches, and confronted white power on the streets of their neighborhoods.

A new, angrier and younger leadership arose in such areas as Brooklyn's predominantly black Ocean Hill–Brownsville district, where the new cry was black power, not nonviolence, and the new spokesmen owed allegiance only to the masses they led. Stokely Carmichael was a leader in the Black Power movement and became chair of SNCC and head of the Black Panther Party. He rejected the goal of integration, arguing instead that it was time for black people to control their destinies. He called on African Americans "to unite, to recognize their heritage, to build a sense of community." That meant, he insisted, that blacks should "define their own goals [and] lead their own organizations." Sensing that the civil rights movement was taking a radical turn away from the church and Christian principles, some black church leaders responded with a theology for Black Power. In 1967, a group of black clergymen, aware of the black consciousness developing among their people, left a meeting of the National Council of Churches and formed a coalition of black ministers, later to be called the National Committee of Black Churchmen. In a manifesto, they provided Black Power with a theology rooted in the Christian gospel:

> Black Theology is a theology of black liberation. It seeks to plumb the black condition in the light of God's revelation in Jesus Christ, so that the black community can see that the gospel is commensurate with the achievement of black humanity. . . . The message of liberation is the revelation of God as revealed in the incarnation of Jesus Christ. Freedom IS the gospel. Jesus is the Liberator![25]

While the National Committee of Black Churchmen sought a Christian vehicle for channeling the anger of Black Power advocates, other blacks rejected Christianity altogether as the religion of white oppression. The most powerful spokesman of that view was Malcolm X, who since the early 1950s had been a follower of Elijah Muhammad and the Nation of Islam. During the early 1960s he became a critic of the civil rights movement because of its integrationist goals. While many in the movement were encouraged by the increasing support of whites, Malcolm X saw continuation of white dominance of black men and women. He wrote:

> I can't turn around without hearing about some "civil rights advance"! White people seem to think the black man ought to be shouting "hallelujah"! Four hundred years the white man has had his foot-long knife in the black man's back—and now the white man starts to wiggle the knife out, maybe six inches! The black man's supposed to be grateful? Why, if the white man jerked the knife out, it's still going to leave a scar!

Malcolm X called Christianity the religion of slave-owners and oppressors, and identified it with the white race and its racist attitudes toward black people. He preached a message of hatred toward whites and scoffed at the notion that Christianity was a bond that crossed race lines. In 1964 he went on a hadj to Mecca, where he experienced the brotherhood of all pilgrims, regardless of race. When he returned to America, he broke with Elijah Muhammad because of the latter's heretical racist views, views that had caused orthodox Muslims to shun the Nation of Islam. Malcolm preached a new message: the problem was not white people but an unjust society built on racial discrimination rather than on brotherly love.[26]

Beyond Christian and Muslim critiques of American society and politics, blacks of the 1960s invoked America's civil religion to demand equality and justice. In a speech at Central State College in Wilberforce, Ohio, on March 19, 1965, Judge

Raymond Pace Alexander, a forthright spokesman for the civil rights cause, called on blacks to claim what America had promised at its conception. Declaring that the denial of civil rights to blacks was not a "black" problem but an "American" problem, he equated the current civil rights movement with the nation's founding. Blacks of the 1960s sought what the patriots of 1776 demanded: "basic human rights in a society organized and dedicated to the proposition that all men are created equal and endowed with the inalienable rights of free men in a free society." The truths that Jefferson wrote about in the Declaration of Independence were no less true in the 1960s, despite their having been denied to blacks over the intervening 190 years: "We hold these truths to be self-evident—that all men are created equal, that they are endowed by their Creator with certain inalienable rights; that among these are life, liberty, and the pursuit of happiness." The civil rights revolution, Alexander concluded, is an extension of the American Revolution, and the success of the former would complete the latter.[27]

Consequences: Predictable and Unintended

Predictably, white Mississippians responded to civil rights advocates as "outside agitators" and mounted a militant defense of their segregated society that included a call for Christians to do their Christian duty. The Ku Klux Klan was eager, as always, to defend the race and "God's Will" against "miscegenation." Sam Bowers, who headed the White Knights of the KKK, called on his members to maintain a "Solemn, determined Spirit of Christian Reverence" in meeting the challenge. But the Klan was only a small part of the defense white Mississippians mounted. Following the *Brown v. Board of Education* decision of 1954, the state legislature had formed the State Sovereignty Commission as an official watchdog for outside agitators; in 1964, the commission provided policemen and Klan members with license plate numbers and other information to help them identify civil rights workers. In addition, most towns boasted a White Citizens Council consisting of leading businessmen who threatened the employment of blacks participating in the civil rights movement. And white churches did their part in isolating their parishioners from the outside agitators by posting deacons and elders at the entrances to their sanctuaries before and during Sunday worship services. While some liberal Southern Baptist ministers took forceful stances against racial discrimination both in society and within their congregations, most led their parishioners in defending segregation as a biblically sanctioned plan of God. A 1963 *Time* magazine piece described Southern Baptists as constituting the "rearguard of the civil-rights battle," with many of them believing that "segregation derives from the law of God."[28]

Equally predictable, while many white Christians in the South were openly hostile to the civil rights movement and many others across the country indifferent to it, many Protestant, Catholic, and Jewish organizations actively supported it. The National Council of Churches had a long history of denouncing racial segregation. Its predecessor organization, the Federal Council of Churches, had declared in 1946 that it "renounces the pattern of segregation in race relations as unnecessary and undesirable and a violation of the Gospel of love and human brotherhood." In 1963, the general board of the National Council of Churches called upon the church to "confess her sin of omission and delay, and to move forward to witness to her essential belief that every child of God is a brother to every other." Similarly, Catholic bishops of the United States issued a pastoral letter to be read in every Catholic church, declaring that "the conscience of the nation is on trial," and calling for equal access and opportunity in housing, education, employment, and public facilities. In January 1963, 650 Protestant, Catholic, and Jewish leaders convened as the National Conference on Religion and Race, giving the impression that religious organizations constituted a united front against racism. However, those white leaders who spoke out against racial discrimination in 1963 represented a small minority of the nation's hundreds of thousands of ministers, priests, and rabbis. Apathy, indifference, and prejudice were pervasive; members of many congregations agreed with the sentiments expressed by James Cardinal McIntyre, archbishop of Los Angeles, who thought that "Negroes had little cause for complaint, and ruled civil-rights agitation out of order." One group of fundamentalist Protestants voiced outright hostility toward the civil rights movement and the National Council of Churches. Led by the Reverend Carl McIntire, a preacher and radio evangelist on the far right, they organized the segregationist American Council of Christian Churches. Claiming ten million members, the organization railed against civil rights agitation as part of a communist plot to subvert American values.[29]

One explanation for the failure of white Protestant churches to fight for justice regardless of color is what historian John Lee Eighmy calls the "cultural captivity thesis."[30] According to that perspective, southern white churches both reflected and reinforced the racist views of the region's culture and therefore failed to meet the great moral challenges of slavery, abolitionism, and the fight for civil rights. While failing to account for the courageous whites who did stand up for freedom and equality for all and did so in the name of the gospel, the thesis does underscore the powerful influence of "southernism" as a cultural template for interpreting the church's mission. Thus while professing belief in the biblical injunction to love one's neighbor as oneself, the vast majority of white churches, nonetheless, continued to close their doors to black worshipers. Recently historians have applied the captivity thesis to black churches, as well, to condemn some prominent black ministers who, rather than leading the march against the evil of segregation, protected the scraps of privilege that the oppressive system of racial injustice had thrown them. In the words of historian Paul Harvey, many white and black churches in the South, when "compelled to choose between Christ and culture, . . . chose culture."[31]

The civil rights movement succeeded in gaining recognition of equal rights for all Americans, regardless of color, in public accommodations, education, employment, and political participation. Moreover, the Civil Rights Act of 1964 and the Voting Rights Act of 1965 contained enforcement provisions that in effect ended de jure segregation. While no one claimed that those pieces of legislation broke down all racist barriers and ended discrimination, they did provide legal recourse for black Americans to claim their inalienable rights.

But the civil rights movement also had unexpected consequences. First, the movement's success diminished the power of black churches by making the federal government the guarantor of rights and opportunities. With Lyndon Johnson's War on Poverty and Great Society, more and more black people sought secular solutions in the realms of poverty, education, job training, medical care, and social security. Long denied access to those secular institutions that white Americans had long enjoyed, blacks could and did avail themselves of opportunities that traditionally all-black institutions, including black churches, could never offer. In the mid-1970s, black ministers recognized the church's need to reclaim its place in black society. Rev. James Cone, a professor at Union Theological Seminary in New York, acknowledged in an article published in 1977 that the civil rights movement had changed the church. Black Power had challenged the church's claim to be the central agency for the struggle for freedom. And black churches were finding it difficult to situate Black Power within a Christian context. The black church faced a dilemma: to reject Black Power was to balk a popular grassroots tide that refused to return to the old days of acquiescence and accommodation, but to reject the traditional church was to reject the best of Christianity as taught by Martin Luther King, Jr. Cone asserted that how the church resolved that dilemma would determine its continued place in the unfinished struggle for liberation.[32]

Second, the civil rights movement contributed to what was a more, not less, segregated society. Whites accelerated their flight to suburbs. To avoid court-ordered busing to enforce equal opportunity in education, many whites organized "Christian" academies, which had all the earmarks of "segregation academies." Churches, especially in the South, continued to be segregated as whites abandoned churches in racially mixed town cores and inner cities and built larger ones in the segregated suburbs. The new segregation undermined King's dream that "the sons of former slaves and the sons of former slaveowners will be able to sit down together at a table of brotherhood."[33]

Third, the civil rights movement led to a realignment of the political parties as the "Solid South" abandoned the Democratic Party—the party that had, albeit reluctantly, championed civil rights. In 1968, Democrats claimed only Texas in the South, while Republicans carried Virginia, the Carolinas, and Florida, and the rest of the South voted for the arch-segregationist George Wallace. Then, in 1972, the entire South joined the rest of the country in giving Republican Richard Nixon a landslide win. The shift of white southerners to the Republican Party meant the infusion of millions of white evangelicals into the GOP. By the late seventies the so-called Religious Right would demand that Republicans support a return to "traditional" moral values. Ironically, in mounting their campaign for a moral revolution, leaders of the Religious Right found inspiration in the successes of the civil rights movement that most of them had vigorously opposed.

The Rise of the "Religious Right":
The Reagan Revolution
and the "Moral Majority"

O n May 1, 2005, Rev. Jerry Falwell called on his congregation at the Thomas Road Baptist Church in Lynchburg,
Virginia, to reclaim America. The fundamentalist pastor
dubbed his plan "Massive Spiritual Aggression" and defined it
as a "Biblical, non-violent, lawful and offensive strategy which
I believe the Lord gave me many years ago as a plan to take
America back." For too long, he asserted, the church in
America had been on the defensive, and the result had been
the loss of moral authority in families, schools, and government. Now was the time to "take back our children . . . take
back our schools . . . take back our government . . . take back
our Judeo-Christian culture." In addition to reaffirming the
nation's "Judeo-Christian culture," Falwell urged Christians to
emulate the New Testament church: "The New Testament
church in the Scriptures was never on the defense. It was always
charging the gates of Hell."[1]

Falwell has been instrumental in mobilizing conservative
Christians into what has become known as the Religious Right.
Like all labels, "Christian Right" fails to identify its constituent
members. While critics label the Christian Right as narrow
and backward, supporters see the movement in a more positive
light—as born-again, evangelical Christians who take seriously
Christ's charge to spread the gospel to the entire world. Surveys
identifying religious affiliations and beliefs rely upon self-

reporting, and those surveys provide some generalizations about individuals most likely to align themselves with the Christian Right. They come primarily from the following denominations: Missouri Synod Lutheran, Southern Baptist Convention, Churches of Christ, and Assemblies of God. The Christian Right attracts few supporters and many critics from the so-called mainline Protestants: Congregationalists, Methodists, Presbyterians, Lutherans, Episcopalians, Disciples of Christ, American Baptists, Unitarians, and Friends. While black Protestants and Roman Catholics might support Christian Right positions on certain issues, such as abortion, they do not tend to identify with them in general. Both the Princeton Religion Research Center's Religion in America Study and the Pew Charitable Trust's Survey on Religious Opinions find that about 40 percent of Americans describe themselves as "born-again" evangelicals. Their strongest presence is in the South, where almost 60 percent of respondents said they were born-again, and in the Midwest, where almost 40 percent gave the same reply. They tend to come from small-town and rural communities. And their college attendance percentage was almost half that of those who did not label themselves born-again. Household income of born-again respondents was also less than half that of others.[2]

The Religious Right pursues a moral agenda focused primarily on family, education, and sexuality. On other issues, its members do not differ markedly from those of other religious groups. For instance, on the question of legalizing marijuana, both evangelical Protestants and mainline Protestants oppose the measure in about the same percentages. The two groups show similar preferences regarding public spending on health education, the environment, and the poor. And they are roughly in accord in their views of extramarital sex. One issue that demonstrates significant difference between the two groups is that of homosexuality. Conservative Protestants view homosexuality as a lifestyle choice, rather than a biological predisposition, by a ratio of two to one over liberal Protestants. On the question of whether pornography leads to a breakdown in morals, almost two-thirds of conservatives answer in the affirmative, while only one-third of liberals offer the same response. On the controversial issue of abortion, differences center on the conditions under which abortion should be legal. There is general agreement on legalizing abortions for birth defects, the health of the mother or child, and rape. The two sides disagree on other reasons, including unwanted pregnancy, inability to afford care of the baby, and refusal to marry. On the question of the Supreme Court's rulings on prayer and Bible reading in public schools, about three-quarters of evangelical Protestants disapprove, compared to fewer than 60 percent of mainline Protestants.[3]

For some, the Christian Right is engaged in a culture war pitting Christians against humanists. Gary DeMar is president of American Vision, an organization whose motto is "Equipping & Empowering Christians to Restore America's Biblical Foundation." Like Falwell, he and his followers believe that America's Christian heritage is rooted in biblical truths, truths that humanists have pushed aside. He framed the contest this way: "The critical issue of our day is the relationship of Christ and His Word to our political and legal system in the United States. Who has jurisdiction over every aspect of American society, Jesus Christ or the State? Is this to be a Christian nation or a humanistic nation?" Cofounder of the Moral Majority Tim LaHaye sees a great contest between Christians and humanists over the minds of the nation's children. In 1980, he wrote, "I am concerned that the 50 million children who will grow up in America during the next generation will have access to the truth, rather than the heresies of humanism."[4]

While many conservatives applauded Falwell's call to arms, other evangelicals contested it as a distortion of true evangelicalism. At the same time that Falwell called on his followers to "take back" the culture, evangelical minister and author Jim Wallis urged believers to "Take Back the Faith" that had been "Co-opted by the Right." Leader of the Sojourners, a group of evangelicals who couple faith in God's transcendence with commitment to social justice, Wallis charged the Religious Right with getting the "public meaning of religion mostly wrong—preferring to focus only on sexual and cultural issues while ignoring the weightier matters of justice." To Wallis, the gospel of the New Testament commands Christians to feed the poor and work for peace, not to champion capitalist greed and American patriotism as the Religious Right is wont to do.[5]

Until Falwell's May 2007 death, Falwell and Wallis opposed each other in a religious marketplace deeply divided since the 1970s, when Falwell organized his Moral Majority movement. Each was evangelical. Each stressed faith and transcendence. But when they expressed the public meaning of their respective faiths, they were poles apart. At least through the presidential election of 2004, the Religious Right has been able to point to more influence in the political arena. Falwell and others have been able to mobilize their conservative base and keep it united to a far greater extent than have those sympathetic with Wallis's views. In fact, before 2004, it was difficult to detect an organized Religious Left (see chapter 8); rather, the opposition shares little other than distaste for the Religious Right. Moreover, the Democratic Party has not welcomed the Religious Left with open arms in a manner comparable to the Republicans' embrace of the Religious Right. In addition, members of the Religious Right have proven to be better communicators, both in the sense of delivering a consistent, understandable message and in that of exploiting modern media to the fullest to reach a mass audience. Liberals tend to be too wordy as they try to qualify their comments, and consequently rarely generate the kind of sound bites that politicians and reporters like. Finally, the Left's commitment to diversity and toleration means that they often stand with unpopular religious outsiders and social minorities.

The political influence of the Religious Right is surprising in light of the history of fundamentalists since the Scopes trial, when conservative evangelicals in general and fundamentalists in particular disengaged from politics. In part, they stayed on the sidelines because they believed that they should concentrate on other endeavors, such as evangelistic enterprises, including revivals and missions. They believed that it was more important to concern themselves with eternal salvation than with mundane politics. Yet at the same time it bothered them to watch American culture become captive to "secular humanism" in the period between 1925 and the mid-1970s. Public education at every level taught the nation's young people that science, not faith in God, held the key to human progress. Moreover, in the view of religious conservatives, the U.S. government seemed to be antagonistic to the Christian faith. As evidence, they pointed to the Supreme Court case, *Engel v. Vitale* (1962), in which the Court banned organized, officially sponsored and mandated prayer in public school. Writing for the majority, Justice Hugo Black argued that a governmental agency's act of dictating that a particular prayer be read to all students amounted to the establishment of one faith in violation of the establishment clause of the First Amendment. In his dissenting opinion, Justice Potter Stewart made the case that Falwell and other Christian conservatives would often repeat: banning prayer in public schools violated the "spiritual heritage of our Nation," as well as denying free exercise to those who wished to pray.[6]

It was the radical politics of the sixties that most disturbed conservative Christians. They were appalled at the cultural assault on the nation's Christian heritage that was mounted in the 1960s when a radical countercultural movement attacked what conservatives deemed sacred while embracing that which they held to be a sacrilege. In supporting the civil rights struggle and protesting the Vietnam War, young insurgents attacked the nation's moral authority and its white, male, upper-class culture. Feminists exposed American culture as a convenient structure erected by males for males, and their critique extended to the Judeo-Christian faith, which, they pointed out, rested on a firm patriarchal structure. Marriage itself came under attack by those who saw it as an exploitative institution that held women in subordination. The counterculture viewed the sexuality and sexual behavior promulgated by the Judeo-Christian culture as violating the right of all individuals to express themselves with freedom, unencumbered by ancient customs and patriarchal authority. The sixties encouraged young people to "do their own thing" and "let it all hang out," which meant ignoring or defying institutional norms that promoted conformity. What was particularly disturbing to Falwell was that many Christians endorsed these attitudes. Liberal Christians embraced the notion of "situation ethics," as more enlightened than living by a fixed moral code such as the Ten Commandments. Mainstream Christians were too willing to conform to modern secular culture where individual freedom reigned supreme, even when that culture made a mockery of God's revealed law. Many of these liberals, conservatives charged, sided with the "proabortion" forces that fought against laws restricting abortion as a violation of a woman's constitutional right to privacy—a view that the Supreme Court upheld in the landmark case *Roe v. Wade* (1973).

Responding to the sixties, a group of fundamentalists met in the early 1970s and organized a movement aimed at restoring America's Christian heritage. Falwell, along with Tim and Beverly LaHaye, Charles Stanley, and D. James Kennedy, launched the Moral Majority with a mission of "organizing evangelical leaders who will boldly engage the culture." Its political aim was set forth in a platform that was "pro-life, pro-traditional family, pro-national defense and pro-Israel." Though fundamentalists had been barely visible in national public affairs over the previous several decades, they had been far from idle. While remaining out of politics, they built an institutional base that was now primed to mobilize its millions of followers for political action. After the mainstream culture ridiculed their stance in the Scopes trial, fundamentalists established their own Bible colleges, publishing houses, mission agencies, and denominations. It was these entities that would enable the Moral Majority to build a grassroots political organization, register voters, rally support for specific causes and candidates, and get out the vote. Following Ronald Reagan's victory in the 1980 presidential race, Falwell and the Moral Majority boasted of their success: "The Moral Majority backs the presidential candidacy of Ronald Reagan and helps sweep him into office in dramatic fashion. In addition, 12 liberal Democrat senators and several liberal House members are also defeated, launching a new wave of political activity within the evangelical community. The political landscape is spectacularly altered."[7]

While Falwell's assessment of the Moral Majority's influence on national politics is open to interpretation, there can be no doubt that the Religious Right had become a political force to be reckoned with and would continue to be so into the twenty-first century. This chapter examines the roots of conservative Christian resurgence, first in the religious culture, and second in the political arena. It explores how a conservative movement made effective use of modern communications to organize and mobilize its base, recruit new members, and convey its message to politicians. It concludes by looking at the dissatisfaction within the Right and opposition from without.

Sex, Feminism, and Family Values

To many outside the Moral Majority, the group speaks a strange and disturbing language, one that appeared to be anti-intellectual, antiscience, and antimodern. But Professor Susan Harding, an outsider, discovered in her study of the Moral Majority that the words of Falwell, LaHaye, Stanley, and others not only made sense to their constituents but for them represented the truth. While outsiders might regard many of their utterances as "odd or ill-considered," to those inside the movement they were powerful and inspiring. Insiders lived in a "world generated by Bible-based stories," and the words of their leaders had "the creative quality of the Bible itself."[8] So when Falwell talked about taking America back from liberals who had denounced its Christian heritage and desecrated its moral values, he was bringing the story of Exodus to the United States. Confident followers looked to the Holy Ghost for deliverance just as the Children of Israel had followed the cloud to the Promised Land.

Ironically, it was a liberal Democrat who introduced the language of "born-again" Christianity into America's political culture. Jimmy Carter, the successful presidential candidate in 1976, brought with him deeply held convictions rooted in his Southern Baptist faith, a faith that was biblical, personal, and evangelical, but not fundamentalist. While presidents before him had been relatively private about their personal religious beliefs, Carter was a practicing born-again Christian who attended worship services regularly and read the Bible daily. He did not hesitate to talk about his personal faith nor to be seen carrying a Bible to church. In the words of one scholar, "President Jimmy Carter helped make it respectable to be 'born again.' " Moreover, following the Watergate scandal in the Nixon years, Americans seemed to pay more attention to the president's character, and thought it dangerous to separate morals from politics.[9] Many southern evangelicals had been more upset by Nixon's crude and sometimes blasphemous language revealed in his secret tapes than by the cover-up of the Watergate break-in or the obstruction of justice.

While divisions within American religious life have a long history, a new chasm opened in the second half of the twentieth century. Theological and ethnic differences receded in importance while a gap between liberals and conservatives surfaced that exposed distinctions in basic values. On their side of the divide, liberals embraced "the values of openness, pluralism, diversity, and mutual tolerance of differences." They subordinated theology to morality, and their ethics "emphasized love, relationships, peace, justice, inclusiveness, tolerance of minorities, and acceptance of varieties of lifestyles and expressions of sexuality." They were heirs to those eighteenth-century liberal Christians who found their religious beliefs compatible with the secular notions of the Enlightenment. Opposing them were conservatives, who traced their lineage to the Pietists of the Great Awakening. Where liberals espoused the moral relativism of situation ethics, conservatives found ethical absolutes grounded in biblical revelation. They supported traditional Christian and Jewish teachings on such questions as "family, sexuality, discipline, and the importance of moral law." In addition, they were deeply patriotic, advocating a strong military against godless communism, and law and order at home against social deviants and criminals.[10]

The counterculture of the sixties represented to conservatives the results of a culture that had turned its back on moral values grounded in God's immutable law. However, the view from within the counterculture was quite different, and, indeed, many inside the youth culture viewed their cause as a "moral-religious quest." In their critique of American mainstream culture, they saw a society that had made gods of science and technology, and they saw a government and economy that reduced people to objects. This depersonalized culture perpetuated the "myth of objective consciousness," but it was hardly objective in its concerns and in its use of resources. Rather, it served the religions of power and wealth, fueling "self-interested nationalism" and business profits. Those who dared oppose this dominant culture, argued Theodore Roszak in his influential *The Making of a Counter Culture*, whether American black laborers or Vietnamese peasants, found themselves dehumanized and either controlled or eliminated. Such a culture mocked the nation's civil religion, especially the cherished ideals of liberty and justice for all.[11]

Conservative Christians rejected the counterculture's critique of America and were appalled at the response of mainline Protestants. As conservatives saw it, liberal Christians were so busy promoting ecumenism and embracing secularization that they had lost their distinctive Christian voice. As an example of the liberal perspective, conservatives pointed to Harvey Cox's *The Secular City: Secularization and Urbanization in Theological Perspective* (1965). Rather than challenging secular culture, the Harvard Divinity School professor wrote, Christians should follow the lead of the "world" and let the world set the church's agenda. In the sixties, the world led liberals to confront the very issues raised by the counterculture: war, materialism, racial injustice, nationalism, and poverty. In trying to address those issues, liberal Christians strove to be "relevant," to demonstrate that they were not mired in tradition and theology but were concerned about solving real problems with love and empathy. Though American Catholics continued to hear a strict message from the Vatican on questions of sexuality, especially those of abortion and birth control, they also heard a new message after the Second Vatican Council completed its work in 1965. Like liberal Protestants, Catholics tried to make religion more relevant. One major change was to abandon Latin as the language of the Mass in favor of the vernacular. And the Church of Rome made several major statements that were similar to those voiced by the National Council of Churches, including a denunciation of nuclear weapons and the suggestion that the United States had not done enough to address poverty. Moreover, Catholics in Latin America embraced the radical tenets of liberation theology, with its Marxist economic analysis, demanding radical social, political, and economic reform.[12]

A number of widely publicized local movements gave impetus to the rise of what was labeled the New Christian Right. In each instance, opposition manifested itself in grassroots campaigns against cultural practices that threatened traditional social and moral values. In the mid-1970s, the wife of a fundamentalist minister denounced most of the books adopted for English classes by the Kanawha County School Board in the Kanawha Valley of West Virginia. She claimed the books were "disrespectful of authority and religion, destructive of social and cultural values, obscene, pornographic, unpatriotic, or in violation of individual and familial rights of privacy." Many of her neighbors in the conservative mining region agreed with her and joined in a massive boycott of the schools. Sympathetic miners waged wildcat strikes, teachers mounted their own strike, and picketers blanketed the community until the school superintendent resigned and the board established a textbook adoption procedure that enabled parents to screen out offensive books. The Kanawha Valley action inspired similar campaigns around the country, empowering parents, especially conservative Christians, to demand that schools reflect traditional moral values.[13]

A second local grassroots campaign, in Dade County, Florida, was aimed at curbing gay rights. In 1977, the Dade County Commission passed an ordinance prohibiting discrimination against gays in housing, employment, and public accommodations. The ordinance inspired conservatives to form a protest organization, called Save Our Children, which opposed a provision that required private schools, including Christian academies, to hire homosexuals as teachers. Local ministers, assisted energetically by the popular singer Anita Bryant, mounted a vigorous campaign calling for a referendum on the ordinance. By a two-to-one margin, the ordinance was defeated, and, again, the action inspired similar protests against gay rights around the country.[14]

A third grassroots conservative campaign took place in hundreds of local communities in an effort to defeat ratification of the equal rights amendment to the Constitution. Passed by Congress in 1972, the amendment prohibited sexual discrimination by states and the federal government. After twenty-two of the needed thirty-eight states ratified it, conservatives, led by Phyllis Schlafly, mounted a "Stop-ERA" campaign that succeeded in killing the amendment three states short of the number required. Analyses of the successful campaign indicate that religion played a significant role. With the exception of Tennessee and Texas, all of the southern states rejected the amendment, reflecting the region's heavy concentration of fundamentalist churches and high levels of church attendance. Churches provided many of the leaders and activists in the campaign. Similarly, the states with concentrations of Mormons defeated the measure, with church leaders and members organizing against a measure they considered to be anathema to the traditional family.[15]

Mobilizing the Religious Right

The success of conservative Christians in these local battles over family and moral values caught the attention of political strategists within the Republican Party. Having lost the White House to the Democrats and Jimmy Carter in 1976, Republicans looked for a way to capitalize on what appeared to be widespread conservative dissatisfaction over the country's moral drift. The political activists who became the architects of a strategy to turn local conservative religious protest into a national moral campaign had no ties to the evangelicals they hoped to lead. They were political professionals who saw an opportunity to unite religious and secular conservatives and thus expand the base of the Republican Party. They were Howard Phillips of the Conservative Caucus, John Dolan of the National Conservative Political Action Committee, Paul Weyrich of the National Committee for the Survival of a Free Congress, and Richard Viguerie, a fund-raiser for a number of conservative causes.[16]

These political operatives found many evangelicals receptive to the idea of joining with secular conservatives to oppose liberal policies. The issue that Weyrich was able to exploit was the threat to Christian schools' tax-exempt status. From the mid-1960s, fundamentalist and evangelical churches, particularly in the South, established private schools as an extension of their education programs. Many opponents, with good reason, viewed these institutions as "segregation academies," designed as alternatives to public schools then under federal desegregation mandates. Parents insisted that the schools were a response to the "secular bias" of public schools, underscored by court decisions banning school-sponsored prayer and daily Bible reading. They also found the curriculum objectionable, especially the teaching of evolution, history courses that "distorted" America's heritage and values, and sex education courses. Moreover, these parents did not want their children exposed to the "hedonistic youth culture" that prevailed in public schools. Therefore, they organized Christian schools that provided "a well-ordered atmosphere in which religious beliefs, patriotic sentiments, and conservative behavioral patterns were reinforced rather than challenged." New textbooks provided specifically Christian content. One Christian math text taught addition by asking students to calculate how many people were saved at a revival on successive nights. Critics charged that the narrowly focused curriculum did not prepare students for the modern world, but defenders pointed out that students in Christian schools performed as well as those in public schools, or better.[17]

Architects of the Christian Right as a national political movement seized on the threat of federal government interference in the Christian schools to mobilize fundamentalists and evangelicals in the 1970s. Administrators and board members of the academies had engaged in running battles with state school boards over matters such as curriculum and teacher certification. They were therefore wary of the new federal Department of Education established under Jimmy Carter's administration. But their primary fear was that the Internal Revenue Service would revoke their tax-exempt status. A federal district court in 1972 ruled that a school that practiced segregation no longer qualified as a charitable institution under the tax code. Then, in 1975, the IRS revoked the tax-exempt status of fundamentalist Bob Jones University of Greenville, South Carolina, because the school denied admission to blacks until 1971, and thereafter forbade interracial dating. Seeing the federal government as determined to impose secular standards on Christian schools, school officials sought help from sympathetic Republican political operatives in Washington.[18]

Ironically, liberal political strategists provided the blueprint that Paul Weyrich deployed in helping conservative Christians use their political clout to defend their schools. Weyrich recalled the moment he realized how conservatives could effectively make their voices heard. He attended a political strategy session run by liberals who were attempting to get disparate groups to work toward a common cause. "They had all these different groups, including religious groups," Weyrich recalled, "networking with people on the hill, formulating strategy for offering amendments, and then executing that strategy with media, with demonstrations, with lawsuits, with studies, with political action, by targeting people—all the different elements of the political process." He realized that that same strategy was a workable formula for organizing and mobilizing the millions of conservative Christians who perceived the federal government as a threat to their values. Among his first steps was to establish a "low-profile policy analysis organization" that would be able to formulate position papers on conservative issues and show sympathetic lawmakers a version of the Republican Party very different from Richard Nixon's. Thus, with funds provided by Colorado brewer Joseph Coors, the Heritage Foundation began churning out papers offering a conservative alternative to Nixon's views on welfare, foreign policy, and economics.[19] Under Weyrich's leadership, the Heritage Foundation agreed to take up the issue of government interference in Christian schools. His challenge, however, was to convince conservative Christians, many of whom had theretofore been reluctant to engage in national politics, to become activists in the fight for their cause.

The greatest challenge was among southern theological conservatives, and by the 1950s the South was the base of American evangelicalism. While many northern evangelicals in the early 1900s had reconciled science and faith and had embraced modernity, southern evangelicals retreated into a culture that emphasized personal salvation instead of social transformation. To most, Christianity's central imperative was to be "born again," to experience a life-changing conversion, after which the newly redeemed creature would seek to live a moral life and work for the salvation of others. There was no sense of duty to remake the social order; that was up to God in his own time and way. Thus southern evangelicals chose not to engage in political affairs, certainly not as activists. Some did, however, join various fringe groups that promised to defeat the enemies of "true" Christianity and restore morality. Studies of such extremist organizations as the Ku Klux Klan and virulent anticommunist groups show that southern evangelicals were overrepresented.[20]

Southern evangelicals made their political clout known in 1976 when they supported the Democratic presidential candidate, Jimmy Carter, a devout Southern Baptist who openly declared during the campaign that he was a "born-again" Christian. *Time* magazine heralded 1976 as the "Year of the Evangelical," signifying the coming-out of evangelicals, in particular southern evangelicals, in American politics. With the help of southern evangelicals, Carter and the Democrats reclaimed the South, winning all of the region's electoral votes, after Nixon and the Republicans had swept the South in 1968 and 1972. Carter was well suited to burnish the image of evangelicals, whom most of the country regarded as backward, uneducated extremists. He was well educated and thoroughly modern, with his technical expertise in nuclear energy. Thus he appealed to voters outside the South as a moderate, reasonable candidate while appealing to his evangelical neighbors as a fine Christian. But the image was fleeting, and the Democratic hold on the South was short-lived—in large part because of the disaffection of white evangelicals.

The centerpiece of Carter's presidential campaign was government reorganization. Labeled a "technocrat" by some, he was interested in streamlining the federal government so it could deliver services and uphold laws more efficiently. He thought that some agencies, such as the Department of Health, Education, and Welfare, were too bloated and diffused. Moreover, he believed that some issues, such as education and energy, deserved separate cabinet-level departments. In addition, Carter promised to address what he considered to be one of the nation's most challenging social problems, the decline of the American family. Just before the election in November 1976, he told the National Conference of Catholic Charities that he intended to convene a White House Conference on the Family in order to place the issue at the forefront of the national agenda.[21]

When President Carter began implementing his liberal policies, he incensed conservative evangelicals. First, he supported the establishment of the Department of Education as a cabinet position, a move that angered white southerners in general and evangelicals in particular. Southern whites had resented federal involvement in education since *Brown v. Board of Education* in 1954. Local control of public schools was almost sacred in the United States as a whole and especially in the South. Southern school boards played an important role in maintaining the South as a segregated society by establishing separate schools for blacks and whites. After the court decision declared those schools to be inherently separate and unequal, school boards and governors defied federal authority to force integration. In 1955, the Little Rock, Arkansas, school board agreed to pursue a policy of "gradual integration," but when nine black students attempted to enroll in Central High School in 1957, Arkansans rose up in protest, and Governor Orval Faubus ordered the National Guard to prevent their entry. To uphold the Constitution, President Eisenhower sent troops from the 101st Airborne Division to protect the minority students. As white southerners saw it, the use of federal force to integrate schools was a violation of states' rights, an assault on state sovereignty. Similarly, conservatives viewed Jimmy Carter's new Department of Education in the same light: federal violation of states' rights. Evangelicals, in particular, saw it as an agency empowered to control or undermine Christian academies by forcing them to comply with federal civil rights and curriculum guidelines. The issue was financial as well as theological. If the federal government could take away the academies' tax-exempt status, then parents would face much higher tuition fees. Bill Billings, a leader in promoting Christian academies, explained, "If the Christian schools were to lose their tax-exempt status, . . . their tuition could conceivably double. When it becomes not just a moral or a conservative/liberal issue, but a pocketbook issue, you definitely take an interest." Parents indeed took an interest and became activists in opposing Carter and the Democrats.[22]

In addition to alienating evangelicals over the issue of education, Carter lost their support when they realized that his view of the family was far different from theirs. In a 1979 statement kicking off National Family Week, President Carter made clear his inclusive definition of family. "We are a nation of families," he said. "All families are important, but the extended family, the foster family, and the adoptive family play a special role by relieving the isolation of those who lack the comfort of a loving nuclear family." His press secretary, Jody Powell, was even more expansive: "When I think of family," he stated, "I don't just think of my wife and my mother and my daughter and my grandchildren. I think of hundreds of people—cousins and aunts and uncles and now two sets of in-laws and all that." He explained that Carter thought of family in the "broad sense" of the diverse ways that Americans take care of each other. To conservative evangelicals, Carter was trying to redefine family in opposition to the biblical conception. They wanted to limit its meaning to "people related by blood, adoption, or marriage, and to establish the basic unit of husband, wife, and children as the norm." Beverly LaHaye recalled how conservative evangelicals felt betrayed by the White House conference, especially by Carter's willingness to include homosexuals. As a result, she claimed, by the 1980s, homosexuals "were driving in, because they wanted to be part of the whole definition of the family. And we objected to that."[23]

That Carter had lost much of the evangelical support that had helped him win the presidency was illustrated at a breakfast he hosted for a group of prominent conservative ministers. Included in the group were Jerry Falwell, Oral Roberts, Rex Humbard, Jim Bakker, Charles Stanley, and Tim LaHaye. Recognizing that he needed to shore up support among conservative evangelicals, the president had the previous day addressed four thousand members of the National Religious Broadcasters, and he hoped to follow up with a more personal appeal for support from that group's most visible leaders. But when his guests pressed for clear answers to some pointed questions, he equivocated. He gave a vague response to their query about his views on abortion and hedged when asked about the small number of evangelicals in his administration. Tim LaHaye summed up the ministers' assessment of the president, asking

[w]hy he [Carter] as a Christian and a pro-family man, as he protested to be, was in favor of the Equal Rights Amendment in view of the fact that it would be so

harmful to the family, and he gave some off-the-wall answer that the Equal Rights Amendment was good for the family. Well, I knew when he said that that he was out to lunch. We had a man in the White House who professed to be a Christian, but didn't understand how un-Christian his administration was.[24]

Paul Weyrich sensed that conservative evangelicals' frustration with Carter's views on education and the family was much broader than that expressed by a few leaders. He believed that there was a huge group of parents "out there in real America, . . . real, true grassroots Americans" who were ripe for the Republicans' picking. Weyrich described the moment that a political lightbulb flashed on for him about mobilizing and organizing conservative evangelicals for the GOP:

Wait a second—these folks are numerous and they're out there and they're not organized. Let's get them in, let's get them organized, and let's get them voting, and see what happens.[25]

As a politico, Weyrich knew how to count, and he knew that the number of conservative evangelicals was huge and that they were discontented with liberal policies. In 1957, a religious census estimated that there were fifty-eight million Protestants in America and that twenty-four million of those were classified as fundamentalists. After the volatile 1960s, evangelical-fundamental Protestants represented the fastest-growing segment of American Protestants. In its 1977–1978 poll, the Gallup organization defined an evangelical as one who "(1) has had a born-again experience (i.e., committed his life to Jesus Christ at some point in time); (2) believes in a literal interpretation of the Bible; and (3) has encouraged someone else to believe in Jesus Christ." By that definition, the Gallup Poll counted fifty million evangelicals, ten million of whom were technically fundamentalists.[26] The decreased number of fundamentalists signaled not so much a change in theological perspective as a blurring of the line between the terms "fundamentalist" and "evangelical." Nonetheless, the number was huge and represented an attractive target to Republican organizers.

To understand the Christian Right's political activism, one must first understand its goals and frustrations. The overarching objective was to restore America's status as a Christian nation. All of the constituent groups cite that goal as their primary mission. Jerry Falwell wished to "take America back" to its Christian heritage and thus rescue it from what he saw as its decades-long usurpation by the secular humanists. Pat Robertson's speeches are filled with calls to "reclaim America," to "take back our nation," and to "restore our Christian heritage." The National Association of Evangelicals states its mission as that of "recapturing America for our children." Robertson denounced the doctrine of "separation of church and state" as a liberal, anti-Christian ploy to keep God out of public life. He repeatedly points out that the phrase is not to be found in the Constitution. All of the conservative groups share a "restorationist rhetoric" reflecting their desire to go back to a time when America was a Christian nation. In doing so, they create a "useful past," an enterprise that serves more to buttress their claims than to illuminate the founding period. As "proof" for their argument, they quote the founders. In the preface to his book of quotations from the founders' writings on religion, James Hutson describes the process:

> What better way to prove that the Founders were grounded in and instructed by Christian principles than by calling the most important of them to the witness stand and letting them testify in their own words to the

importance of Christianity in their lives? All quote book compilers employ this strategy, invariably focusing on Washington, Jefferson, Madison, Franklin, Adams, and a handful of lesser luminaries, culling statements from their writings that attest to the beneficent influence of Christianity on their lives and on the public welfare, and presenting these pronouncements in serial form. On the basis of the evidence offered, they assume that only the most perverse reader could deny that Christianity was the formative force in the founding of the United States.[27]

In George W. Bush, the Religious Right found a born-again Christian who, unlike Jimmy Carter, spoke their language and subscribed to their views. Far more than Reagan or George H. W. Bush, George W. Bush believed that religious groups should participate actively in public life and should receive their fair share of public funds. In describing religious initiatives, Bush and his administration preferred the label "faith-based" to "religious." By that phrase, they sought to differentiate between Americans with strong ties to their religious faith and those who were more secular and humanist. Further, they sought to portray those who opposed religious involvement in public affairs as being opposed to faith itself and thus violators of religious freedom.

The results of his "faith-based initiatives" have been dramatic in some cases, as illustrated by the Heritage Community Services of Charlestown, South Carolina, a small offshoot of an antiabortion pregnancy crisis center. In the mid-1990s, the "deeply conservative" organization operated its abstinence education program on a shoestring annual budget of about $55,000, a sum that restricted its outreach to the local community. Ten years later, thanks to almost $3 million in federal grants from the Bush administration, the agency has expanded its services to middle and high schools throughout South Carolina, Georgia, and Kentucky. Heritage is but one of many faith-based organizations that have benefited from President Bush's determination to direct federal funds to conservative causes. He and other conservatives argued that for years, under the Democratic Party's control, federal funds had flowed primarily to liberal religious groups and their social services. For decades mainline organizations such as Catholic Charities, the Salvation Army, and Lutheran Social Services had received most of the billion dollars a year granted to social service agencies. Further, Democrats sent millions to Planned Parenthood to promote birth control. Thus when Bush was elected, he promised his conservative constituents that they would receive their fair share. He created the Compassion Capital Fund, which distributed almost $150 million from 2002 to 2005, in order to "expand the role that faith-based and community groups play in providing social services to those in need." Critics claimed that the program violated the doctrine of separation of church and state. The administration countered by pointing out that the only thing new was a fairer distribution of funds, and that federal monies would fund social, not religious, services. The ten cabinet-level departments that distributed the funds encouraged conservative religious organizations to apply for federal money to finance Head Start, subsidized housing, and abstinence education programs.[28]

Critics from the Left and the Right worry that funding ideologically based organizations leads to abuse. Liberals point to the December 12, 2002, executive order that exempted religious groups receiving federal funds from complying with certain civil rights statutes and permitted discriminatory hiring practices that would enable the groups to employ no one outside their faith. Further, liberals charge that the "faith-based" monies constitute nothing other than a "slush fund" for conservative special-interest groups, such as Pat Robertson's Operation Blessing, which has received more than $20 million from the Compassion Fund and the Agricultural Department. Conservatives also express concerns about faith-based politics. Representative Mark Edward Souder of Indiana voiced consternation that the federal drug program had "gone political," explaining that the administration could not sell it to its Republican supporters unless it could show that the funds would benefit conservative social service organizations. Grover Norquist, president of Americans for Tax Reform, called faith-based grant making "corrupting":[29] "The danger is that any group that gets money from the government will end up serving the interests of the state rather than the constituencies they are trying to serve. . . . The guy who writes the check writes the rules."[30]

In addition to supporting "faith-based" domestic programs, President George W. Bush also defines his foreign policy in religious terms. In a March 11, 2004, address to the National Association of Evangelicals, he declared that America is a nation on a "mission," a mission to stamp out terrorism in the world. Employing another term dear to evangelicals, he said that the country was "called" to rid the world of evil and spread freedom and democracy.[31] A central theme of the president's reelection campaign was that of America as God's agent of freedom. "Freedom isn't America's gift to the world," he told audiences, "It's the Almighty God's gift to each man and woman in this world." Viewing the world in moral terms of good and evil, the administration drew sharp lines among nations, identifying Iraq, Iran, and North Korea as an "axis of evil." While defining "good" as God's gift of freedom, Bush, in detailing what freedom meant, offered a description that sounded like American civic liberalism: decent health care, good education, responsive government.[32] Not since Woodrow Wilson had an American president espoused a "missionary" diplomacy.

In addition to enjoying the support of sympathetic presidents, the Religious Right has seen a shift within the Supreme Court that makes it more favorably inclined to conservative causes. As a result of Republican presidents' appointments of conservative justices, the Supreme Court, beginning in the 1980s and continuing to the present, has chipped away at the separationist doctrine adopted by an earlier, more liberal Court. President Ronald Reagan moved the Court to the right with his appointment of William Rehnquist as chief justice in 1986 and by naming Antonin Scalia and Anthony Kennedy as justices. President George H. W. Bush's nomination of Clarence Thomas put another conservative on the bench, and President George W. Bush moved the Court further to the right by nominating John Roberts as chief justice and Samuel Alito as justice. The Court's conservative majority has adopted an accommodationist doctrine toward religion in the public square. In *West Side Community School v. Mergens*, (1990) the Court ruled unconstitutional a public school's prohibition of a Christian students' club from meeting in the school building after hours, as did other student organizations. Although a school employee would have to be assigned for custodial purposes, public expense was minor and, the justices decided, did not involve an undue entanglement of government in religion. In *Rosenberger v. The University of Virginia* (1995), the Court ruled against the university's denial of funds to *Wide Awake*, a student periodical that presented a "Christian perspective." The Court held that the funds came from mandatory student fees, and that denial of a share of those to the group constituted a violation of free speech and risked "fostering a pervasive bias or hostility to religion."[33] While applauding these first steps in dismantling the wall of separation, the

Religious Right waits impatiently for the Court to overturn *Roe v. Wade*, the case that for many religious conservatives symbolizes America's godless drift.

Opposition to the Religious Right

Religionists and secularists alike have opposed the Religious Right's claims on several fronts. Some oppose the exclusivism of any group that purports to speak for all Americans on moral issues. They maintain that "morality and virtue are not issues that belong exclusively to the religious right or, for that matter, to religion." They are matters that are the concern and responsibility of all citizens. Influenced by secular as well as religious ideas, and fearing that religion would divide people, the founders "made no constitutional provision for the national government to instruct its citizens in matters of moral and religious conscience." They did not believe that the federal government existed to create moral citizens; rather, they believed that moral citizens created a democratic society. Morality was essential to democracy. A free, independent society could not work without compassion, mercy, honesty, and integrity. Nor could it function unless the people possessed a "sense that social injustices suffered by their neighbors were social wounds to the entire community." Republican virtue demanded that citizens pursuing their self-interest also consider the impact of their actions on others.[34] Moral instruction belonged to families, schools, and religious institutions, all of which operated outside the jurisdiction of the government.

Some oppose the Religious Right on the same grounds on which Americans have objected to religious activists throughout American history: that they become the party of "religious correctness." Isaac Kramnick and Laurence Moore, historians who coined the phrase, maintain that religious correctness is any group's claim that it represents the one true faith. Armed with that certainty, the group or coalition seeks official sanction for its moral code and standards. Barred from gaining constitutional recognition by the framers of "godless politics," advocates of religious correctness then enter the political arena to achieve the recognition and power that others refuse to endorse in the free, competitive religious marketplace. Some detractors suggest that the advocates of the Religious Right present themselves as victims when they seek government protection and support. The image of "the evangelical as victim" is not part of the portrayal that the Religious Right promotes; nonetheless, some see that notion as a dominant theme in the movement's rhetoric. Barry Lynn of Americans United for Separation of Church and State rejects the idea that evangelicals and fundamentalists are victims of anti-Christian bigotry in the United States. "What they are really complaining about," he asserts, "is the failure of government to help them promote their faith." Political scientist Matthew Moen agrees that the Religious Right has adopted the rhetoric of "victimization," and sees it as "a clever and calculated ploy to tap the reservoir of positive sentiment for victims of American society." Evangelicals have a long history of regarding the "world" as the enemy and persecutor of Christians. They point to the New Testament as sure evidence that to be a Christian is to be persecuted, and the Christian Right finds evidence on every hand that American "secular humanists" are waging a systematic war against the Christian faith.[35] Kramnick and Moore point out that when proponents of religious correctness enter the political arena, they should shed their mantle of victimization and expect the same kind of bare-knuckle treatment that any other political activist encounters in special-interest politics.[36] They echo the sentiment of James Madison, who viewed religious groups as interests groups, and his hope that the jealousies of each would cancel out the aggrandizements of the others.

Some religious groups contest the Religious Right's specific list of moral issues. Some are false issues, they claim. For instance, they note that students attending public schools are not forbidden to pray; at any time they can pray in silence. The only prohibition is that against school-sponsored or state-sponsored prayer. Some have pointed out that the kind of prayer the Religious Right advocates is that which Jesus taught his disciples to shun. Rather than making a show of one's faith through public prayer—prayer in the streets—one should retire to one's closet and pray in private. Others question the inconsistency in the Religious Right's position as "pro-life" advocates. While labeling abortion of fetuses as murder, they do not question the deaths of enemy soldiers and civilians in America's wars, nor do they have any qualms about state-sponsored executions of convicted criminals. Some opponents of religious correctness object to the ungenerous, sanctimonious attitude of the Religious Right toward people they label sinners. Again, the charge is that of a narrow definition of sinful behavior. While viewing homosexuals as sinners, for example, evangelicals rarely speak out against venal businessmen.

While attacks from liberal religionists and secularists are to be expected, defections on the part of some high-profile supporters of the Religious Right have exposed fissures within the movement. In 1999, Paul Weyrich, who played a pivotal role in linking interests of the Religious Right with those of the Republican Party, stated in an open letter to conservatives, "I believe that we probably have lost the culture war." While he thought that the battle should continue, he concluded that political activism was not the best means. In fact, he stated, "I know that what we have been doing for thirty years hasn't worked, that while we have been fighting and winning in politics, our culture has decayed into something approaching barbarism."[37] That same year Cal Thomas, conservative newspaper columnist and early supporter of the Moral Majority, and Ed Dobson, onetime assistant to Jerry Falwell, reached a similar conclusion. In their book, *Blinded by Might*, they declared the Moral Majority a failure as a political force. According to Dobson, the Religious Right had failed to stem the tide of crime, homosexuality, pornography, and abortion: "[E]very plank of our [Moral Majority] platform we have failed from a legislative and judicial perspective." Thomas said it was time for religious conservatives "to admit that because we are using the wrong weapons, we are losing the battle." Like Weyrich, Dobson and Thomas did not abandon the moral positions enunciated by the Religious Right, but they called for a change of tactics, one centered in homes, churches, and communities, not in the corridors of power. What most rankled conservatives about their book was Thomas's rejection of the idea that America enjoys "most favored nation" status with God, or that it was once a "Christian nation." Thomas asserted that the Christian Right "set America apart and above all other nations. This is heresy." He and Dobson called on Christians to change America's culture by being obedient to divine law, not by engaging in electoral politics, which, they contended, has promoted Christian arrogance, not moral reformation.[38]

Though not a well-known national figure, Rev. Gregory Boyd, pastor of a thriving megachurch in Maplewood, Minnesota, is representative of a growing number of clerics who are distancing themselves from the Religious Right. A conservative who is sympathetic with many of the Right's moral positions, Boyd began to resist the frequent and insistent urgings of political activists to use his church to promote conservative issues and candidates in the 2006 congressional campaign. He was asked to announce an antigay rally, introduce a conservative candidate from his pulpit, and erect an antiabortion display in the lobby. He refused each time out of a conviction that the church was becoming so embroiled in the "world" that it was losing sight of its spiritual mission. In a series of six sermons called "The Cross and the Sword," he said that "the church should steer clear of politics, give up moralizing on sexual issues, stop claiming the United States as a 'Christian nation' and stop glorifying American military campaigns." Hardly a liberal—he is antiabortion and antihomosexuality—Boyd fears that the political battle to win the culture war could cost the church its soul. "When the church wins the culture wars, it inevitably loses," he proclaimed in a sermon. "When it conquers the world, it becomes the world. When you put your trust in the sword, you lose the cross." While most of Boyd's congregation remained in the church after his public defection from the Religious Right, about one thousand of the five thousand members departed.[39]

Former Republican senator John Danforth is critical of the Religious Right primarily because of what he considers to be its negative influence on the GOP. An ordained Episcopal minister and a Republican moderate, Danforth published a book that appeared during the congressional campaign of 2006, which describes religion as a "divisive force in the United States today." Further, he "accuses the religious right and its political supporters of creating a sectarian party." He declares that Republican leaders have tried so hard to please their most conservative constituents that they have proven to be "neither humble Christians nor effective politicians." Richard Land, a prominent conservative within the Southern Baptist Convention, dismisses Danforth by saying that he was part of the problem with the Republican Party before it reached out to the Religious Right.[40] Danforth and Land represent the two sides in the struggle within the GOP over the influence of the Religious Right. Danforth wants less; Land wants more.

On the eve of the 2006 congressional election, Dick Armey, Texas congressman and former House majority leader, blamed the zeal of certain elements of the Religious Right for the party's loss of public support. In particular, he singled out James Dobson, founder and president of Focus on the Family, and other "self-appointed Christian leaders" who had, in Armey's view, exerted far too much influence within the party. He thought that the Right's insistence on making the Republican Party partisans in the Terri Schiavo right-to-die case was just one of many examples of the party's caving in to people like Dobson. He said that Dobson and "his gang" were "bullies" and "thugs" who tried to blackmail the party into following their narrow agenda. Further, Armey contended, they divided religious supporters. They have split "the conservative Christian movement into two camps: those who want to 'practice their faith independent of heavy-handed government' and 'big government sympathizers who want to impose their version of "righteousness" on others.' "[41]

Defenders of the Religious Right were quick to respond. Judge Roy Moore, former chief justice of the Alabama Supreme Court, who defied a court order to remove a Ten Commandments monument from the court building, disagreed with Armey's assessment. He pointed out in a *Washington Times* editorial that the same Religious Right that Armey criticized was responsible for Republican victories in 2000 and 2004. Moore blamed President Bush for straying from "our Godly heritage"—which for Moore means Christian heritage—when the president proclaimed at a press conference that "Christians and Muslims worship 'the same God.' "[42]

Though they might denounce its aims and values, critics concede that the Christian Right is more effective in presenting its message than are liberal Christians. Part of the problem lies in the sedate, rational approach of the more liberal denominations. They recognize the complexities of modernity and resist "biblical simplification." Such an approach, however, has little appeal for those who seek certainty amid ambiguity and simplicity amid complexity. Conservatives are revivalists and see themselves as an extension of the long heritage of American revivalism. Revivals appeal to audiences' emotional needs and claim to offer nothing less than a new life for those who undergo a spiritual new birth. In fearful, uncertain times, revivals provide hope and security, on the one hand, and, on the other, a scapegoat on which to blame one's troubles.[43]

The Christian Right has demonstrated impressive skills in building new megachurches, modern communications networks, and effective lobbying organizations. Dissatisfied with the mainstream media that conservative Christians believed expressed humanist ideas and ridiculed Christian principles, the Religious Right has developed an alternative media that advances its views. In particular, they have been savvy in their exploitation of such new media as cable television and the Internet. Ralph Reed and the Christian Coalition took the lead in demonstrating to conservative Christians how to organize at the grassroots level to exert political influence. Without question, the Religious Right has found effective ways to get its message to conservative Protestants. The bigger challenge that the Religious Right faces is how to extend its influence. Widening the circle means packaging its message to make it palatable to persons who do not share the hard-edged notions of fundamentalism. But many within the Religious Right do not want any compromise in their message; their goal is to "take America back," and that means a transformation of the country into a Bible-based republic.[44]

One of the aims of the Religious Right is mass evangelism, and one of the expressions of that goal is the emergence of the megachurch. As evangelical congregations grew in size, and as their memberships came to reflect a higher socioeconomic status, they sought bigger arenas for reaching larger audiences. Inspired by Billy Graham's "crusades" that filled such venues as Madison Square Garden and by Robert Schuller's Crystal Cathedral in Garden Grove, California, conservative Protestants in the late 1970s began building enormous edifices that would seat thousands and even tens of thousands. In architecture and services, these new churches marked a departure from "traditional" churches. Looking more like theaters or convention centers, these structures borrowed heavily from secular architecture to provide light and comfort for worshipers. Snack bars and contemporary music make megachurches more appealing to younger members. Pastors employ the latest electronics equipment from Ipod streaming to multimedia presentations to communicate to audiences within the building and to those outside. Ironically, while preaching a conservative, backward-looking message, Religious Right pastors are modern and forward-looking in their delivery of that message. They consciously make their churches look like such secular venues as shopping malls to attract people from secular society. And they organize their churches along business lines, conceiving of pastors as entrepreneurs and CEOs. One writer on the megachurch phenomenon explains the approach succinctly: "The typical traditional church is no place for the unchurched."[45]

While the Religious Right has claimed credit for the resurgence of the Republicans, as well as the "Reagan Revolution," the evidence suggests that religious conservatism is but one of several explanations. Changing views toward American social and moral values are undeniable influences in the electoral shifts beginning in the 1990s. Voters indicate in exit interviews that cultural values as well as pocketbook concerns shaped their electoral choices. Some analysts are skeptical of the role of religion in American politics, suggesting that in a society that measures national and personal success by the standard of the "almighty dollar," economics and economic expectations dominate in influencing voting patterns. In their analysis of the election of 1992, when Democrats shattered the Republicans' coalition, and that of 1994, when the Republicans demolished Democratic control of Congress, Ruy Teixeira and Joel Rogers found nonreligious factors to be persuasive. They conclude that "the chief cause of voter volatility lies in declining living standards and the persistent failure of either political party to successfully address this problem." In particular, they identify "Non-College-Educated Whites" as the pivotal group of voters whose shifting loyalties explain electoral shifts.[46] Religious sociologist Kenneth Wald also advocates caution in accepting at face value the claims made by any religious group on the electoral process. First, he points out the difficulty of assessing impact when the religious identity of voters is not always clear. Second, he does find that evangelicals have made a difference "on some measures." However, he concludes in the third place, "the Religious Right does not seem to have been the principal cause of these changes." Perhaps the biggest impact of the Religious Right, according to Wald, is voter turnout. When evangelicals turn out in large numbers, as they did in 1994, the Republican Party has been the beneficiary.[47] When they do not, as in 1998, Democrats are the winners. The message is that politicians who ignore evangelicals do so at their peril.

Reemergence of the "Religious Left"? America's Culture War in the Early Twenty-first Century

For most of its first three decades as a political force, the Religious Right faced little concerted, organized opposition from a coalition on the religious left. While individuals from liberal Christian organizations as well as liberal Jews attacked the Right, there was minimal coordination. Moreover, most religious liberals were Democrats, which meant they were members of a party reluctant to promote any religious movement that could be defined as exclusive, or that could be accused of trying to create a religious establishment. However, a succession of electoral failures culminating in the reelection of George Bush in 2004 inspired some liberal leaders to organize a Religious Left that would offer an alternative moral vision and agenda to that of the Religious Right.

Though situated at opposite ends of the religious-political spectrum, the Religious Left and the Religious Right share a long history. Their contestation in promoting rival moral visions for the nation dates at least to the modernist-fundamentalist controversy early in the twentieth century. Each has experienced moments of success in shaping public policy, and each has been relegated to the sidelines when the other has had a dominant presence in national politics. Further, each has shaped its present coalition and agenda in response to dissatisfaction with secular politicians' lack of regard for spiritual sensitivities and moral concerns. The present Religious Left is the successor of the liberal Protestants, Catholics, and Jews who for almost forty years between 1932 and 1968, an era dominated by Democratic administrations and congressional majorities, had a prominent voice in influencing liberal politics and policies. Then, when the Religious Right and the Republican Party forged a successful partnership in the 1970s, religious liberals vacated the national stage for the next thirty years as the Religious Right claimed to be the nation's moral conscience.

At about the same time in the 1970s when Jerry Falwell issued his call for the "moral majority" to rise up and take back an America that had gone astray, Michael Lerner was making his own assessment of the country's moral and political landscape. A liberal social activist and psychotherapist turned rabbi, Lerner, like Falwell, viewed with dismay what he saw in the sixties. To be sure, he was troubled by different concerns: rather than focusing on abortion and *Roe v. Wade*, he protested the denial of basic civil rights to African Americans; instead of calling for a stronger national defense, he spoke out against American policy in Vietnam, where hundreds of thousands were slaughtered; and while Falwell lauded the Invisible Hand that guided American free enterprise, Lerner decried the destruction of the earth's environment by corporations seeking ever higher profits. Both men were lifelong Democrats, but both had also grown disenchanted with the party.

While Falwell walked away from the Democrats into the open arms of the Republican Party, Lerner remained in the fold, where he hoped to find political support for his moral vision. He was to be disappointed, although he initially saw encouraging signs. Democratic leaders embraced feminists and environmentalists, and Lerner hoped that they would welcome "liberal and progressive forces, . . . end the cold war, and devote America's massive resources to promoting social and economic justice." He hoped that the party would become a great moral force that would call on the nation to expand the founding ideals of liberty and justice for all. Instead, the Democratic Party, Lerner lamented, had departed from its long tradition of fighting for those enduring values and had become the mouthpiece of baser interests. Rather than offering the nation a moral vision, it lowered its sights and, in the words of its most successful politician of the last quarter of the twentieth century, reminded the faithful that "it's the economy, stupid." Ironically, millions of Democrats left the party, including those whose economic interests were far better served by Democratic than Republican policies. At a loss to explain why such an important, and seemingly natural, part of the party's base would depart, Lerner sought reasons.[1]

Operating under the aegis of the Institute for Labor and Mental Health, Lerner and his researchers discovered what he called a "spiritual crisis" in the country. As they interviewed middle- and working-class men and women across the nation, they discovered a common theme: disillusionment with the promise of their jobs and emptiness in the American Dream. Over and over they heard people say that they wanted more than their jobs gave them; they wanted to find some meaning in life beyond themselves and their material well-being, and they wanted to feel that they were making a contribution to humankind. Lerner acknowledged that Falwell and the Moral Majority had addressed that yearning. Though he disagreed almost completely with Falwell's moral vision, Lerner nonetheless believed that the conservative minister had struck a responsive chord, and that, in turn, the Republican Party had become for millions the party that took their values seriously. Rather than dismiss the Religious Right as part of a vast "right-wing conspiracy," Lerner and others who shared his concern began to speak of a new vision offered by the Religious Left. While the Religious Left had long been active in American politics, primarily within the Democratic Party, it now faced a new challenge: how to reach a skeptical party as well as a skeptical public.

The "reemergence" of the Religious Left suggests a comeback of sorts by what had once been a force in American politics but had a much-diminished presence since the rise of the Religious Right in the 1970s. For most of the twentieth century, spanning the period from the Progressive Era of the early 1900s to the civil rights movement of the 1960s, the Religious Left was the dominant religious voice in the public square. It appealed to white Protestants from almost all denominations, as well as to liberal Catholics, blacks, Jews, and "people who say they are 'spiritual' but not affiliated with an organized faith." But since the 1970s, the Religious Left has been marginalized by the rise of the Moral Majority and other conservative Christians on the right, and by "the rise of a secular, liberal, urban elite" on the left "that was not particularly comfortable with religion."[2] Thus the new Religious Left is seeking to reclaim its prominence in defining a moral vision for the nation. This chapter examines the brief history of the reemergent Religious Left as it seeks to influence America's political culture as well as neutralize the Religious Right in electoral politics.

Defining the Religious Left

Like the Religious Right, the Religious Left defies easy definition. First, there is no monolithic entity to which adherents belong—no "card-carrying" members. Individuals and groups identify with the Religious Left in support of specific issues; thus there is a fluid quality to its makeup, a certain ebbing and flowing based on particular interests. Second, the label, again like that of the Religious Right, is a partisan designation

that draws all the slings and arrows of political and ideological opponents. Having spent almost three decades blasting
the various manifestations of the Religious Right, the Religious
Left surely expected the attacks it has endured. Third, true
believers insist on self-identification, explaining to the world
that they are "progressive" and "compassionate" Christians
who follow Christ's example of working for social justice and
world peace. According to a July 2006 survey of American attitudes toward religion conducted by the Pew Charitable Trust,
only 7 percent identified with the "religious left" political
movement. Though not that much smaller than the 11 percent
who identified with the "religious right," the Religious Left is,
according to the survey, "considerably less cohesive in its political views than the religious right." A far larger number of those
polled, 32 percent, identified themselves as "liberal or progressive Christians."[3]

The designation "Religious Left" arose out of partisan politics, especially the presidential election of 2004. Steven Waldman, founder of Beliefnet, a leading faith and spirituality Web
site, and contributing editor of the *Washington Monthly*, has
been a close observer of religion and presidential politics, and
he has attempted to evaluate the Religious Left's chances of
swaying evangelicals. Arraying evangelicals on a continuum according to their leanings in the 2004 election, Waldman identifies three groups. First are the "fundamentalists," whom he
identifies with the likes of Jerry Falwell, Pat Robertson, and
James Dobson. He calls them "solidly Republican" and esti-
mates that they account for about 15 percent of the total electorate. Second, there are "moderates," about 9 percent of voters, most of whom voted for George Bush because of foreign
policy, abortion, and gay marriage, though a sizable minority
supported John Kerry because of economic interests. Third are
"liberal" evangelicals, who make up about 3 percent of the

electorate and tend to vote Democratic because of their concerns regarding the environment and poverty. The Religious Left hopes to retain the loyalty of the last group, make serious inroads in the middle group, and possibly sway a few from the first. Joining liberal evangelicals in the Religious Left are their liberal counterparts among mainline Protestantism, African American Protestants, Catholics (especially Latino Catholics), and Jews. According to political scientist John Green's research, the Religious Left accounted for about 40 percent of the Kerry vote.[4]

In his book *The Left Hand of God*, Michael Lerner explains why "the Religious Left" is an apt description for the group he supports. He contends that most people of faith have two impulses, each contending for attention and each directing behavior. He calls these the Right and the Left Hand of God. The Right Hand, he contends, warns that the "world is a place in which everyone is going to exercise power over you, dominate you, control you unless you dominate and control them first." The Left Hand is predisposed toward a world of hope that tells people "that this fearful view isn't right, that this isn't who they were born to be, that there is something deeply screwed up about such a world."[5]

While critical of the Religious Right and its "unholy" alliance with the political Right, Lerner points out that many "very decent Americans" are drawn to the Religious Right because "it is the only voice that they encounter that is willing to challenge the despiritualization of daily life," and to call for "a life that is driven by higher purpose than money." Lerner expresses an appreciation for "their willingness to state their objectives clearly and honestly," and sees that candor and openness as "a refreshing change from the diet of mush that often emerges from the Democratic Party." Though he sees the Religious Right's political agenda as posing a "huge danger to

American society," Rabbi Lerner acknowledges that it succeeded in mobilizing millions behind a clear message. He recalls Paul Weyrich's clarion call in 1980: "We are talking about Christianizing America. We are talking about simply spreading the gospel in a political context." Lerner debated Weyrich that year and found him "a powerful advocate for a frightening worldview, that I hoped would remain marginal in America." But the evidence twenty-five years later indicates that the Religious Right has succeeded in following the advice of Jerry Falwell, who said, "Get them saved, get them baptized, and get them registered."[6] Lerner calls for progressive Christians to enter the political arena and offer people a spiritual choice. In 2005, he helped organize the Network of Spiritual Progressives, an umbrella group of liberals that he hopes will become the institutional expression of the Religious Left, and that can become for the Democratic Party and the Green Party what the Religious Right has been for the Republican Party: a movement that "energizes and provides intellectual, political, and spiritual inspiration." He is under no illusion that this organization will appeal to "hard-core fundamentalists or those who have made an idolatry of their worship of the free market," but he does think it will appeal to millions who suffer from the "despiritualized" world and wish to challenge the "ethos of selfishness and materialism in daily life."[7]

Thus Spiritual Progressives—or, as they have been dubbed in the secular press and by the Religious Right, the Religious Left—seek to offer American voters a spiritual alternative to both secular materialism and the Religious Right. They agree with the Right that Americans have lost their way by abandoning their spiritual heritage, but they disagree with the Right's interpretation of that heritage and their moral vision. Like the Religious Right, they face the challenge of voicing a spiritual message that will have wide appeal without being heard as sectarian; or, stated differently, they face the dilemma of being nonpartisan in partisan politics.

The rise of the Religious Left was predicated in part on the belief that the Religious Right was weakening. At the same time, its leaders hope to emulate the success of the Religious Right by mobilizing people of faith who want to see a spiritual dimension in the public square, but who are opposed to the Religious Right's particular moral agenda. Further, there is a tacit recognition that the Religious Right has evolved into what Kevin Phillips has called the "First American Religious Party," having as its overall goal the creation of an "American Theocracy." Though such rhetoric ignores earlier attempts to establish a "Christian" or "orthodox" party such as that in the nineteenth century led by Ezra Stiles Ely, it does indicate a radical shift in America's religio-political landscape. Before the 1960s, party alignments and voting patterns tended to be governed by denominational, ethnic, and regional affiliations. In the Midwest, according to Phillips, "Yankee Congregationalists, Swedish Lutherans, and Welsh Methodists were overwhelmingly Republican, while German and Irish Catholics, Wisconsin Synod Lutherans, and Southern Baptists were lopsidedly Democratic." Neither party enjoyed a sizable advantage among religious voters. However, that changed after 1972 when President Richard Nixon's appeal to the "silent majority" lured large numbers of conservative religionists from the Democratic Party, whose presidential candidate, George McGovern, was vilified by Republicans as promoting immorality and weakness. Indeed, Republicans labeled McGovern the "triple-A candidate—Acid, Amnesty and Abortion."[8] That attack succeeded in galvanizing conservative religious opinion against the Democrats, and it helped launch Jerry Falwell's organization of the Moral Majority and the rise of the Religious Right.

The Religious Left faces twin challenges: that of questioning the Religious Right's claim to be "the" political voice of people of faith, and that of reversing the Democratic Party's secular orientation. Political analyst William Schneider describes the existing party alignment: "Since 1980, religious Americans of all faiths—fundamentalist Protestants, observant Catholics, even Orthodox Jews—have been moving toward the Republican Party. At the same time, secular Americans have found a home in the Democratic Party." In attempting to reinject religion into the Democratic Party, the Religious Left faces a daunting mission: convince religious voters that they have a legitimate alternative to the Religious Right without scaring secular Democrats who either dismiss religion altogether or relegate it to the individual and the private sphere.

Who are the constituent members of the Religious Left? Perhaps the most accurate portrayal has come from members of the secular press who cover religion. In depicting the nascent movement, the press has offered more of a mosaic than a portrait, but they have nonetheless identified some of the groups and leaders who are most active in organizing the Religious Left. Just as the press tends to reduce the Religious Right to a few highly visible leaders, such as Jerry Falwell and Pat Robertson, so have reporters compiled a roster of individuals who represent the Religious Left. At the top of the list is Michael Lerner, whom reporters characterize as "long time political activist" and author of the best-selling *The Left Hand of God.* Jim Wallis shares the spotlight with Lerner. Wallis is the founder of the "poverty-fighting coalition Call to Renewal" and author of *God's Politics.* Other prominent leaders of the Religious Left include George Lakoff, founder and fellow of the Rockridge Institute, which is "dedicated to strengthening our democracy by providing intellectual support to the progressive community." But, like the Religious Right, the Religious Left is more than a couple of high-profile leaders; it is a coalition of diverse organizations. The following enumeration of leaders and the organizations they head gives some idea of that diversity and the orientation of constituent groups. Rev. Lennox Yearwood Jr. is chairman and CEO of the Hip-Hop Caucus in Washington, D.C., "a national coalition of pop culture, social, political and youth organizations." Tim Carpenter is national director of Progressive Democrats of America, which is a co-sponsor of the Conference on Spiritual Activism. Ron Sider is president and founder of Evangelicals for Social Action, an organization that promotes social justice issues among evangelicals. Ahmed Nassef is executive director of the Progressive Muslim Union of North America. Alexia Kelley is executive director of the Catholic Alliance for the Common Good. And Iva Caruthers is general secretary of the Samuel DeWitt Proctor Conference, a network dedicated to the African American faith community and the needs of those it serves.[9] The roster of activists includes pastors, academics, and public servants. Some of the more notable pastors are Robin Meyers, pastor of Mayflower Congregational Church in Oklahoma City, Oklahoma, and author of *Why the Christian Right Is Wrong: A Minister's Manifesto for Taking Back Your Faith, Your Flag, Your Future*; Jan Linn, copastor of the Disciples of Christ Congregation, Spirit of Joy Christian Church in Minneapolis, and author of *Big Christianity: What's Right with the Religious Left*; and Sister Joan Chittister, a Benedictine nun, lecturer, and writer, who is particularly active on peace issues. Professors who identify with the Religious Left include Tony Campolo, professor emeritus at Eastern University in St. Davids, Pennsylvania; Leigh Eric Schmidt, a professor of religion at Princeton University and author of *Restless Souls: The Making of American Spirituality from Emerson to Oprah*, which links American interest in spirituality with political liberalism; Michael N. Nagler, professor emeritus at the University of California, Berkeley, founder of the Peace and Conflict Studies program there, and author most recently of *The Search for a Nonviolent Future: A Promise of Peace for Ourselves, Our Families and Our World*; and Randall Balmer, evangelical professor of American religious history at Barnard College and Columbia University, and author of *Thy Kingdom Come: How the Religious Right Distorts the Faith and Threatens America*. The best-known political figure associated with the Religious Left is former Republican senator and UN ambassador John C. Danforth, who is also an Episcopal priest and author of *Faith and Politics: How the "Moral Values" Debate Divides America and How to Move Forward Together*. The common goal of these leaders and their organizations is to promote issues of peace and social justice in a political culture where, they fear, only voices of secularists and the Religious Right are being heard. Secularists, they charge, ignore spiritual needs altogether, and the Religious Right preaches a gospel of fear and division.

The Network of Spiritual Progressives (NSP) recognizes the diverse interests and emphases of its constituent organizations, while at the same time inviting all to make common cause in support of a progressive moral vision for America. The NSP sets forth its views in a manifesto that is equally critical of the Religious Right and of the dominant secular culture. It opens with a rejection of the overriding values of the political and social institutions that define America. It charges secular leaders with ignoring the spiritual dimension of human existence and advancing the illusion that the world of power and wealth is the "real world." Further, it rejects the place of religion in America as defined by secularists: relegated to the lives of individuals and families, consigned to weekends, and separated from issues and decisions of the political and business arenas. The NSP approaches politics from a different perspective from

that of materialist liberals. The organization's core vision statement underscores its spiritual approach: "We will unashamedly
use and learn from the language and practices of spiritual communities. The spiritual life can give us a level of mindfulness,
focus, and calm so that we can re-center ourselves and discover
what we truly value." Translated into specific objectives, the
NSP seeks through "spiritual politics" to work for the following
moral vision: "Interdependence and Ecological Sanity," an environmental commitment that takes seriously the biblical injunction to be good stewards of the earth's human and material
resources; a "New Bottom Line in Our Economic and Social
Institutions" that would broaden the definitions of efficiency
and productivity to include a commitment to expand time for
family, community, and spiritual exploration; "Supporting the
Struggles for Social Justice and Peace"; "Peace, Justice and Reconciliation for Israel and Palestine"; and a "Spiritual Movement" that recognizes the spiritual component to be at the
center of public as well as private life and promotes "an inner
life that is also an interconnected life with other human beings
and with the Unity of All Being."[10]

In addition to crafting a core vision of spiritual politics, the
NSP has drawn up a "Spiritual Covenant with America" that
differentiates its aims from those of secular liberals and religious conservatives. The covenant incorporates promises to
"Support Families," restore "Personal Responsibility," build
"Social Responsibility," "Educate for Values," institute a "Single Payer National Health Care System that transforms how
we understand health," serve as "Stewards of the Environment," build a safer world and a rational approach to immigration through a strategy of "generosity and non-violence," and
seek "separation of Church, State and Science." For each component of the covenant, the organization differentiates between
its promise and that found in the "Liberal Agenda" and in

the "Conservative Agenda." For example, in the final clause, regarding the relation between church and state, the NSP charges liberals with "mistakenly confus[ing] the separation of Church and State with the separation of spiritual values from the state." And they charge conservatives with trying "to privilege Christian values in the public sphere." The NSP pledges to protect society from the fundamentalist aim of imposing a particular religion on everyone, while at the same time avoiding a "First-Amendment Fundamentalism" that tries to keep all values out of public life.[11]

Fending Off Attacks

Perhaps the strongest evidence of the Religious Left's emergence as a political force is the opposition that it has generated. Indeed, the Religious Left faces challenges from two fronts. First, and most predictable, the Religious Right and the political Right have been quick to dismiss it as an ultraliberal front for the Far Left in American society. Never known for subtlety, conservative radio talk show host Rush Limbaugh characterized members of the Religious Left as moral relativists who reject the absolutes of the Christian faith. On the April 27, 2005, broadcast of the *Rush Limbaugh Show*, he said:

> I would submit to you that people on the left are religious, too. Their God is just different. The left has a different God. There's a religious left in this country. . . . And, the religious left in this country hates and despises the God of Christianity and Catholicism and whatever else. They despise it because they fear it, because it's a threat, because that God has moral absolutes. That God has right and wrong, that God doesn't deal

in nuance, that God doesn't deal in gray area, that God says, "This is right and that is wrong."[12]

Writing in Jerry Falwell's *National Liberty Journal* in 2005, assistant to the chancellor of Liberty University Edward Hindson delivered a scathing attack on the Religious Left that forecasts its failure. Claiming that "Left-Wing Christians Just Don't Get It," Hindson dubbed the Religious Left the "furious faithful" who are "upset by the political influence of Christian conservatives." To Hindson, the latest liberal protest is part of a pattern. He claimed that since "evangelicals woke up from their political slumber in 1980 and rallied behind the candidacy of Ronald Reagan, liberal religious elements have screamed in protest that conservative Christians were trying to take over America." He concluded by predicting that the Religious Left will fail in all of its efforts to wrest control from the Religious Right. To Hindson, it is a simple matter: "Conservative religion is on the rise and liberal religion is in demise. The 'mainline' has now become the sideline! This trend is not going to change because liberals have little or no evangelistic fervor." Further, he noted that even the *Economist* could see that in 2004 "Middle America" found an "overtly religious party" preferable to an "overtly secular one." Hindson concluded that the *Economist* writer understood what liberals refuse to admit, that "America is still overtly religious at her grassroots core."[13]

Former secretary of the interior in the Reagan administration James Watts labeled the Religious Left an arm of ultraliberal political operatives who wish to give their initiatives a moral patina. In particular, he saw the Religious Left as extreme environmentalists who use religion to defend their stance. He warned, "Never underestimate the political impact of the twisted charges by extreme environmentalists now advanced by the religious left to divide the people of faith."[14]

Judge Roy Moore of Alabama indicts the Democratic Party for abandoning religious principles altogether. He reminded them that as recently as 1949, Democratic leaders had publicly embraced the nation's religious heritage. He quoted President Harry Truman's declaration in his inaugural address of that year: "The American people stand firm in the faith which has inspired this nation from the beginning. . . . We believe that all men are created equal because they were created in the image of God. From this faith we will not be moved." But since that time, Moore claimed, the Democratic Party "has adopted a more liberal social philosophy and a warped morality defined by abortion, homosexuality and what the definition of sex 'is.' "[15]

Conservative religious, media, and political leaders portray the emergence of the Religious Left as a desperate attempt to reclaim religious influence for the Democratic Party. In announcing the debut of a liberal Christian group, the Christian Alliance for Progress, the *Washington Times* interviewed a number of conservatives who accused the organization of advancing old liberal causes under a new name. Tony Perkins, president of the Family Research Council, predicted that the Religious Left will have no impact on the Religious Right and, if anything, will result in the Right's gaining new members. In his words, "an organization created under a new name to reach a particular group with the same worn-out policy positions that have been rejected by values voters is not going to get them anywhere." The *Times* noted that the Christian Alliance "specifically supports abortion rights and homosexual 'marriage,' arguing that the latter is part of a biblical call for equality and justice." Such stances link the New Left with the Old Left, another chapter in a long history of espousing big government while attacking "corporate interests."[16]

Conservative groups accelerated their criticism of the Religious Left after the Democrats won majorities in both houses of Congress in November 2006. Writing in the *American Family Association Journal*, news editor Ed Vitagliano offered a critique of the "Evangelical Left" in February 2007. He noted that the Left is seeking political power the same way that the Right gained it, and he condemned liberal leaders as hypocritical for warning against the Religious Right's "imminent theocratic takeover" while at the same time inviting political liberals like Bill Clinton and Barack Obama to their pulpits. Further, Vitagliano argued, the Left attacks the Right for being too narrow in making one's stance on abortion and same-sex marriage a litmus test for one's authenticity as a Christian while promising a "broader, . . . more Biblical political agenda" that turns out to be a narrow list of liberal causes, such as advocacy for the "minimum wage, racial injustice and global warming."[17]

Jerry Falwell weighed in against the Religious Left by attacking the group's claim that its faith is biblical and Christian. In particular, he characterized the Left as not believing in the Bible as divine revelation and a reliable guide in all matters, and in embracing a religious pluralism that includes non-Christian and anti-Christian sentiments. Of Jim Wallis, one of the Left's most visible spokesmen, who insists that he is an evangelical, Falwell had this to say:

> I've never believed that Jim Wallis was an evangelical. I've asked him on talk shows if he believes the Bible is the infallible word of God—well, that's the cornerstone of evangelical Christianity—and he's never been willing to say publicly that he does. I've asked him the question: Do you believe Christ is the only way to heaven? And he's never been willing to say yes. All evangelicals will say "yes" quickly to that question.[18]

The Religious Left faces opposition from secular interests as well as from the Religious Right. Indeed, humanists—or nontheists, as they are often referred to in religious circles—have joined the debate over moral issues. Long a favorite whipping boy for Christian conservatives, "secular humanists" have weighed in on the debate and refuse to grant exclusive authority regarding moral matters to concerned Christians or religionists from either the Left or the Right. If 2008 is going to be the "Year of the Bible," as some evangelicals proclaim, the Bible will have to share the stage with a number of works that challenge biblical claims, and thus challenge both the Religious Right and the Religious Left. Several self-avowed humanists have published best sellers since the 2004 presidential election, not only attacking the long-held claim that religion, especially Christianity, is the foundation of morality, but charging that morality as taught and practiced by many Christians is immoral. Writing in the wake of September 11, 2001, Stanford Ph.D. student Sam Harris wrote a book attacking not only the Muslim fundamentalists who carried out the murderous missions of that day but moderate Christians as well, charging that religionists of all stripes promote the fear and submissiveness that enable a wide spectrum of immoralities to flourish in the name of God. His book, *The End of Faith: Religion, Terror, and the Future of Reason*, questioned the most basic assumptions of Christianity in general and evangelicals in particular, and soon became a best seller. Other humanists manifestos soon appeared, including Daniel Dennett (professor of cognitive studies at Tufts University), *Breaking the Spell: Religion as a Natural Phenomenon*; Richard Dawkins (Oxford biologist), *The God Delusion*; and David Shermer (science historian), *Why Darwin Matters: The Case against Intelligent Design*. In his provocative polemic against all religion, Christopher Hitchens expresses his view that faith has no place in politics because it perpetuates ignorance and violence. Instead, he prefers the "finer tradition" of reason and calls for a "New Enlightenment."[19] As the Religious Left attempts to move the Democratic Party toward its moral vision, it faces influential voices who offer not only a nonsectarian position, but a nonreligious stance.

Selling the Vision to the Democratic Party

Religious coalitions exercise their influence on American public life in different ways and at different times. Sometimes, as during the last quarter of the twentieth century, the Religious Right operated near the center of the political arena and did so in a very noisy way. However, for much of the 1930s through the 1960s, conservative Christians experienced a period of political quietism, choosing instead to influence public life in ways that those outside their circles would hardly notice. For religious liberals, a similar pattern occurred, though the timing was different. From the 1930s through the 1960s, liberals were active near the center of political power, working for peace and justice causes through electoral politics, legislative lobbying, and public demonstrations. Then, in the 1970s, the Religious Right pushed mainline Protestants to the political sidelines. But just as religious conservatives were hardly idle during their long time out of politics, religious liberals also found alternative public roles to play while outside the national spotlight. As Robert Wuthnow and John Evans point out, "to speak of churches playing a public role is . . . broader than to talk about religion and politics."[20] The political process represents but one avenue for exerting public influence. Coalitions play an important educative role by holding meetings for the purpose of discussing controversial social problems, disseminating information in the community on social issues, cooperating with nonprofit community groups for improving the lives of all citizens, and joining corporate boards in an effort to influence company policies for the public good.

Political scientist Laura Olson notes that while the mainline liberal clergy have been less visible in recent decades on the national political stage, they have, nevertheless, been actively engaged in politics. As the Religious Right gained direct influence in the Reagan and the Bush White House and Republican Congresses, religious liberal activists have shifted their attention to addressing social problems at the local level. In part, they have followed that course simply because Republicans have pushed policy authority on many issues away from Washington and down to the state and local levels. In that sense, they have joined the Religious Right in establishing local faith-based organizations to fight for social and economic justice. In particular, they have tackled the problems of poverty and urban blight that have spread in major cities whose human and fiscal resources have been undercut by middle-class migration to the suburbs.[21]

But while shifting their activism to the local level, mainline Protestants have maintained an institutional presence in Washington despite their being eclipsed by the Religious Right during Republican rule. Each of the major mainline Protestant churches has a lobbying arm located on Capitol Hill to coordinate its national advocacy efforts and to fight for liberal policies. These groups pursue "peace and justice" agendas that include "advocating human rights at home and abroad, working to preserve the environment, questioning U.S. use of military force, and above all else fighting for the disadvantaged." They lobby members of Congress and their staff, file amicus curiae briefs in federal cases, and participate in "action networks" to communicate with the public about policy issues.[22] Through these means, the Religious Left rather quietly offers an alternative moral vision to that of the Religious Right.[23]

But in the summer of 2004, the Religious Left took the national stage in bold and noisy ways reminiscent of the early days of the Moral Majority. In a full-page ad in the *New York Times* during the Republican National Convention, the Religious Left announced its return to national politics and declared its readiness to challenge the Religious Right's dominance in defining the nation's moral agenda. John Podesta, president of the Washington-based Center for American Progress and former chief of staff to President Clinton, underscored the historical significance of the moment: "What we're seeing in this campaign is a reinvigoration of the progressive religious voice." What remains to be seen, more cautious observers noted, was whether such assertions had "real political muscle" behind them. It is inevitable that the Religious Left would be compared to the Religious Right as a political force. Mark O'Keefe of the *Christian Century* wrote, "[T]he Religious Left has been overshadowed in recent decades by a highly organized Religious Right employing high-tech communication and old-fashioned political strategies to energize grassroots voters." By comparison, the Religious Left has yet to demonstrate the "institutional breadth and structure that translate into real political power." In its *New York Times* ad, the Religious Left proclaimed in bold letters: "God is not a Republican. Or a Democrat." While appealing in a Democratic stronghold like New York City, the sentiment might not have much impact in Middle America, according to Podesta, who points out that there is no "nationwide organization backing this up."[24]

At the same time the ad appeared, former president Bill Clinton chose the nondenominational Riverside Church in New York to challenge the Religious Right's claim to represent America's religious heritage. It was there, early in the twentieth century, that Harry Emerson Fosdick had championed the modernist vision of Christianity, while thundering against fundamentalists. In midcentury, William Sloane Coffin advocated peace and justice initiatives from the pulpit. And it was there that Martin Luther King, Jr., launched his anti–Vietnam War campaign.[25] Within that tradition, Clinton declared from the Riverside pulpit that "[p]olitical involvement dictated by faith is not the exclusive province of the right wing." It remains to be seen whether, like Fosdick and Coffin, Clinton will see his progressive beliefs expressed in public policy. Certainly, Clinton's remarks came at a time when the Religious Left was struggling to reclaim its political voice.[26]

As campaigning for the fall 2006 midterm elections got under way, Democrats made overtures to religious voters. Some influential party leaders tried to change their party's position, or at least its perceived position, toward religion in the public square. Illinois senator Barack Obama joined fellow party members Hillary Rodham Clinton and Howard Dean in suggesting that Democrats engage more openly religious issues that concern large numbers of Americans. In an interview with ABC, Obama opined, "Over the long haul, I think we make a mistake when we fail to acknowledge the power of faith in the lives of the American people, and join a serious debate about how to reconcile faith with our modern, pluralistic democracy." He said that for too long Democrats have remained on the sidelines when religion and politics were discussed, thus contributing to "America's religious gap [that] has been manipulated by the likes of such evangelical conservative leaders as Rev. Jerry Falwell and broadcaster Pat Robertson." He called on secularists to approach discussions of religion and politics with a more open mind, contending that they might discover that their values are not as different from those of religious people as they might have assumed. Besides, he added, "Secularists are wrong when they ask believers to leave their religion at the door before entering into the public square." At the same time, he warned Democrats about inauthentic displays of religious concern. "Nothing is more transparent," he said in a CNN interview, "than inauthentic expressions of faith: the politician who shows up at a black church around election time and claps—off rhythm—to the gospel choir."[27]

After regaining majorities in both houses of Congress in November 2006, Democrats openly extended a hand to the Religious Left. On December 2, incoming Senate majority leader Harry Reid invited Rev. Jim Wallis to give the Democratic response to President Bush's weekly radio address. Mark Tooley, director of the United Methodist Committee at the Institute on Religion and Politics, recognized the invitation as a part of the Democratic Party's strategy to gain strength among evangelicals. Writing in the neoconservative *Weekly Standard*, Tooley called Wallis, head of the progressive evangelical coalition Sojourners and author of the best-selling *God's Politics*, a "once angry-toned 1960s street activist [who] has in recent years attempted to become the chief spokesman for the evangelical left." Tooley concluded that his "radio stint in the place of congressional Democrats suggests he may have finally succeeded." Wallis defended his radio response as a nonpartisan opportunity to address important issues. "I work hard to maintain my independence and non-partisanship," he explained, "and didn't want to be perceived as supporting one party over the other." He said that it was an opportunity to get his message out to millions of people, adding that he would have accepted a similar Republican invitation. He stressed that he was not speaking "for the Democratic party, but as a person of faith who feels the hunger in America for a new vision of our life together, and sees the opportunity to apply our best moral values to the urgent problems we face." Tooley noted, however, that Wallis hit the usual Democratic liberal notes "about an 'anti-poverty agenda' that reduces 'the gap between rich and poor,' about extricating U.S. troops from a 'disastrous' war in Iraq, about protecting the 'earth and the fragile atmosphere' from global warming."[28]

While questioning whether Wallis was the right religious spokesperson for Democrats, Tooley thought it was a smart political ploy to reach out to the growing evangelical demographic. The Religious Right had demonstrated the potency of courting people of faith by allying with the Republican Party; now the Democratic Party was hoping that the Religious Left would draw in evangelical voters. But Tooley was skeptical that a social activist, as he called Wallis, could lure evangelicals who define themselves "by their personal faith in Jesus Christ and the authority of the Bible," not by their stand on social issues. Further, Tooley claimed, Wallis and the Religious Left are out of touch with times. They are throwbacks, recalling the "early 20th-century Social Gospel advocates who rejected 'fundamentalism' in favor of progressive social reform." They now belong to the churches of "declining, liberal mainline Protestantism, whose demographic implosion cleared the way for evangelical predominance."[29] Tooley's commentary summarized the conservative interpretation of Democratic attempts to forge alliances with evangelicals: whether politicians or religionists, Democrats are out-of-touch liberals.

Other conservatives are not as quick to dismiss the Religious Left as a force within American politics. David Klinghoffer, senior fellow in the conservative think tank the Discovery Institute, called the Religious Left a "fast-emerging" group that is taking on its "longer established competitor, the Religious Right." While he is clear in preferring the ideas of the Right, Klinghoffer thinks that the growing appeal of the Religious Left signals an important turn in American politics away from a secularist to a religious orientation. He noted of the Religious Right and the Religious Left: "[T]hese two Bible-citing political movements equally have woken up to the realization that there is something intrinsically American about using the Bible as a guide to practical politics. That's good news, and a blow to secularist orthodoxy." Klinghoffer has been among those predicting that the 2008 presidential campaign will be the "Year of the Bible." But while the Left and the Right share that Bible, their differences far outweigh their commonalities, as witnessed by the best-selling books published by Religious Left leaders, including Rabbi Michael Lerner's *The Left Hand of God: Taking Back Our Country from the Religious Right*, Rev. Jim Wallis's *God's Politics: Why the Right Gets It Wrong and the Left Doesn't Get It*, and former President Jimmy Carter's *Our Endangered Values: America's Moral Crisis*. Klinghoffer hastened to point out to his *National Review* readers that those books deal with the intersection of religion and politics as they relate to such "Left-ward" issues as poverty, race, the environment, and sex, adding that "Spiritual" as used in these works should not be deemed a "synonym for good, true, or even credible." He concluded his assessment of the rising Religious Left by asking whether it was a movement that could connect "at the grassroots level." And yet—noting that one of its constituent groups, the NSP, had recently staged a "Religious Left teach-in" in Washington, D.C., and attracted a large crowd—Klinghoffer declared that "something important is percolating." He seemed to welcome the Religious Left to the national debate over virtue and values, and suggested that the country's moral course would be determined through the exchange between two religious coalitions composed largely of evangelical Christians.[30]

However, early in the campaigning for the 2008 presidential race, neither Christianity nor the Bible was the dominant religious question. Instead, it was Mormonism and the Book of Mormon. Mitt Romney, former Massachusetts governor seeking the Republican nomination, was forced to defend his Mormon faith. As John Kennedy learned in 1960, many voters deem America to be a distinctively Protestant "City on a Hill." Some conservative evangelicals, in particular, are offended by the Church of Latter Day Saints' claim to be the true chosen people of God. Some go so far as to consider Mormonism a "non-Christian cult" based on what they deem to be a spurious revelation contained in the Book of Mormon.[31]

Leaders of the Religious Left soon discovered that it was one thing to draft a list of broad principles but another to translate those principles into specific policy goals that would enjoy the wide support of its constituent members and appeal to the Democratic Party. A group of twelve hundred members of New Religious Left organizations from thirty-nine states gathered in May 2006 at the All Souls Unitarian Church in Washington, D.C., to "to wrest the mantle of moral authority from conservative Christians" and plan how they would take their message to those in power. After "rousing" speeches by Rabbi Michael Lerner and Sister Joan Chittister, participants split into groups of fifty or so to discuss specific issues and how they would present them to members of Congress the following day. Yet in the session on ethical behavior, including sexual behavior, the group said almost nothing about abortion or same-sex marriage; rather, urged by Rev. Ama Zenya of First Congregational Church in Oakland, California, they talked about their spiritual values and how "to practice fully our authentic being." A Washington lawyer, Kimberly Crichton, reminded the group that their mandate was to discuss specific legislation and specific policy matters. Mr. Zenya replied, "What we envisioned this time is saying we are a religious voice." What we are doing, he added, was primarily "relationship-building [and] consciousness-raising," rather than policy drafting, prompting one gentleman in the front pew to respond to Crichton by saying, "[T]he answer is, no."[32]

After observing the conference's difficulty in defining a set of specific position statements, one outside observer noted that the Religious Left's esteem for pluralism might be its biggest stumbling block. The reporter noted that "liberal believers have so far been unable to approach, even modestly, the success of the religious right and command the attention of Congress." The problem was not low turnout—the conference enjoyed high attendance from across the country—but high regard for pluralism: "for letting people say what they want, how they want to, and for trying to include everyone's priorities, rather than choosing two or three issues that could inspire a movement." One of the movement's leaders, Tony Campolo, conceded at the end of the conference, "We didn't get on the same page with everyone, and it is about getting on the same page." He explained that the problem lay in the nature of liberals: "The thing about the left is that they want everybody to feel good."[33]

In addition to agreeing upon a set of specific moral positions, the Religious Left faces the challenge of how best to influence the Democratic Party, a party wary of any effort to penetrate the wall separating church and state and uneasy with religious language in the public square. Lerner thinks that the Democratic Party might well win elections in the short term because of failed Bush administration policies, but he believes that without embracing "progressive spiritual" policies, the party will continue to witness the slide of intellectual and political energy to the Right. Lerner does not underestimate the job of convincing secular Democrats that the party should embrace the NSP's Spiritual Covenant with America, especially, he writes, as "many on the Left, to be blunt, hate and fear religion."[34]

The relationship between the Religious Left and the Democratic Party is a delicate one at best. On the one hand, Democratic leaders agree that the overwhelming majority of evangelicals voted in 2000 and 2004 for the Republican Party, and that one part of their strategy to win back the White House in 2008 must be to woo some of those voters away from the GOP. Recognizing that the Republicans beat them in part by becoming the party of "faith," some Democrats search for ways to engage with religion. For certain Democrats, it is primarily a problem of perception that the party can correct by shaking off its secular image. Others seek opportunities to stake out a more culturally acceptable way of discussing the explosive issues of same-sex marriage and abortion. And still others welcome the reemergence of the Religious Left and its social agenda. In his postelection analysis in November 2004, Al From, director of the Democratic Leadership Council, declared, "You can't have everybody who goes to church vote Republican; you just can't." The problem for Democrats is how to woo church members without alienating other constituents in the party. Some conservative evangelicals who supported George Bush ventured that it would not take much for Democrats to appeal to some churchgoers. Richard Land, president of the Ethics and Religious Liberty Commission of the Southern Baptist Convention, suggested that Democrats could win members of his church "if the party demonstrates a greater friendliness to religious beliefs and even modestly softens its support for abortion rights." Democrats, however, are divided on what stance the party should take toward religion. One group dismisses or minimizes the need for change, arguing that the polls overstate the importance of conservative Christians in the 2004 election because of "poorly framed surveys." Another group concedes that Democrats need to find a new way to talk about issues, a way to "rephrase their positions in more moral and religious language." Still others believe that the party must do more than make a linguistic shift; it must acknowledge that the Republicans have occupied the middle on the hot social issues like abortion, and that if Democrats wish to win back many religious traditionalists, the party should "publicly welcome opponents of abortion into its ranks and perhaps even bend in its opposition to certain abortion restrictions." From said, "I want to win some people who are pro-life, because they probably agree with us on a lot of other things." Such an open-arms approach is likely to meet stiff resistance by many Democrats, especially abortion rights groups, including those that blocked Pennsylvania governor Robert Casey from speaking at the 1992 Democratic convention because he was an observant Catholic.[35]

Discussions about staking out a new position on the issue of abortion reveal the splits among Democrats concerning the influence of religion on the party's platform. Elizabeth Cavendish, interim president of NARAL Pro-Choice America, contends that the party "needs more religious language, . . . but not new positions." She and others claim that the incidence of abortion fell during the Clinton administration while rising in the Bush era, concluding from that comparison that Democrats can shift the debate from abortion rights to abortion frequency. They think that the Clinton formulation—that abortion should be "safe, legal, and rare"—gives them a sensible and defensible stance. Other Democrats want to reach out to religious antiabortion voters. Representative Rosa DeLauro of Connecticut is a Catholic who wants the Democratic Party to declare, "We would like to see fewer abortions and we want our children to learn good values." She thinks that the party could appeal to many Catholic voters by emphasizing the religious imperatives behind "pushing for real health care reform, reluctance before [going to] war and alternatives to abortion, such as adoption." Representative DeLauro said: "An over-whelming number of Democrats are people of faith. We need to be more explicit and more public about our convictions and our beliefs."[36]

Former professor of political theory at the University of Maryland, deputy on domestic affairs in the Clinton White House, and now fellow at the Brookings Institute William A. Galston offered a systematic and sustained discussion of the role of religion in the Democratic Party at a mid-2006 Pew Forum entitled "Religion, Moral Values and the Democratic Party." He first called for Democrats to broaden "the religious issues agenda," rather than continuing the discussion of religion and politics as it has been "narrowly conducted over the past generation, primarily on the agenda put forth by the Religious Right." Second, he thinks the party should do more than merely hire a "different language consultant" to talk about religion; rather, he thinks the party ought to discuss in moral terms such substantive issues as war, poverty, and social justice. Third, and perhaps most critical to Democratic success, Galston argued, was to change the way the party addressed the question of abortion: "[T]he fundamental turn that the party has to make in talking about abortion is a movement away from the idea that it's morally neutral to the idea that it is a misfortune, and even when necessary a regrettable necessity, and therefore it is something to be minimized." What that would do, he contends, is to bring back to the party large numbers of white Catholics whose historic commitment to issues of social justice is at the heart of the Democratic agenda.[37]

Some Democrats object to injecting more religion into the party. They fear that a "faith-based" approach makes them look more like the Bush-led Republican Party, where faith is narrowly defined by a conservative agenda. Representative Jerrold Nadler of New York is a Jew who is skeptical of the importance of faith in voter behavior. He argues that there is little evidence that more Americans' votes were "based on faith" in 2004 than in 2000. Further, if President Bush pushes for federal funding of social services engaged "on the basis of faith," Democrats should oppose this effort on the basis of discrimination. Nadler's argument is a call for Democrats to defend the party's stance on religious liberty that originated with Thomas Jefferson, a position that opposes sectarian intrusions into the public square.[38]

Mainline Protestant political activists also face opposition from fellow believers who worry about mixing religion and politics. Some question whether the church and the clergy ought to be involved in politics in the first place. Liberal clergy are torn on the question of engaging in politics. On the one hand, they embrace the doctrine of separation of church and state that constrains their involvement. On the other, they are loath to allow the Religious Right to define the national moral agenda.

Democratic leaders are also conflicted over a greater religious influence within the party. They welcome religious groups that may bring in new voters by offering an acceptable alternative to those disenchanted with the Religious Right and the Republican Party. Party leaders seeking new language for addressing social issues invite those who can speak the language of faith in a genuine way that convinces religious voters that the Democrats understand their spiritual longings and can translate those into policy statements. One of the criticisms of Democratic candidate John Kerry during the 2004 presidential campaign was that even when he began to talk about religion and his own experiences as a Catholic, his statements did not have the ring of authenticity. By contrast, even Democratic critics who disagreed with what he had to say acknowledged that President Bush spoke the language of faith with conviction. But Democrats are wary about religious influences and leaders within their party. They have long valued the separation of church and state and think that the Jeffersonian wall has served the nation well by checking sectarian control. Democrats trumpet their party as the party of diversity, and many within it worry about adopting stances that cater to particular religious sensitivities, whether softening language on abortion to lure Catholics and conservative Protestants or adopting radical policy statements such as those offered by the Religious Left.

As the Religious Left attempts to influence the Democratic Party by combating the Religious Right and offering an alternative moral vision that will appeal especially to "people of faith," it faces opposition similar to that confronting the Religious Right. The Right has dismissed the separation of church and state as a myth and claimed that the United States was founded as a Christian nation. They have vigorously promoted an agenda aimed at "reclaiming" that religious heritage, arguing that it is a nonsectarian legacy. The Religious Left and other critics, however, point out that the Religious Right's vision is highly partisan, and that indeed it is striving to make the GOP a religious party and the nation a theocracy. However, the Religious Left courts analogous opposition as it tries to convince the Democratic Party to give a "spiritual dimension" to its policy positions.[39]

As Americans discuss the future and the United States' place in the world, they do so within a polarized political culture where increasingly conservatives talk to conservatives and liberals talk to liberals but the two rarely engage each other in serious dialogue. Some political scientists note the balkanization of the electorate as seen graphically on election-night maps showing the red (Republican) versus the blue (Democratic) states. Republicans dominate the South and the West and are overwhelmingly preferred in rural regions. Democrats prevail in cities and on the coasts. Red and blue zones, then, become "one-party fiefdoms" with little opposition. While the electorate is riven by economic issues, particularly government spending and taxation, it is also split along a cultural divide. Indeed, the politicization of religion contributes to polarization. There is little evidence that the Religious Right and their opponents engage in serious, open-minded discussion of such controversial issues as prayer in public schools. Rather, they vilify each other in most unchristian and irreligious ways on cable television stations, clear-channel radio stations, and Internet Web sites devoted to partisan diatribe rather than to a fair exchange of ideas.[40] The Pew survey before the 2006 elections indicates that many Americans are "uneasy" with the current mix of religion and politics. Religious conservatives think that liberals are too secular; religious liberals think that conservatives are too "assertive" in pushing their religious agenda.[41]

Some critics of the current state of religion in American politics are speaking out against the politicization of religion—by religious people of all political stripes. Writing from the perspective of a professing, practicing Catholic, historian Garry Wills argues that there is no such thing as a "Christian politics." He notes that Jesus told Pontius Pilate, who tried him under the authority of the Roman Empire: "My reign is not of this present order. If my reign were of this present order, my supporters would have fought against my being turned over to the Jews. But my reign is not here." From that and other passages, Wills concludes that Christ was the original advocate of separation of church and state, and that he did not engage in partisan politics. He charges those who present moral issues to the public as if they were Christian in origin are distorting the New Testament. He indicts those who support public prayer and display of religion with violating Jesus' injunction: "When you pray, be not like the pretenders, who prefer to pray in the synagogues and in the public square, in the sight of others. In truth I tell you, that is all the profit they will have. But you, when you pray, go into your inner chamber and, locking the door, pray there in hiding to your Father, and your Father who sees you in hiding will reward you" (Matt. 6:5–6). Wills notes that Jesus was the victim of "every institutional authority in his life and death," and regrets that Republicans and Democrats are again victimizing him for partisan purposes.[42]

The politicization of religion and the polarization that it has promoted return us to where we began. The delegates to the Constitutional Convention in 1787 avoided religious discussion because they knew that religion as a force in public affairs was divisive. While they believed that religion was important in the culture as a means of building the moral character of citizens, they thought religion and the country would be best served if sectarian religion had no place in the political arena. Further, they knew that, given the country's pluralist culture, any expression of religion offered as a guide to national policy would be labeled sectarian and would be contested as such. Two hundred and twenty years after the new republic's birth, critics of both the Religious Right and the Religious Left think the delegates were wise to keep religion out of national politics.

NOTES ▨

INTRODUCTION

1. Samuel Williams, *The Influence of Christianity on Civil Society* (Boston, 1780), 9, 20–21.
2. Amy Sullivan, "The Good Fight: How Much Longer Can the Religious Left Remain Politically Neutral?" *Washington Monthly,* March 2005.
3. Williams, *The Influence of Christianity on Civil Society,* 20–21.
4. Ezra Stiles Ely, *The Duty of Christian Freemen to Elect Christian Rulers* (Philadelphia, 1828), 11–13.
5. See James Rohrer, "Sunday Mails and the Church-State Theme in Jacksonian America," *Journal of the Early Republic* 7 (Spring 1987): 65.
6. See, for example, the following works written by political scientists: Kenneth Wald, *Religion and Politics in the United States,* 4th ed. (Lanham, MD, 2003); John Green, *The Diminishing Divide: Religion's Changing Role in American Politics* (Washington, DC, 2000); Geoffrey Layman, *The Great Divide* (New York, 2001); Allison Calhoun-Brown, *Religion and Politics in the United States,* 5th ed. (Lanham, MD, 2006); Robert Booth Fowler, Allen D. Hertzke, Laura R. Olson, and Kevin R. de Dulk, *Religion and Politics in America: Faith, Culture, and Strategic Choices,* 3d ed. (Boulder, CO, 2004); James Reichley, *Faith in Politics* (Washington, DC, 2002). Historians writing on religion and politics in the past twenty years have also concentrated on the Religious Right; see, for example, Garry Wills, *Under God: Religion and American* (Norwalk, CT, 1990).
7. See Robert Wuthnow, *Restructuring of American Religion: Society and Faith Since World War II* (Princeton, 1988).

8. Robert Bellah, Richard Madsen, William Sullivan, Ann Swidler, and Steven Tipton, *Habits of the Heart: Individualism and Commitment in American Life* (Berkeley, 1985), 22.

9. Alexis de Tocqueville, *Democracy in America*, trans. and ed. Harvey Mansfield and Delba Winthrop (Chicago, 2000), 280.

10. Chris Beneke, *Beyond Toleration: The Religious Origins of American Pluralism* (Oxford, 2006), especially 163–164.

11. *New York Times*, April 16, 2006.

CHAPTER ONE
Providential and Secular America: Founding the Republic

1. Samuel Sherwood, *A Sermon Containing Scriptural Instructions to Civil Rulers, and All Freeborn Subjects* (New Haven, 1774), vi, 11, and 27.

2. Ibid., 24.

3. See Fred Anderson, *The People's Army: Massachusetts Soldiers and Society in the Seven Years War* (Chapel Hill, NC, 1996), particularly chapter 7, "Victory Comes from the Lord: Providentialism and the New Englanders' Understanding of Warfare."

4. For immigration and pluralism, see Sally Schwartz, *A Mixed Multitude: The Struggle for Toleration in Colonial Pennsylvania* (New York, 1988).

5. For English roots of anti-Catholicism, see Arthur Marotti, *Religious Ideology and Cultural Fantasy: Catholic and Anti-Catholic Discourses in Early Modern England* (South Bend, IN, 2005). For American manifestations of anti-Catholicism, see Jay Dolan, *In Search of American Catholics: A History of Religion and Culture in Tension* (New York, 2002).

6. See Beneke, *Beyond Toleration*, 6–7.

7. For discussion of the significance of religion in the Revolutionary generation, see James Hutson, *Religion and the Founding of the New Republic* (Washington, DC, 1998).

8. Cited in Ellis Sandoz, ed., *Political Sermons of the American Founding Era, 1730–1805*, 2 vols. (Indianapolis, 1998), 1:91. For insightful analysis of Puritan rhetoric in the Revolutionary period, see Harry Stout, "Rhetoric and Reality in the Early Republic: The Case of the Federal-

ist Clergy," in *Religion and American Politics from the Colonial Period to the 1980s*, ed. Mark Noll (New York, 1990), 62–76.

9. Nathan Hatch, *The Democratization of American Christianity* (New Haven, 1989), especially chapter 2, "The Crisis of Authority," 17–48.

10. Ibid., 35, 44–46, and 180–182.

11. For different interpretations of the Enlightenment and religion, see Peter Gay, *The Enlightenment: The Rise of Modern Paganism* (New York, 1995), and Jonathan Sheehan, *The Enlightenment Bible: Translation, Scholarship, Culture* (Princeton, 2005).

12. See Garry Wills, *Inventing America: Jefferson's Declaration of Independence* (New York, 1978).

13. For discussion of republicanism, see J.G.A. Pocock, *The Machiavellian Moment: Florentine Political Thought and the Atlantic Republican Tradition* (Princeton, 1975); Bernard Bailyn, *The Ideological Origins of the American Revolution* (Cambridge, MA, 1967); and Gordon Wood, *The Creation of the American Republic, 1776–1787* (Chapel Hill, NC, 1969).

14. Thomas Jefferson to Dr. Thomas Cooper, February 10, 1814, in *The Writings of Thomas Jefferson*, ed. Albert Ellery Bergh, Library Edition, Issued under the Auspices of The Thomas Jefferson Memorial Association (Washington, DC, 1903), 14:85–97.

15. See Joseph Story, "Christianity a Part of the Common Law," *American Jurist and Law Magazine* 9 (1933): 346–348.

16. Julian Boyd, ed., *The Papers of Thomas Jefferson*, 28 vols. (Princeton, 1955), 12:15.

17. Pauline Maier discusses the canonization of American civil documents in *American Scripture: Making the Declaration of Independence* (New York, 1997).

18. Robert Bellah, "Civil Religion in America," *Journal of the American Academy of Arts and Sciences*, "Religion in America" issue, 96, no. 1 (Winter 1967): 1–21.

19. Jonathan Edwards, *A History of the Work of Redemption* (Philadelphia, [1773]), 281–282.

20. Edmund Morgan, *Puritan Political Ideals, 1558–1794* (Indianapolis, 1965), iii.

21. Analysis based on documents from the conventions. Max Farrand, ed., *The Records of the Federal Convention of 1787*, 3 vols. (New Haven, 1911), and Jonathan Elliot, ed., *The Debates in the Several*

State Conventions on the Adoption of the Federal Constitution, 5 vols. (Philadelphia, 1961).

22. Farrand, *Records of the Federal Convention*, 1:451.

23. Ibid., 1:451–452.

24. Ibid., 3:531.

25. W. W. Hening, ed., *Statutes at Large of Virginia*, 13 vols. (Richmond, 1823), 12:84–86.

26. Cited in Isaac Kramnick and R. Laurence Moore, *The Godless Constitution: The Case against Religious Correctness* (New York, 1996), 29.

27. Farrand, *Records of the Federal Convention*, 3:122.

28. Ibid., 3:310.

29. See text of *Federalist* No. 10 in *Federalists and Antifederalists: The Debate over Ratification of the Constitution*, ed. John Kaminski and Richard Leffler, 2d. ed. (Lanham, MD, 1998), 26–32.

30. Robert Rutland and William Rachal, eds., *The Papers of James Madison*, 8 vols. (Chicago, 1973), 8:298–304.

31. Philip Kurland and Ralph Lerner, eds., *The Founders' Constitution*, 4 vols. (Chicago, 1987), 4:643.

32. Ibid.

33. Cited in Stephen Weeks, *Church and State in North Carolina* (Baltimore, MD, 1893), 59.

34. Elliot, *The Debates in the Several State Conventions on the Adoption of the Federal Constitution*, 4:197–199 and 215.

35. For representative arguments supporting a Bill of Rights, see Kaminski and Leffler, eds., *Federalists and Antifederalists*, 152–165.

36. This discussion rests heavily on Frank Lambert, " '. . . [or] Jefferson and No God': Campaigning for a Voter Imposed Religious Test in 1800," *Journal of Church and State* 39 (Fall 1997): 201–221. See also Frank Lambert, *The Founding Fathers and the Place of Religion in America* (Princeton, 2003), 265–287.

37. Paul Ford, ed. *The Works of Thomas Jefferson*, 12 vols. (New York, 1905), 9:457.

38. Thomas Jefferson, *Notes on the State of Virginia*, ed. William Peden (Chapel Hill, NC, 1982), 158.

39. Cited in L. H. Butterfield, *Elder John Leland* (Worcester, MA, 1953), 198–199.

40. Noble E. Cunningham, Jr., "Election of 1800," in *History of American Presidential Elections, 1789–1968*, ed. Arthur M. Schlesinger, Jr., 4 vols. (New York, 1971), 1:124, 139.

41. Tunis Wortman, *A Solemn Address, To Christians & Patriots, Upon the Approaching Election of a President of the United States* in Sandoz, *Political Sermons of the American Founding Era, 1730–1805,* 2:1488, 1493.

42. John Mitchell Mason, *The Voice of Warning to Christians,* in Sandoz, *Political Sermons of the American Founding Era, 1730–1805,* 2:1466.

43. Philip Hamburger, *Separation of Church and State* (Cambridge, MA, 2004), 111–112.

44. Charles Francis Adams, ed., *The Works of John Adams, Second President of the United States,* 10 vols. (Boston, 1856), 9:636–637.

45. Ibid., 10:387.

46. Lester Cappon, ed., *The Adams-Jefferson Letters: The Complete Correspondence between Thomas Jefferson and John Adams,* 2 vols. (Chapel Hill, NC, 1959), 2:406, 509, and 512.

47. Cited in Richard Beale Davis, "The Abbé Correa in America, 1812–1820: The Contributions of the Diplomat and Natural Philosopher to the Foundations of Our National Life. Correspondence with Jefferson and Other Members of the American Philosophical Society and with Other Prominent Americans," *Transactions of the American Philosophical Society* (1955), 178.

CHAPTER TWO
Elusive Protestant Unity: Sunday Mails, Catholic
Immigration, and Sectional Division

1. Barbara Cross, ed., *The Autobiography of Lyman Beecher,* 2 vols. (Cambridge, MA, 1961), 1:252.

2. Ibid., 1:336–337.

3. Mark Noll, David Bebbington, and George Rawlyk, eds., *Evangelicalism: Comparative Studies of Popular Protestantism in North America, the British Isles, and Beyond, 1700–1990* (New York, 1994), 6.

4. Daniel Walker Howe, "Religion and Politics in the Antebellum North, in Noll, *Religion and American Politics,* 130–131.

5. Mark Noll, *America's God: From Jonathan Edwards to Abraham Lincoln* (New York, 2002).

6. See ibid.

7. See Hatch, *The Democratization of American Christianity,* 4.

8. See Nancy Cott, *The Bonds of Womanhood: "Woman's Sphere" in New England, 1780–1835* (New Haven, 1977).

9. See Christine Stansell, *City of Women: Sex and Class in New York, 1789–1860* (Champaign-Urbana, IL, 1987).

10. See Leonard Richards, *Shays' Rebellion: The American Revolution's Final Battle* (Philadelphia, 2003).

11. See Thomas Slaughter, *The Whiskey Rebellion: Frontier Epilogue to the American Revolution* (New York, 1988).

12. Paul Newman, *Fries' Rebellion: The Enduring Struggle for the American Revolution* (Philadelphia, 2005).

13. Alexis de Tocqueville, *Democracy in America*, ed. Richard Heffner (New York, 1956), 152.

14. Tocqueville, *Democracy in America*, trans. and ed. Mansfield and Winthrop, 501 and 505.

15. Frances Trollope, *Domestic Manners of the Americans*, ed. John Larson (St. James, NY, 1993), xii–xiii, xviii–xix, and 20–21.

16. Kramnick and Moore, *The Godless Constitution*, 131–133.

17. Cited in Stout, "Rhetoric and Reality in the Early Republic," 62–63.

18. Jasper Adams, *The Relation of Christianity to Civil Government in the United States* (Charleston, SC, 1833), 7, 16–17, and 22.

19. Daniel Dreisbach, ed., *Religion and Politics in the Early Republic: Jasper Adams and the Church-State Debate* (Lexington, KY, 1996), 154–155.

20. Eugene Genovese and Elizabeth Fox-Genovese, "Slaveholders and the Bible," in *Major Problems in American Religious History*, ed. Patrick Allitt (New York, 2000), 188–190.

21. Jay Dolan, "Catholic Charity and Protestant Suspicions," in Allitt, *Major Problems in American Religious History*, 183–185.

22. Cited in George Fredrickson, "The Coming of the Lord: The Northern Protestant Clergy and the Civil War Crisis," and Mark Noll, "The Bible and Slavery," in *Religion and the American Civil War*, ed. Randall Miller, Harry Stout, and Charles Reagan Wilson (New York, 1998), 113–114.

23. Hatch, *The Democratization of American Christianity*, 3–4.

24. Ibid., 4–5.

25. See Ellen Eslinger, *Citizens of Zion: The Social Origins of Camp Meeting Revivals* (Knoxville, TN, 1999).

26. Paul Johnson, *A Shopkeeper's Millennium: Society and Revivals in Rochester, New York, 1815–1837* (New York, 1978), 100.

27. Cited in Frank Lambert, *Inventing the "Great Awakening"* (Princeton, 1999), 91–92, 96.

28. See Terry Bilhartz, *Urban Religion and the Second Great Awakening* (Rutherford, NJ, 1986).
29. Howe, "Religion and Politics in the Antebellum North," 131–132.
30. Charles Finney, "Sinners Bound to Change Their Own Hearts," in *Sermons on Important Subjects*, 3d ed. (New York, 1836), 7.
31. For a discussion of evangelical benevolence, see Charles Foster, *An Errand of Mercy: The Evangelical United Front, 1790–1837* (Chapel Hill, NC, 1960), 47–49, and 127.
32. See William Addison Blakely, ed., *American State Papers Bearing on Sunday Legislation* (Washington, DC, 1911), 176.
33. Kramnick and Moore, *The Godless Constitution*, 131.
34. Blakely, *American State Papers Bearing on Sunday Legislation*, 179.
35. Kramnick and Moore, *The Godless Constitution*, 133–134.
36. Ibid., 135–136.
37. Blakely, *American State Papers Bearing on Sunday Legislation*, 314–316.
38. Kramnick and Moore, *The Godless Constitution*, 136–141.
39. Ibid., 142–143.
40. John Bassett, ed., *Correspondence of Andrew Jackson*, 13 vols. (Washington, DC, 1929), 4:447.
41. James Hitchcock, *The Supreme Court and Religion in American Life*, 2 vols. (Princeton, 2004), 1:32–33.
42. See Jody Roy, *Rhetorical Campaigns of 19th Century Anti-Catholics and Catholics in America* (New York, 1999).
43. Robert Swiegenga, "Ethnoreligious Political Behavior in the Mid-Nineteenth Century: Voting, Values, and Cultures," in Noll, *Religion and American Politics*, 153–159.
44. Roy, *Rhetorical Campaigns of the 19th Century Anti-Catholics and Catholics in America*, 3.
45. Orestes Brownson, *The American Republic: Its Constitution, Tendencies, and Destiny* (Detroit, 1895), 192 and 212.
46. Noll, "The Bible and Slavery," 43–44.
47. John McKivigan, *The War against Proslavery Religion: Abolitionism and the Northern Church* (Ithaca, NY, 1984), 20–21, 27, 31, and 143.
48. Cited in James Moorhead, "Social Reform and the Divided Conscience of Antebellum Protestantism," *Church History* 48 (December 1979), 424.

49. Ronald Walters, *The Antislavery Appeal: American Abolitionism after 1830* (New York, 1984), 39–41.

50. See Mark McGarvie, *One Nation under Law: America's Early National Struggles to Separate Church and State* (DeKalb, IL, 2004). For discussion of tension between religion and slaveholding, see chapter 6, 131–151.

51. Genovese and Fox-Genovese, "Slaveholders and the Bible," 189.

52. Kurt Berends, " 'Wholesome Reading Purifies and Elevates the Man': The Religious Military Press in the Confederacy," in Miller, Stout, and Wilson, *Religion and the American Civil War*, 142–143.

53. Ibid., 145.

54. Fredrickson, "The Coming of the Lord," 121.

55. Ibid., 122.

56. Roy Basler, ed., *The Collected Works of Abraham Lincoln*, 13 vols. (New Brunswick, NJ, 1953), 13:333.

CHAPTER THREE
The "Gospel of Wealth" and the "Social Gospel":
Industrialization and the Rise of Corporate America

1. See Hamlin Hill, ed., *Mark Twain: The Gilded Age and Later Novels* (New York, 2002).

2. The classical discussion of the Puritans' theological interpretation of wilderness is Perry Miller, *Errand into the Wilderness* (Cambridge, MA, 1956).

3. For Jefferson's moral views of agriculture, see his 1785 letter to John Jay in Boyd et al., *The Papers of Thomas Jefferson*, 8:426–427.

4. For firsthand accounts of religious life among the Lowell girls, see Benita Eisler, ed., *The Lowell Offering: Writings of New England Mill Women, 1840–1845* (New York, 1977).

5. Hill, *Mark Twain*, 46, 66–67.

6. Ibid., 201–205.

7. Ibid., 206.

8. An engaging biography of Carnegie is Joseph Wall, *Andrew Carnegie* (Pittsburgh, 1989).

9. Andrew Carnegie, *The Gospel of Wealth and Other Timely Essays* (Garden City, NY, 1933), 3–4.

10. "Our Church-Erection Interests," *United Brethren Review* 5, no. 2 (April 1894): 179–18.

11. Russell H. Conwell, *Acres of Diamonds* (Old Tappan, NJ, 1960), 20–24.

12. Bruce Barton, *The Man Nobody Knows: A Discovery of the Real Jesus* (Indianapolis, 1925), 8–9.

13. For Rockefeller's attitudes toward organized labor, see Ron Chernow, *Titan: The Life of John D. Rockefeller, Sr.* (New York, 1998).

14. For relations between industry and regulation, see Mansel Blackford, "Businessmen and the Regulation of Railroads and Public Utilities in California during the Progressive Era," *Business History Review* 44 (Autumn 1970): 307–319.

15. George Marsden, *The Soul of the American University: From Protestant Establishment to Established Nonbelief* (New York, 1994), 4, 265.

16. Dwight Moody, *Heaven: Where It Is, Its Inhabitants, and How to Get There* (Chicago, 1995), 11.

17. This excerpt comes from Moody's sermon on the Ten Commandments. For the full text, see the Web site, http://www.fbinstitute.com/moody/The_TenCommandments_Text (accessed June 11, 2007).

18. Bruce Eversen, *God's Man for the Gilded Age: D. L. Moody and the Rise of Modern Mass Evangelism* (Oxford, 2003), 107.

19. Ibid., 3–4.

20. George Marsden, *Religion and American Culture* (Belmont, CA, 2001), 126.

21. Cited in James Findlay, "Moody, 'Gapmen,' and the Gospel: The Early Days of Moody Bible Institute," *Church History* 31 (September 1962): 324, 326.

22. Cited in William Ellis, *"Billy" Sunday: The Man and His Message* (n.p., 1914), 147.

23. Rebecca Edwards, *New Spirits: Americans in the Gilded Age, 1865–1905* (New York, 2006), 180.

24. Marsden, *Religion and American Culture*, 166.

25. Albert Raboteau, *Slave Religion: The "Invisible Institution" in the Antebellum South* (Oxford, 1978), 128–129.

26. See Milton Sernett, ed., *Afro-American Religious History: A Documentary Witness* (Durham, NC, 1985), 239–240.

27. Edwards, *New Spirits*, 173.

28. Walter Rauschenbusch, *A Theology for the Social Gospel* (New York, 1918), 161.

29. Susan Curtis, *A Consuming Faith: The Social Gospel and Modern American Culture* (Baltimore, 1991), 139.
30. Elizabeth Burt, ed., *The Progressive Era: Primary Documents on Events from 1890 to 1914* (Westport, CT, 2004), 26–27.
31. Rauschenbusch, *A Theology for the Social Gospel,* 110–111.
32. Ibid., 111.
33. Robert Wiebe, *The Search for Order, 1877–1920* (New York, 1967), 137.
34. Michael McGerr, *A Fierce Discontent: The Rise and Fall of the Progressive Movement in America, 1870–1920* (New York, 2003), 66.
35. Norman Risjord, *Populists and Progressives* (Lanham, MD, 2005), 14–15.
36. McGerr, *A Fierce Discontent,* 66.
37. Curtis, *Consuming Faith,* 157–161.
38. McGerr, *A Fierce Discontent,* 80.
39. See Noll, *America's God.*
40. Robert Crunden, *Ministers of Reform: The Progressives' Achievement in American Civilization, 1889–1920* (Urbana, IL, 1984), 8.
41. McGerr, *A Fierce Discontent,* 68.
42. Risjord, *Populists and Progressives,* 83.
43. Wiebe, *The Search for Order,* 137, 207.

CHAPTER FOUR
Faith and Science: The Modernist-Fundamentalist Controversy

1. While most scholars date the rise of historical fundamentalism in the United States in the early twentieth century, many recognize earlier expressions of fundamentalism. See, for example, Ernest Sandeen, "Fundamentalism and American Identity," *Annals of the American Academy of Political and Social Science* 387 (1970): 56–65.
2. Joel Carpenter, "Fundamentalist Institutions and the Rise of Evangelical Protestantism, 1929–1942," *Church History* 49 (March 1980): 64.
3. Bradley Longfield, *The Presbyterian Controversy: Fundamentalists, Modernists, and Moderates* (New York, 1991), 9–10.
4. Ibid., 11.
5. Robert Handy, "Protestant Theological Tensions and Political Styles in the Progressive Period," in Noll, *Religion and American Politics,* 282.

6. For discussion of Christian realists, see Heather Warren, *Theologians of a New World Order: Rheinhold Niebuhr and the Christian Realists, 1920–1948* (New York, 1997).

7. See R. A. Torrey and Alan Dixon, eds., *The Fundamentals: A Testimony to the Truth* (Grand Rapids, MI, 2003).

8. Ferenc Szasz, *The Divided Mind of Protestant America: 1880–1930* (Tuscaloosa, AL, 2002), 15–17.

9. Ibid., 17, 30–31.

10. Ibid., 34.

11. Ibid.

12. Ibid., 35.

13. Ibid., 36.

14. Ibid., 338–39.

15. See Allitt, *Major Problems in American Religious History,* 259–261.

16. Ibid., 261–263.

17. Cited in Lambert, *The Founding Fathers and the Place of Religion in America,* 160.

18. Cited in Benjamin Franklin, *The Autobiography and Other Writings,* ed. Kenneth Silverman (New York, 1986), 255.

19. Marsden, *The Soul of the American University,* 265.

20. Ibid., 268 and 272.

21. Ibid., 4–5.

22. George Marsden, *Fundamentalism and American Culture: The Shaping of Twentieth-Century Evangelicalism, 1870–1925* (New York, 1980), 242 n. 20.

23. Ibid., 17.

24. See Robert Cherny, *A Righteous Cause: The Life of William Jennings Bryan* (Norman, OK, 1994).

25. For a biography that captures Bryan's spirituality, see Michael Kazin, *A Godly Hero: The Life of William Jennings Bryan* (New York, 2006).

26. For a recent account of the Dayton trial, see Edward Larson, *Summer for the Gods: The Scopes Trial and America's Continuing Debate over Science and Religion* (Cambridge, MA, 1998).

27. See Marsden, *Fundamentalism and American Culture,* 184–187; see also Szasz, *The Divided Mind of Protestant America,* 117–118.

28. Szasz, *The Divided Mind of Protestant America,* 119; and Marsden, *Fundamentalism and American Culture,* 187.

29. *New York Times,* July 22, 1925.

30. Mark A. Noll, "Science, Theology, and Society: From Cotton Mather to William Jennings Bryan," in *Evangelicals and Science in Historical Perspective*, ed. David Livingstone, D. G. Hart, and Mark Noll (New York, 1999), 99.
31. Marsden, *Fundamentalism and American Culture*, 11.
32. Ibid., 100.
33. James Hutson, ed., *The Founders on Religion: A Book of Quotations* (Princeton, 2005), 190–191.
34. Cited in Marsden, *Religion and American Culture*, 205.

CHAPTER FIVE
Religious and Political Liberalism: The Rise of
Big Government from the New Deal to the Cold War

1. Wuthnow, *Restructuring of American Religion*.
2. See U.S. Bureau of Economic Analysis, May 26, 2005, at the agency's Web site, www.bea.gov (accessed January 8, 2007).
3. While secularization theory has come under attack in recent years, it continues to have defenders. See Frank Lechner, "The Case against Secularization: A Rebuttal," *Social Forces* 69 (June 1991): 1103–1119; Gerald Marwell and N. J. Demerath, III, "Secularization by Any Other Name," *American Sociological Review* 68 (April 2003): 314–316. Proponents of the secularization theory point out that secularization is not just the decline of religion in a society but the decline of religious authority in society. See Mark Chaves, "Secularization as Declining Religious Authority," *Social Forces* 72 (March 1994): 749–774.
4. Roger Finke and Rodney Stark, *The Churching of America, 1776–1990: Winners and Losers in Our Religious Economy* (New Brunswick, NJ, 1992), 17–21.
5. For a view of NAE history as presented by the organization today, see its Web site at http://www.nae.net/index.cfm?FUSEACTION=nae.history (accessed June 11, 2007).
6. See Henry Pratt, "The Growth of Political Action in the National Council of Churches," *Review of Politics* 34 (July 1972): 323–341.
7. http://mb-soft.com/believe/txn/liberali.htm (accessed June 11, 2007).
8. *Christian Century*, January 4, 1933, 34.
9. *Catholic Action*, Social Action Number, June 1938.

10. Coolidge's Puritan heritage is captured in William Allen White, *A Puritan in Babylon: The Story of Calvin Coolidge* (1946; Phoenix, AZ, 2001).

11. Samuel Rosenman, ed., *The Public Papers and Addresses of Franklin D. Roosevelt*, 13 vols. (New York, 1950), 8:1.

12. Quotations taken from "Harry Truman Speaks," compiled by Raymond Geselbracht and posted on the Truman Presidential Museum and Library Web site, http://www.trumanlibrary.org/speaks.html (accessed June 11, 2007).

13. Robert Alley, ed., *The Constitution and Religion: Leading Supreme Court Cases on Church and State* (New York, 1999), 47, 54, and 59.

14. Ibid., 82–85, 165, 171, and 179.

15. See Warren, *Theologians of a New World Order*.

16. Philip Goff, " 'We Have Heard the Joyful Sound': Charles E. Fuller's Radio Broadcast and the Rise of Modern Evangelicalism," in *Embodying the Spirit: New Perspectives on North American Revivalism*, ed. Michael McClymond (Baltimore, 2004), 148–150.

17. Ibid., 150.

18. Ibid., 152–153.

19. Ibid., 153.

20. Laurence Moore, *Religious Outsiders and the Making of Americans* (New York, 1987), 150–151, 164–165.

21. See William G. McLoughlon, *Modern Revivalism: Charles Grandison Finney to Billy Graham* (New York, 1959), 79 ff., 225, 489.

22. The statement is found on the World Council of Churches Web site, http://wcc-coe.org/who/histor-e.html (accessed June 11, 2007).

23. See http://www.bwanet.org (accessed June 11, 2007).

24. Benton Johnson, "Theology and the Position of Pastors on Public Issues," *American Sociological Review* 32 (June 1967): 439.

25. Wald, *Religion and Politics in the United States*, 151–153.

26. Allitt, *Major Problems in American Religious History*, 335–337.

27. Cited in Finke and Stark, *The Churching of America*, 201.

28. Paul Boyer, *By the Bomb's Early Light: American Thought and Culture at the Dawn of the Atomic Age* (New York, 1985), 183–184.

29. Ibid., 211–212.

30. Ibid., 211–218.

31. Ibid., 202–203.

32. Ibid., 219.

33. Marsden, *Religion and American Culture*, 220 and 226–227.

34. For discussion of the "religion" of America, see Marvin Frankel, *Faith and Freedom: Religious Liberty in America* (New York, 1994), 42.
35. John F. Kennedy, "Address to the Ministers of Houston," in *The Annals of America*, 18 vols. (Chicago, 1968), 17:589–591.
36. See Marsden, *Religion and American Culture*, 224–225.
37. Ibid., 238.

CHAPTER SIX
Civil Rights as a Religious Movement: Politics in the Streets

1. Politics out-of-doors has a long tradition in Anglo-American history and has provided a forum for the disaffected to voice grievances when institutional channels are either unavailable or unresponsive. For a discussion and case study, see Carl Prince, "The Great 'Riot Year': Jacksonian Democracy and Patterns of Violence in 1834," *Journal of the Early Republic* 5 (Spring 1985): 1–19.
2. See Moore, *Religious Outsiders and the Making of Americans*. In particular, see discussion of black churches and black culture, 173–200.
3. Cited in Sernett, *Afro-American Religious History*, 431.
4. Cited in Allitt, *Major Problems in American Religious History*, 362.
5. Cited in Sernett, *Afro-American Religious History*, 434–435.
6. Cited in Lambert, *Inventing the "Great Awakening"*, 142.
7. W.E.B. DuBois, "Of the Faith of the Fathers," in Allitt, *Major Problems in American Religious History*, 313–314.
8. Ibid., 310–319.
9. Benjamin Mays and Joseph Nicholson, "The Genius of the Negro Church," in Allitt, *Major Problems in American Religious History*, 338–340.
10. Ibid., 340–343.
11. Robert Miller, "The Attitudes of American Protestantism toward the Negro, 1919–1939," *Journal of Negro History* 41, no. 3 (July 1956): 215–217.
12. Cited in Sernett, *Afro-American Religious History*, 441.
13. For the story of Jordan's activism, see Dallas Lee, *The Cotton Patch Evidence: The Story of Clarence Jordan and the Koinonia Farm Experiment* (San Francisco, 1971).
14. *Christian Century*, June 21, 1928, 785. Italics found in the source.
15. Miller, "The Attitudes of American Protestantism toward the Negro, 1919–1939," 218–220.

16. Cited in Paul Harvey, *Freedom's Coming: Religious Culture and the Shaping of the South from the Civil War through the Civil Rights Era* (Chapel Hill, NC, 2005), 169.

17. Ibid., 169.

18. Ibid., 170.

19. Ibid., 170–171.

20. Ibid., 171–175.

21. Cited in Beth Schweiger and Donald Mathews, eds., *Religion in the American South: Protestants and Others in History and Culture* (Chapel Hill, NC, 2004), 319.

22. Harvey, *Freedom's Coming*, 178–179.

23. Ibid., 192.

24. Gayraud Wilmore, *Black Religion and Black Radicalism* (Garden City, NY, 1972), 231.

25. Ibid., 263–265.

26. Sernett, *Afro-American Religious History*, 413.

27. See Frank Hale, ed., *The Cry for Freedom: An Anthology of the Best That Has Been Written on Civil Rights since 1954* (New York, 1969), 248–250.

28. Benjamin Muse, *The American Negro Revolution: From Nonviolence to Black Power, 1963–1967* (Bloomington, IN, 1968), 51.

29. Ibid., 48–52.

30. See John Lee Eighmy and Samuel Hill, *Churches in Cultural Captivity: A History of the Social Attitudes of Southern Baptists* (Knoxville, TN, 1987).

31. Schweiger and Mathews, *Religion in the American South*, 285.

32. Sernett, *Afro-American Religious History*, 477–479.

33. The Southern Christian Leadership Conference, *The SCLC Story in Words and Pictures* (Atlanta, 1964), 50–51.

CHAPTER SEVEN
The Rise of the "Religious Right": The Reagan Revolution
and the "Moral Majority"

1. http://www.trbc.org/new/falwellsermons.php (accessed June 11, 2007).

2. For the Pew report published August 30, 2005, see the Pew Forum on Religion and Public Life Web site, http://pewforum.org/docs (accessed June 11, 2007).

3. Glenn Utter and John Storey, *The Religious Right: A Reference Handbook* (Santa Barbara, CA, 1995), 86–91.

4. Ibid., 94, 102.

5. Jim Wallis, *God's Politics: Why the Right Gets It Wrong and the Left Doesn't Get It* (New York, 2005), 3–4.

6. Alley, *The Constitution and Religion*, 171–176.

7. See the Moral Majority Coalition's time line at http://www .moralmajority.us/index.php?option=com_content&task=view&id= 5&Itemid=29 (accessed June 11, 2007).

8. Susan Harding, *The Book of Jerry Falwell: Fundamentalist Language and Politics* (Princeton, 2000), x–xi.

9. Marsden, *Religion and American Culture*, 272.

10. Ibid., 48–249.

11. Ibid., 249–250.

12. Ibid., 252–259.

13. Wald, *Religion and Politics in the United States*, 205–206.

14. Ibid., 206.

15. Ibid., 206–207.

16. Ibid., 208.

17. William Martin, *With God on Our Side: The Rise of the Religious Right* (New York, 1996), 168–169.

18. Ibid., 169–170.

19. Ibid., 170–172.

20. Wald, *Religion and Politics in the United States*, 203.

21. Martin, *With God on Our Side*, 173–174.

22. Ibid., 173.

23. Ibid., 178.

24. Ibid., 189.

25. Cited in ibid., 175.

26. David Bromley and Anson Shupe, *New Christian Politics* (Macon, GA, 1984), 35.

27. Hutson, *The Founders on Religion*, ix–x.

28. *Washington Post*, March 22, 2006.

29. Ibid.

30. Ibid.

31. *Progressive*, March 17, 2004.

32. See *Time* On-Line Edition at http://www.time.com/time/columnist/ klein/article/0,9565,1154170,00.html, posted January 28, 2006 (accessed June 11, 2007).

33. Alley, *The Constitution and Religion*, 232, 392.

34. Kramnick and Moore, *The Godless Constitution*, 130–131.

35. Justin Watson, *The Christian Coalition: Dreams of Restoration, Demands for Recognition* (New York, 1997), 3.

36. Kramnick and Moore, *The Godless Constitution*, 20.

37. The letter is posted on the Web site of the National Center for Public Policy Research; see http://www.nationalcenter.org/Weyrich299.html (accessed June 11, 2007).

38. For a review of the book, see *Christian Century*, May 19, 1999. Cal Thomas and Ed Dobson, *Blinded by Might: Can the Religious Right Change America?* (Grand Rapids, MI, 1999).

39. *New York Times*, July 30, 2006. Boyd has published his thoughts on religion and politics in *The Myth of a Christian Nation: How the Quest for Political Power Is Destroying the Church* (Grand Rapids, MI, 2006).

40. *Washington Post*, September 28, 2006. Danforth's book is *Faith and Politics: How the "Moral Values" Debate Divides America and How to Move Forward Together* (New York, 2006).

41. *Washington Post*, November 6, 2006.

42. *Washington Times*, November 24, 2006.

43. Utter and Storey, *The Religious Right*, 105.

44. Linda Kintz and Julia Lesage, eds., *Media, Culture, and the Religious Right* (Minneapolis, 1998), 295–307.

45. Anne Loveland and Otis Wheeler, *From Meetinghouse to Megachurch: A Material and Cultural History* (Columbia, MO, 2003), 114–131.

46. See Amy Astell, ed., *Unraveling the Right: The New Conservatism in American Thought and Politics* (Boulder, CO, 1998), 228.

47. Wald, *Religion and Politics in the United States*, 235–239.

CHAPTER EIGHT
Reemergence of the "Religious Left"? America's Culture War in the Early Twenty-first Century

1. Michael Lerner, *The Left Hand of God: Taking Back Our Country from the Religious Right* (San Francisco, 2006), 40.

2. *Washington Post*, May 20, 2006.

3. See http://pewforum.org/docs/index.php?DocID=153; survey results posted on August 24, 2006 (accessed June 11, 2007).

4. http://www.slate.com/id/2139365/ (accessed June 11, 2007).

5. Lerner, *The Left Hand of God*, 50.

6. Ibid., 6–8.

7. Ibid., 3–4.

8. Kevin Phillips, *American Theocracy: The Peril and Politics of Radical Religion, Oil, and Borrowed Money in the 21st Century* (New York, 2006), 182–184.

9. See May 1, 2006, posting, "The Religious 'Left' Reasserts Itself," http://www.religionlink.org/tip_060501.php (accessed June 11, 2007).

10. For the core vision of the Network of Spiritual Progressives, visit http://www.spiritualprogressives.org/ (accessed June 11, 2007).

11. For the Spiritual Covenant with America, see http://www .spiritualprogressives.org/ (accessed June 11, 2007).

12. Posted at http://mediamatters.org/items/200504280002 (accessed June 11, 2007), a Web site that monitors "misinformation" in the conservative media.

13. *National Liberty Journal*, July 28, 2005.

14. *Washington Post*, May 21, 2005.

15. Ibid.

16. *Washington Times*, June 23, 2005.

17. *American Family Association Journal*, February 2007. For the online version, see http://www.afajournal.org/2007/february/ 0207religious _left.asp (accessed June 11, 2007).

18. *Washington Post*, November 26, 2006.

19. Christopher Hitchens, *God Is Not Great: How Religion Poisons Everything* (New York, 2007); see especially 253–277.

20. Robert Wuthnow and John H. Evans, eds., *The Quiet Hand of God: Faith-Based Activism and the Public Role of Mainline Protestantism* (Berkeley, CA, 2002), 3.

21. Laura Olson, "Mainline Protestant Washington Offices and the Political Lives of Clergy," in Wuthnow and Evans, *The Quiet Hand of God*, 54–55.

22. Ibid., 55–56.

23. Wuthnow and Evans, *The Quiet Hand of God*, 2–3.

24. *Christian Century*, September 21, 2004.

25. For the history of Riverside as a bastion of Christian liberalism, see Peter Paris, John Cook, James Hudnut-Beumler, and Lawrence Mamiya, eds., *The History of the Riverside Church in the City of New York* (New York, 2004).

26. *Christian Century,* September 21, 2004.

27. *Chicago Tribune,* June 28, 2006. Also see CNN.com, "Obama to Democrats: Woo Evangelicals," June 28, 2006 (accessed June 11, 2007).

28. *Weekly Standard,* December 13, 2006.

29. Ibid.

30. *National Review,* June 2, 2006.

31. *Los Angeles Times,* June 10, 2007.

32. *New York Times,* May 19, 2006.

33. Ibid.

34. Lerner, *The Left Hand of God,* 3–4, 127.

35. *New York Times,* November 17, 2004.

36. Ibid.

37. For transcript of Galston's analysis, see http://pewforum.org/events/index.php?EventID=115 (accessed June 11, 2007).

38. *New York Times,* November 17, 2004.

39. Lerner, *The Left Hand of God,* 5.

40. Steven Hill, "Divided We Stand: The Polarizing of American Politics," *National Civic Review,* January 31, 2006.

41. See http://pewforum.org/docs/index.php?DocID=153; survey results posted on August 24, 2006 (accessed June 11, 2007).

42. Garry Wills, "Christ among the Partisans," *New York Times,* April 9, 2006.

INDEX ▨

209; and Moral Majority, 190; nation as, 78–79; and Network of Spiritual Progressives, 229; and religious conservatives, 157; and Religious Right, 4, 185; and republicanism, 45; and social gospel movement, 97

Family Research Council, 232

Faubus, Orval, 201

Federal Council of Churches (FCC), 103, 139, 145, 153, 179; "Atomic Warfare and the Christian Faith," 154

Federalist, 30

Federalists, 16, 34, 36, 49, 59

feminism, 189, 219

Fermi, Enrico, 131

Finney, Charles Grandison, 56–57, 58, 69, 94, 128; *Lectures on Revivals of Religion*, 57

Florence, republic of, 24

Focus on the Family, 214

foreign policy, 140, 190, 198, 207, 222

Fosdick, Harry Emerson, 138, 238; "Shall the Fundamentalists Win?" 107

Founders: and atomic bomb supporters, 152; and Christianity, 204–5; and civil rights movement, 178; and Enlightenment, 156; Hutson on, 204–5; and King, 162, 163; and morality, 128, 209; and Religious Right, 209; and Sovereignty of God amendment, 72

France, 17

Franklin, Benjamin, 28, 51, 117, 157, 205

freedom: and civil rights movement, 175; of conscience, 19, 20, 35, 44,

53, 62–63, 149; gospel of, 162; and King, 162; and moral codes, 7; Roosevelt on, 141. *See also* religious freedom

freedom marches, 171, 173

freedom songs, 172–73

Freedom Summer (1964), 174

free market, 23, 47, 75, 85, 156

Free Soil Party, 68

free-speech movement, 173

French and Indian War, 17

Freud, Sigmund, 105

Friends, 185

Fries, John, 47

From, Al, 244

Fuller, Charles, 145–46; *Old Fashioned Revival Hour*, 145

fundamentalism: and America as Christian nation, 11; and anti-Christian bigotry, 210; and atomic bomb, 155; beliefs of, 105–6, 107; and Bible, 105, 106, 107; definition of, 106–7; Fosdick on, 107; and Fuller, 146; Lippmann on, 129; and modernists, 105, 106, 118, 121, 122, 136, 218; and Moral Majority, 190; and Network of Spiritual Progressives, 230; as norm, 106; in post–World War II era, 145; and Puritans, 112; and religious conservatives, 12, 147; and Religious Left, 224; and Religious Right, 12; and Republican Party, 222, 226; as response to secular threats, 106; and Scopes trial, 124, 125, 126, 127, 137, 188, 190. *See also* conservatives, Christian; evangelicalism

Mississippi, 178–79; in post–World War II period, 133; and Protestants, 169–70; in South, 160–61, 182–83; and Southern Baptists, 170; and Truman, 142; in white churches, 163, 169, 170, 181. *See also* African Americans; civil rights movement
self-improvement, 85
Senate, *Report on the Subject of Mails on the Sabbath*, 62–63
separation, of church and state: and American Revolution, 1; Baird on, 53; and Baptists, 38; controversy over, 9; and Democratic Party, 64, 243, 248; and disestablishment in Massachusetts, 51; and *Everson v. Board of Education*, 142–43; and Falwell, 3; and George W. Bush, 206; Jackson on, 64; and Jefferson, 143, 248; and Jesus Christ, 249; and Madison, 143; and Network of Spiritual Progressives, 230; and presidential campaign of 1800, 36; and religious conservatives, 138; and religious liberals, 140, 247; Robertson on, 204; and Sovereignty of God amendment, 72; and Sunday mail service, 60, 62–63; Williams on, 1
September 11, 2001, attacks, 234
settlement houses, 99
Seventh Day Baptists, 61
sexuality, 48, 85, 185, 186, 187, 189, 192, 197, 241, 242. *See also* homosexuality
Shays, Daniel, 46
Shays's Rebellion, 46
Sherman, Roger, 29

Shermer, David, *Why Darwin Matters*, 234
Sherwood, Samuel, 14–15
Sider, Ron, 227
Silent Majority, 4
sin, 139, 144, 155, 156
sixties culture, 189–90, 193, 219
slave codes, 164
slavery: and Bible, 67–68, 70–71, 164; and Christian conversion, 92; and Christianity, 163–64, 165, 166; expansion of, 48, 67, 72; and God, 68; and moral decline, 52; and morality, 68; and Protestant disunity, 43–44, 67–73; in South, 52; and Southern Baptists, 169; uprisings against, 164. *See also* African Americans
Smith, Adam, *Wealth of Nations*, 23
Smith, Whiteford, 71–72
social change, 44, 45–46
social contract, 24, 25
social Darwinism, 82, 87, 124
social gospel, 173, 240
social gospel movement, 6, 77, 94–103, 104, 170
social insurance, 139
socialism, 77, 97, 134
social justice: and civil rights movement, 6, 157; and Democratic Party, 246; and Lerner, 219; and McDowell, 100; and National Council of Churches, 137; and Network of Spiritual Progressives, 229; and Religious Left, 222, 228; and religious liberals, 132, 145; and social gospel movement, 6, 94; and Sojourners, 187. *See also* justice